International Journal on Advances in Internet Technology

2017 vol. 10 nr. 1&2

Printed from e-media with permission by:

Curran Associates, Inc.
57 Morehouse Lane
Red Hook, NY 12571

Some format issues inherent in the e-media version may also appear in this print version.

Printed by Curran Associates, Inc. (2018)

International Academy, Research, and Industry Association (IARIA)
412 Derby Way
Wilmington, DE 19810

Phone: (408) 893-6407
Fax: (408) 527-6351

petre@iaria.org

Additional copies of this publication are available from:

Curran Associates, Inc.
57 Morehouse Lane
Red Hook, NY 12571 USA
Phone: 845-758-0400
Fax: 845-758-2633
Email: curran@proceedings.com
Web: www.proceedings.com

The *International Journal on Advances in Internet Technology* is published by IARIA.
ISSN: 1942-2652
journals site: http://www.iariajournals.org
contact: petre@iaria.org

Sponsored by IARIA
www.iaria.org

International Journal on Advances in Internet Technology
Volume 10, Number 1 & 2, 2017

Alessandro Testa, University of Naples "Federico II" / Institute of High Performance Computing and Networking (ICAR) of National Research Council (CNR), Italy
Stephanie Teufel, University of Fribourg, Switzerland
Parimala Thulasiraman, University of Manitoba, Canada
Pierre Tiako, Langston University, USA
Orazio Tomarchio, Universita' di Catania, Italy
Dominique Vaufreydaz, INRIA and Pierre Mendès-France University, France
Krzysztof Walkowiak, Wroclaw University of Technology, Poland
MingXue Wang, Ericsson Ireland Research Lab, Ireland
Wenjing Wang, Blue Coat Systems, Inc., USA
Zhi-Hui Wang, School of Softeware, Dalian University of Technology, China
Matthias Wieland, Universität Stuttgart, Institute of Architecture of Application Systems (IAAS),Germany
Bernd E. Wolfinger, University of Hamburg, Germany
Chai Kiat Yeo, Nanyang Technological University, Singapore
Abdulrahman Yarali, Murray State University, USA
Mehmet Erkan Yüksel, Istanbul University, Turkey

International Journal on Advances in Internet Technology
Volume 10, Numbers 1 & 2, 2017

CONTENTS

Ryo Nishimura, Ryukoku University, Japan
Yoshihiro Okada, Ryukoku University, Japan

Influence of the Perception of Data Security and Security Importance on Customer Usage of Internet Services

Erik Massarczyk, Peter Winzer
Faculty of Design – Computer Science – Media
RheinMain University of Applied Sciences
Wiesbaden, Germany
Email: erik.massarczyk@hs-rm.de, peter.winzer@hs-rm.de

***Abstract*—An increasing customer usage of Internet services with various devices demands a greater effort on data security and privacy issues, because more and more devices are connected and much personal information are spread more widely. However, in many cases the performance of services is more important than the provision of data security. Therefore, it would be necessary to investigate how the user perception of data security influences the usage of Internet services, which will be analyzed with a adjusted combined approach of the Technology Acceptance Model and the second model of the Unified Theory of Acceptance and Use of Technology. To support the analysis of this conceptual relationship, an evaluation of the interrelation between the perceived data security importance and the user behavior is also examined. The aim of this paper is to figure out a possible negative impact of the perception of data security and security importance on the usage of Internet services. The goal of the paper is to prove an influence of data security within an adjusted conceptual model based on the Technology Acceptance Model and the second model of the Unified Theory of Acceptance and Use of Technology. In general, a significant relationship between the perceived data security, perceived data security importance and user behavior of Internet services cannot be found. Particularly, some regressive influences are proved in the perceptions of data security importance and usage of specific services. The primary result of this paper is that from the perspective of customers the general perceived data security is significantly most influenced by the perceived email accounts security.**

Keywords*—*data security; security importance; customer usage; Internet services; mobile Internet.

I. INTRODUCTION

During the last 10 to 15 years, more and more people use Internet services. This development leads to a rising global Internet penetration and data flow [1][2]. Furthermore, most people use mainly services for social media, broadcasting/streaming, gaming and cloud computing. Especially during the last years, people started to use the different services with various devices [3][4]. Due to this application of services the devices get connected among each other. Hence, it can be assumed that the personal user data spread to a larger degree [3]. For the customers of Internet services, it is elusive where the personal data is stored and who gets access to the data, because the smart connected devices cover a wide range of information over geographical boundaries [4][5]. Finally, the usage of Internet services by customers faces the problems of data security and privacy from the user perspective. Personal data include critical information about and intellectual properties. These data are countable assets from which enterprises, companies and also criminals can benefit [6].

In general, the users are responsible for which personal data they spread for the usage of different Internet services. Hurdle free communication, marketing measures and advertisements disclose also more personal data of the users. Furthermore, a lot of people are willing to share their personal data in ignorance of risks of data leakage and data theft to reach higher reputation and more contacts. Out of it, it can be concluded that data security and privacy gets more and more important, because more personal data is disclosed and often the users are not able to examine who gets access to their personal information and who uses them for legal and illegal motives [1]. However, it cannot be distinguished between (a) customers, who disclose their personal information and are not aware of the consequences and (b) customers, who completely know the consequences of data disclosure.

The authors will figure out what the user perception of data security and data security importance is, when they use different Internet services with various devices, especially mobile devices with wireless Internet connections. Moreover, each Internet usage is in direct connection with data security and privacy issues. For these reasons, it needs to be investigated whether a higher perception of data security and trust in a service leads to a preferred usage of this service or device [1]. Accordingly, the authors analyze what the users of Internet services do or not do to prevent unauthorized access to their personal data. Despite the issue that influence factors can possibly impact the user behavior of Internet services, the authors will focus on the relation between the perceived data security and the usage of Internet services. The authors will not deeply analyze the relation and terms of data privacy and the misuse of disclosed data.

Generally, the topic describes a global problem, because all over the world customers distribute information and companies, criminals and others use the data for their advantages. Nevertheless, the authors focused on the current situation in Germany.

In Section II, the term data security, the challenges and the used research models will be described. In Section III, the methodology presents the theoretical approach for conducting the study based on presented research models. Following this section, the authors will present the data analysis and some key results of the survey. In Section V, the authors will critically discuss their results and problems of the survey. In the last Section, the improvements of the current research and the used survey will be described.

II. LITERATURE REVIEW

A. Data Security

Data security means that users want to keep their personal data to themselves. Here, it must be clear for them, who gets access to the personal information. Hence, no one should get access to the user's personal data, who does not have the right permission for the usage [5]. However, a lot of companies use personal data of customers, which customers spread in their Internet services, because a lot of users are not fully aware of the possible risks of sharing information [6][7]. Furthermore, they do not know which huge amount of data they produce and how they can prevent such risks [8]. This behavior could be a problem for residential users, because 56% of Internet services and platforms transmit personal information without permissions to third parties [9]. So, users should be better informed and aware of their personal data. In many cases, persons divulge information, which they may regret in a future situation. Furthermore, the data can be linked to critical personal information like credit card numbers, etc. [6][7].

Otherwise, the users also have to prevent unauthorized accesses by changing the passwords regularly, what the authors also investigate with a survey. If the users lose their access and their data is leaked, the users have to bear negative consequences up to the loss in reputation of image, business partners, relatives and friends [3].

User perspective, company perspective, companies' duties

In general, users fear: (a) capturing of passwords and accounts, (b) blackmails, (c) eavesdropping, and (d) undesired access to personal data from criminals [3]. The users want a secure transmission of data and the services should guarantee integrity, availability and confidentiality of the data and their transmission [10].

B. Challenges

The main challenge for analyzing user perceptions of data security is that all user attitudes and beliefs are completely subjective and depend on demographic (age) and cultural factors, which influence the customers' willingness to share data [6]. These discrepancies also include that each user has his perceptions of risks and prevention of risks. In many cases the people prefer to look for the performance of services instead of the security and data protection measures. To increase the customer caution concerning the disclosure and leakage of private data, services should insert several measures and rules which the customers have to comply with to use the services [11]. Furthermore, services and applications should state information about consequences of misuse and data leakage and insert different messages to make sure that the users understand the impacts of their data distribution. However, it is necessary to investigate what kind of impact the factors have on the individual perception of data security and the influence on the usage of Internet services, especially mobile services. Nonetheless, the authors will focus on the perceived data security of customers and will not evaluate the consequences of data disclosure.

C. Research Model – Technology Acceptance Model and Unified Theory of Acceptance and Use of Technology 2

For the analysis of the relation between the perception of data security and the user behavior regarding Internet services, the authors will use the Technology Acceptance Model (TAM) [12][13]. To support the findings and background research, the authors also use the Unified Theory of Acceptance and Use of Technology 2 (UTAUT2), which can be used to examine the relation of external variables and the user behavior of a new service/innovation [14]. The application of both models enables a consideration of the presented problem below in the way of an organizational and customer perspective. Due to the focus on private customers, the application of the UTAUT2 will be more useful to analyze the user acceptance of Internet services [14]. However, the longer experience and greater research background of the TAM gives the authors some implications about the acceptance and usage of Internet services, especially mobile services. Furthermore, the authors do not limit the questions in the survey for private usage. Thus, the respondents could answer for their business and private usage of services. Therefore, both models (TAM and UTAUT2) can be used for the evaluation of influences between data security issues and the usage of Internet services.

The TAM shall clarify how the customer's individual acceptance of Information Technologies (IT) can be explained and predicted [12][13]. Our paper will focus on the dependence of the usage of mobile Internet services on security issues and the acceptance of new technologies. It is currently known that the perceived usefulness has a positive impact on behavioral intentions, which leads to an actual customer usage [13]. However, perceived usefulness does not cover the user's perception, that the usage of the service will enhance his performance [12].

The UTAUT describes four key concepts (performance expectancy, effort expectancy, social influence, and facilitating conditions), which impact the consumer acceptance and behavioral intention of an innovation or technology [15][16]. Generally, it is known that the behavioral intention normally leads to a usage of the service [17]. Venkatesh et al. expand their own model with the factors hedonic motivation, price, and habit, which are classified as critical influence factors and predictors of consumer behavior and have been introduced in the UTAUT2 [14][15]. The UTAUT2 shall illustrate how the customers accept new technologies [18]. Especially the factors (a) costs, (b) usage advantage, (c) economic effort, and (d) expenditure of time are determining if a customer decides to use or not to use an innovation [18]. In the context of this paper, the habit and experience of usage could be a possible impact factor, which is described at the end of this subchapter. The other possible influence factors are not considered in detail.

Moreover, perceived usefulness and behavioral intentions in the TAM are not able to analyze and to reflect the perceived data security, importance of data security and the adoption of Internet services, especially mobile Internet services.

In consideration of Appendix 1, Escorbar-Rodriguez and Carvajal-Trujillo adapt the UTAUT2 with the external variable trust [19], which is influenced by several further components like perceived security and perceived privacy. As mentioned above, the UTAUT2 also describes different concepts/factors as impact factors on the behavioral intention to use of an innovation or service [14].

The authors analyze the direct relationship of the perception of data security and importance of data security on the actual usage of an Internet service. As displayed in Figure 1, the hypotheses will be directly organized for the relationship of the named factors perceived data security and perceived importance of data security and the use of the Internet services. Before these relationships will be examined, the relation between the both possible impact factors will be measured too. To support the both components and to address possible data security measures by the customers. The password behavior of customers in email and Social Media accounts is analyzed as well. The frequency of password-changes is an indicator for the importance of data security. Therefore, the authors decide to design the conceptual model in the way as it can be seen in Figure 1. The password changing behavior, perceived data security and perceived importance of data security are the external variables, which directly influence the actual usage of Internet services by the customers.

Next to the described external variables, credibility as a further factor could be perceived. This factor includes the users' belief that the used systems and their according attitudes would be free of threats for privacy and security [17]. It is further known that perceived credibility positively influences the behavioral intention to use [20]. Lin et al. have figured out that data security and privacy are the most affecting factors for an acceptance and adoption of a new technology [17]. It must be expected that using mobile Internet services will often imply security or privacy threats [20].

Therefore, the authors examine how the perception of data security and the importance of data security of specific Internet services influence the usage of the services. Furthermore, the component perceived security will be supported by Zhong et al. [22], which uses perceived security as external variable to show the influence on the behavioral intention to use mobile payments.

Normally, the external variable perceived security could additionally cover customer concerns about risk (perceived risk), trust and privacy concerns [21]. The named variables also influence the customer decision of adoption. Here, especially trust plays a major role, because trust describes how the customers perceive the credible and secure information and experiences of the providers [19][23][24][25]. Based on the assumption that perceived risks and trust directly influence the usage processes [26], the customers will reduce their usage if expect a loss of privacy and a higher risk in usage [27]. Therefore, the authors will not exclude these criterions and analyze this the influence of trust as a determinant of usage behavior in a second survey [28][29].

Generally, the aim of the analysis is to illustrate how the customers perceive their data security and how they rank the importance of data security for each Internet service they use.

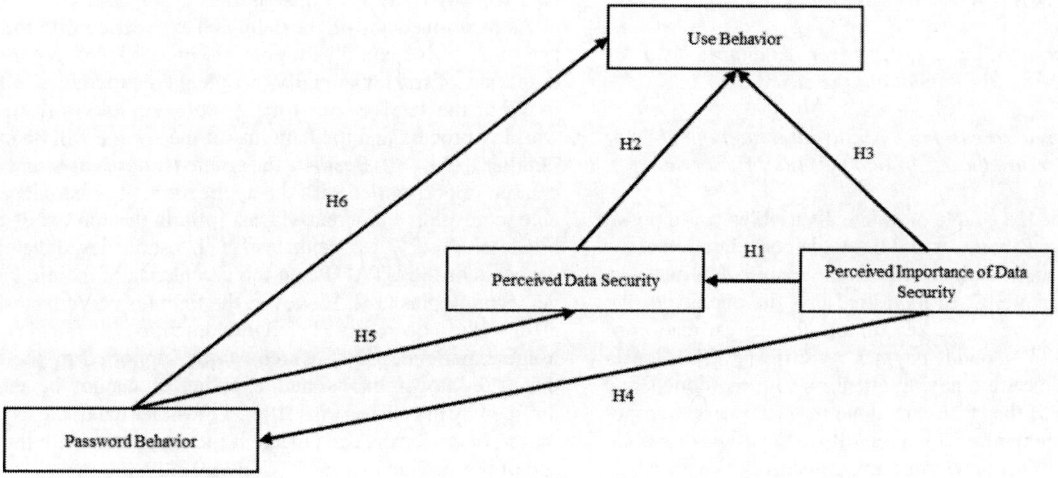

Figure 1. Conceptual Model

In comparison to the presented relationships between the estimation of perceived security, risks and trust and the usage of mobile banking or mobile payments [20][21][22], the authors consider different Internet services for the analysis of the relation between usage of services and the perceived data security and perceived importance of data security. As mentioned in the description of the conceptual model in Figure 1, both named concepts will be supported by the external password changing behavior (for emails and Social Media). Normally, the password changing behavior could be possibly a criterion of the perceived importance of data security but the authors are not sure if the customers perceive the same connection. It can be assumed that customers with a higher awareness of data security will change their passwords more regularly Therefore, the authors will analyze if the password changing behavior fits to the perceived importance of data security. Based on this examination, the authors will test if password changing behavior also relates to the perceived data security and usage behavior.

The research hypotheses of this paper are:

H1: A higher customer perception of importance of data security leads to higher perceived data security.

H2: The customer perception of data security (perceived security) has a directly positive effect on the usage of (mobile) Internet services.

H3: The customer perception of data security importance (perceived importance of data security) has a directly positive effect on the usage of (mobile) Internet services.

H4: A higher customer perception of importance of data security leads to an increasing password changing behavior.

H5: An increased customer password changing behavior leads to a higher perception of data security.

H6: An increased customer password changing behavior leads to an increased usage of (mobile) Internet services.

As mentioned, a couple of external variables could possibly describe security issues and threats in consideration of the usage of Internet services, especially mobile Internet services. For example, Chen identified that the perceived risk can be seen as one of the key drivers for the estimation of uncertainties in mobile payments [20][21][22]. Consequently, customers are paying attention to the products and their providers if they take care about the customers' transactions and personal information security in the usage of mobile payments [22]. This presented relationship is supported by different researches regarding mobile payments as important issues in the trust of services [30][31][32][33][34][35][36][37][38]. Zhong et al. and Abrahão et al. figured out that trust and perceived risk have significant influence on customer acceptance of mobile payments [20][21][22]. In consideration of the mentioned-above factors habit and motivation from the UTAUT2, Lu et al. also illustrate that the usage of mobile payment services is positively influenced by the experience and confidence of the customers [39]. This connection supports the previous descriptions and findings and will be more deeply described in the paragraph below. Moreover, an influence of trust and perceived risk on the acceptance of mobile banking is found too [40][41]. Considering the usage of mobile shopping, trust is also an important influence factor [42]. Besides mobile banking, mobile payments and mobile shopping, the perceived security issues are even higher in mobile telecommunication networks, due to the fact that mobile networks are shared mediums and different persons can use the same mobile radio cell in the same time. This structure makes the system more vulnerable for attacks within the network [43]. Zhou also figured out that especially mobile transactions are critical for the perceptions of trust [28]. The mobile network operators and providers have to take care about these issues and the introduction of security measures can mitigate uncertainties and risks [44][45][46]. The development of trust in a service is a major aim for customers and providers, because the trust in a service increase the customer convenience of the customer and normally leads to a higher performance [26][47]. So, trust needs to be developed [28]. However, especially in mobile banking the customers fear a lack of control, which results in a greater uncertainty [28]. Consequently, the literature conveys the feedback that in several cases trust and the perception of security, risks and uncertainties influence the customer user behavior. All examples and findings demonstrate that possible security issues can significant negatively influence the intention to use mobile Internet services. Therefore, the authors have set the hypotheses that a better perception in data security leads to an increased usage of services.

As mentioned above, the habit and experience with the usage of a service could be a possible impact factor regarding the issues of trust. Generally, people gain experience with a usage of the service over time, people are able to learn the working process and the handling of the service will be more familiar [15][48]. Besides the gained knowledge and increased opportunities with the application, the customers are able to develop an increased trust [46]. In the context of mobile Internet services, Venkatesh et al. test the new developed concepts of the UTAUT2 on the acceptance of mobile Internet technologies [14]. However, the findings of Venkatesh et al. describe a decreasing behavioral intention in case of rising usage experiences [14], which can be supported by the fact that old known habits and experiences cannot be easily dropped by the customers [30]. On the other hand, the expectations of customers can change if the experience with the usage of the service increases. Consequently, the impact of experiences and habits cannot be clearly predicted, due to positive and negative influences on the behavioral intentions of usage. Therefore, the authors decide to not include this variable in this paper. Nevertheless, uncertainties and risks normally base on a lack of experience [49][50][51][52][53].

III. METHODOLOGY

To examine these hypotheses, the authors will use a survey to prove that data security issues have a negative impact on user behavior of mobile Internet services. For the analysis of the individual customer groups, separate cross-sectional surveys ("one-shot surveys") will be conducted within a short period of time [54]. Here, the answers are taken by interviewers in personal oral interviews, thus ensuring completeness and accuracy of the answers. The personal interview will be conducted on the basis of a random quota sample based on the demographic characteristics of gender and age in order to be representative of the local population [55][56]. In general, the interviewers select their test persons at public places like libraries and in the pedestrian zone in Wiesbaden (Germany) to reach a diversified and representative number of test persons. The first survey (440 completed questionnaires) which the authors use to gain information about the mobile data usage have been held in 2016, and was a pre-test, which the authors use to get information from the test persons and to verify whether the posed questions fit to answer the hypotheses and presented concepts. In 2017, another survey run with inclusion of the gained results and information to reach better analyses of the developed concepts.

The data has been analyzed based on quantitative research methods with the statistical program Statistical Package for the Social Sciences (SPSS). After the evaluation of credibility and reliability, which will be tested with the Cronbach's Alpha, the Exploratory Factor Analysis has been done to ensure the validity and to present related groups of perceptions and services. The perceived data security will be queried with the question, how the customers perceive their personal data in the virtual world (5-Point-Likert-scale: very secure to very unsecure). To cover the frequency of (mobile) Internet services usage and the perception of the importance of data security, a 5-Point-Likert-scale (very often to very few and very important to very unimportant) has been implemented [57]. Besides the consideration of the general perception of data security, the authors consider mainly the usage and perception of data security and importance of data security of the services: (a) email, (b) social media, (c) online telephony, (d) online shopping, (e) cloud computing, (f) e-learning, and (g) instant messaging. Other factors, which are included in the survey, are navigation, gaming, online baking, online administration, internet television and video on demand. Based on the fact that the behavioral intention leads in an actual customer usage [13], the analysis of the survey shall present the regression between the external variables perceived data security and user behavior and as well perceived importance of data security and user behavior. Therefore, the authors use the Ordinary Least Square Regression to test the significance of each of the named hypotheses.

IV. DATA ANALYSIS AND RESULTS

A. *Descriptive Results*

56.0% of the asked test persons are female and the group of persons with an age between 20 and 29 years describes an over-representation in this survey with a share of 47.4%. Based on statistical elevations, it can be noted that this age group represents only 12.2% in Germany [58]. Following previous researches activities from ARD/ZDF in 2015, the group of people between 20 to 29 years almost completely uses the Internet [59]. This situation does not comply with the aim to get a representative picture of the German market. But this high proportion of Internet users is able to reach better results for the test of the influence of data security issues on the usage of Internet services, especially mobile services. As mentioned, the most test persons use both Internet services (based on mobile networks as well as on fixed networks). Therefore, they are able to describe the perceptions of usage of services. Contrarily, only a smaller share of elder participants uses the Internet services and so these mostly cannot fully estimate their perceptions of the usage of services, behavior and their security issues. Consequently, the final direction of the data and their representative nature cannot be fully reached and confirmed.

In general, 43.6% of the participants are feeling a data uncertainty. On the opposite, only 3.5% of the interviewed persons are perceiving their data to be very secure. Following these results, which are displayed in Table I, the participants perceive the estimation and importance of data security of the services differently. Services which are related to financial payments are superiorly estimated with a higher importance of data security. In contrast, approximately half of the asked persons perceives the necessity of a high data security in the services email, social media and instant messaging.

TABLE I. Importance of Data Security.

Internet Services	Importance of Data Security
Email	56.3% very high importance
Social Media	45.6% very high importance
Online Shopping	64.3% very high importance
Online Banking	86.0% very high importance
Instant Messaging	47.3% very high importance

Supporting the illustrated perceptions of data security, the authors have included questions about the perceived necessity (a) to change the passwords for email and social media accounts, and (b) to use an anti-virus program. Over two third of interviewees (69.7% for email, 68.5% for social media) have answered that they change their passwords less than once a year. The authors conclude that they normally never change their passwords. However, 84.7% of the persons use anti-virus programs to protect their devices. Generally, the usage of the anti-virus program should not include costs, because 70.9% of the persons use the free version of the anti-virus programs. Following the numbers of McAfee, 14.5% of the German Internet users do not use an anti-virus program

[60]. Based on this study's results, the 15.3% of persons which are not using an anti-virus program indicate a similar and representative relation of the generated data.

B. Reliability and Validity

The results of the reliability and validity analyses are illustrated in Table II. Generally, the examined concepts of Internet service usage and data security are reliable and valid. Following Cronbach, the Cronbach's Alpha values have to be greater than 0.7 to present a good reliability [61][62][63]. This value has been achieved by all questions analyzing the concepts. The consideration of the exploratory factor analysis includes the assessment of Kaiser-Meyer-Olkin criterion, the significance test from Bartlett, and the examination of the cumulative variance [64][65][66][67][68]. All of the combined questions for the analysis of the determined concepts (a) perceived security, (b) security importance, and (c) user behavior (see Figure 1) have reached significant p values ($p<0.05$) in the Bartlett-Test. Furthermore, all concepts boast Kaiser-Meyer-Olkin values above the mark of 0.7 [64][65][66][67][68]. Both tests describe a good validity of the gained data. Moreover, the cumulative variances from all considered concepts are above 50%, which indicate high explanation rates of the variances in the collected data [65][66][67]. Consequently, the reliability and validity of the collected data are proved. Due to the presented differences in the demographics, the asked persons do not completely function as a representative mirror of the situation in the German market.

C. Correlation Analyses

The correlation analyses are divided in two parts. Firstly, the authors will contemplate the correlations of the perceptions of data security in general and in single service considerations. Secondly, the authors also correlate the results of the perceived importance of data security with the results of the perceived data security in general and for the single services. Thirdly, the correlations between the usage of Internet services (fixed-line and mobile) and the perceptions of data security (in general and single view) are considered.

Firstly, the general data security perception does not correlate significantly ($p>0.05$) with the individual perceptions of data security from the single services. In consideration of individual perceptions of the services, customer perceptions of data security for (a) email, (b) social media, (c) online telephony, (d) online shopping, (e) cloud computing, (f) e-learning, (g) instant messaging, and (h) online administration correlate significantly positively ($p<0.05$) with the perceptions of data security of the other services (see Table III and Appendix 2).

The correlation predicts that if a customer perceives a higher data security in the usage of email, social media, instant messaging, and online shopping, they will intensively perceive a higher data security in the other services. Equally, the customer rates the named services with a higher importance of data security.

The consideration of the correlation coefficient follows the classification that high correlation coefficients have Pearson correlation values above 0.5 [69][70]. In Table III, the data security perceptions of the following Internet services correlate strongly with each other: (1) e-learning and online administration (value 0.705), (2) instant messaging and social media (value = 0.601), (3) email and online telephony (value = 0.593), (4) email and online shopping (value = 0.546), and (5) instant messaging and online telephony (value 0.504).

Due to the values above 0.5, the authors assume that a relation between these factors exists. Consequently, the correlations do not indicate a significant connection between the general perceived data security and (a) the perceived data security for the single services and (b) importance of data security for the single services. It is doubtful if the further regression analyses may find significant regressive relationships between the named variables. Nonetheless, the correlations show that each perception of data security for each specific single service correlates positively with each other. This means if a customer perceives one service as more secure, he feels the same for other services. The same relation is valid for the perceived importance of data security.

TABLE II. Results of the Reliability and Validity Tests.

	Reliability – Cronbach's Alpha	Validity – Exploratory Factor Analysis			
		Kaiser-Meyer-Olkin	Bartlett-Test	Cumulative Variance	Highest Loadings
General Combined Usage of Internet Services	α=0.732	0.777	p<0.05	68.5% (6 Factors)	Fixed Video on Demand (0.735)
Fixed Usage of Internet Services	α=0.882	0.854	p<0.05	67.0% (3 Factors)	Email (0.885) Instant Messaging (0.865)
Mobile Usage of Internet Services	α=0.840	0.820	p<0.05	51.3% (2 Factors)	Navigation (0.811) Instant Messaging (0.771) Email (0.713)
Data Security	α=0.837	0.783	p<0.05	67.5% (4 Factors)	E-Learning (0.880) Online- Shopping (0.822) Online Banking (0.820) Online Gaming (0.805)

TABLE III. Correlation Analysis of Data Security Perceptions of selected services.

		Data Security Email	Data Security Online Telephony	Data Security Social	Data Security Online Shopping	Data Security Cloud Computing	Data Security IM	Data Security E-Learning	Data Security Administra-tion
Data Security Email	Correlation by Pearson	1	.593**	.435**	.546**	.427**	.388**	.330**	.400**
	Significance (2-sided)		.000	.000	.000	.000	.000	.000	.000
Data Security Online Telephony	Correlation by Pearson	.593**	1	.485**	.305**	.263**	.504**	.358**	.385**
	Significance (2-sided)	.000		.000	.000	.000	.000	.000	.000
Data Security Social Media	Correlation by Pearson	.435**	.485**	1	.381**	.390**	.601**	.275**	.276**
	Significance (2-sided)	.000	.000		.000	.000	.000	.000	.000
Data Security Online Shopping	Correlation by Pearson	.546**	.305**	.381**	1	.343**	.197**	.264**	.369**
	Significance (2-sided)	.000	.000	.000		.000	.000	.000	.000
Data Security Cloud Computing	Correlation by Pearson	.427**	.263**	.390**	.343**	1	.249**	.345**	.400**
	Significance (2-sided)	.000	.000	.000	.000		.000	.000	.000
Data Security IM	Correlation by Pearson	.388**	.504**	.601**	.197**	.249**	1	.264**	.287**
	Significance (2-sided)	.000	.000	.000	.000	.000		.000	.000
Data Security E-Learning	Correlation by Pearson	.330**	.358**	.275**	.264**	.345**	.264**	1	.705**
	Significance (2-sided)	.000	.000	.000	.000	.000	.000		.000
Data Security Administration	Correlation by Pearson	.400**	.385**	.276**	.369**	.400**	.287**	.705**	1
	Significance (2-sided)	.000	.000	.000	.000	.000	.000	.000	

**. Correlation p=0.01 (2-sided) significant. / *. Correlation p=0.05 (2-sided) significant.

A linkage between the data security perceptions of email services, online shopping and online telephony follows the natural order, due to the fact that the online shopping and online telephony normally need an email account for the receipts of transactions and verification of the user. Therefore, the customers evaluate the same security issues on the named three services. The relations between the assessment of data security of instant messaging and social media and online telephony can also be comprehended. Based on the fact that social media platforms and online telephony providers include instant messaging systems in their service, the customers perceive similarly.

The interrelation of e-learning and online administration can be drawn in the point that both systems are based on platforms which cover personal user behavior and data.

Interestingly, the frequency of changing the email password also significantly correlates positively ($p<0.05$) with all of the individual data perceptions of the specific services. If a customer changes his password more frequently, he will feel safer in the usage of the services and rates the services with higher data security importance. However, a significant correlation between the password changing behaviors and the general perceived data security cannot be found.

It must be predicted that the perceived data security does not depend on the password changing behavior for email and Social Media accounts.

Secondly, the consideration of the usage of Internet services will be divided in the customer fixed-line application and mobile application consideration. In each consideration (mobile and fixed-line), the usage of all Internet services correlates significantly positively ($p<0.05$) with each other (see Appendix 3 and 4). It can be predicted that if a customer chooses to use one service that he will also use other Internet services. Based on the high correlation coefficients over 0.5 (fixed correlation coefficients: 0.5 to 0.7; mobile correlation coefficients 0.2 to 0.6), it can be assumed that the perceptions of data security of the specific services belong to each other and could have a linear relationship [69][70]. However, the usage of the Internet services in the fixed-line network does not correlate significantly with the usage of the Internet services in the mobile network overall. Here, the authors have to assume that the usages of the Internet services within the fixed-line and mobile networks do not directly interact with each other. This relation does not fit with the current status of knowledge, because normally there is a relationship between the usage of Internet services in fixed-line and mobile infrastructures.

The comparison of usage and data security illustrates that the general perception of data security does not correlate significantly ($p>0.05$) with the usage of Internet services (mobile and fixed-line) (see Table IV and V). However, in consideration of the specific Internet services, the authors get some positive and negative correlations. The usage of emails correlates significantly ($p<0.05$, Pearson-value = 0.105) with the perception of data security for emails (see Table VI). Despite a lower correlation coefficient [69][70], it can be assumed that a highly perceived data security could lead to an increased usage of emails. However, the relation between this perception and the fixed usage of this service is quite stronger than the usage of this service in the mobile network. The customer ratings for the security importance are quite similar. Besides a predicted influence of the perception of data security for online shopping (fixed-line and mobile shopping) and the usage of online shopping, the authors find significantly positive correlations between the usage of online shopping and the perception of data security for the services emails ($p<0.05$, Pearson-value = 0.142) and online banking ($p<0.05$, Pearson-value = 0.144) (see Table VI). It can be assumed that a higher perception of data security concerning the safety of online banking and the email accounts could lead to a stronger usage of online shopping. Despite the low correlation coefficients (based on [69][70]), it can be noted that both services could be used if a customer decides to use online shopping platforms. Finally, especially in the usage of mobile Internet services the authors also find significantly negative correlations of social media (SM) and instant messaging (IM) with the data security perceptions of e-learning (SM: $p<0.05$, Pearson-value = -0.158; IM: $p<0.05$, Pearson-value = -0.113) and online gaming (SM: $p<0.05$, Pearson-value = -0.185; IM: $p<0.05$, Pearson-value = -0.153) (see Table VII). Here, it must be predicted that the usage of IM and SM would increase if the users perceive a decreasing data security in online gaming and e-learning. From the current point of view, a coherent argumentation cannot be included. At this point, the authors will consider this relation in the regression analysis in detail.

Additionally, the authors also analyze the correlation between the password changing behavior and the usage of the services. For the mobile and fixed services, the password changing behaviors correlate positively significant ($p<0.05$) with usage of Social Media. The correlation coefficients are spread around the value of 0.100 which mean quite weak correlations [69][70]. The prediction would be that people, which are changing their passwords more regularly, use Social Media more often.

TABLE IV. Correlation Analysis of the General Data Security Perceptions and Fixed Internet Service Usage.

		Data Security
Fix Usage Email	Correlation by Pearson	-.033
	Significance (2-sided)	.509
Fix Usage Surf	Correlation by Pearson	-.026
	Significance (2-sided)	.599
Fix Usage Online Telephony	Correlation by Pearson	.052
	Significance (2-sided)	.334
Fix Usage Video on Demand	Correlation by Pearson	.025
	Significance (2-sided)	.634
Fix Usage IPTV	Correlation by Pearson	-.006
	Significance (2-sided)	.933
Fix Usage Online Shopping	Correlation by Pearson	.014
	Significance (2-sided)	.796
Fix Usage Cloud Computing	Correlation by Pearson	.038
	Significance (2-sided)	.525
Fix Usage Social Media	Correlation by Pearson	-.021
	Significance (2-sided)	.685
Fix Usage Video Telephony	Correlation by Pearson	.009
	Significance (2-sided)	.879
Fix Usage E-Learning	Correlation by Pearson	-.016
	Significance (2-sided)	.791
Fix Usage IM	Correlation by Pearson	-.051
	Significance (2-sided)	.324
Fix Usage Navigation	Correlation by Pearson	.016
	Significance (2-sided)	.756

**. Correlation p=0.01 (2-sided) significant. /*. Correlation p=0.05 (2-sided) significant

TABLE V. Correlation Analysis of the General Data Security Perceptions and Mobile Internet Service Usage.

		Data Security
Mobile Usage Email	Correlation by Pearson	.027
	Significance (2-sided)	.578
Mobile Usage Surf	Correlation by Pearson	-.035
	Significance (2-sided)	.482
Mobile Usage Online Telephony	Correlation by Pearson	-.084
	Significance (2-sided)	.119
Mobile Usage Video on Demand	Correlation by Pearson	.007
	Significance (2-sided)	.899
Mobile Usage IPTV	Correlation by Pearson	-.066
	Significance (2-sided)	.312
Mobile Usage Online Shopping	Correlation by Pearson	-.090
	Significance (2-sided)	.086
Mobile Usage Cloud Computing	Correlation by Pearson	-.081
	Significance (2-sided)	.178
Mobile Usage Social Media	Correlation by Pearson	.013
	Significance (2-sided)	.800
Mobile Usage Video Telephony	Correlation by Pearson	.021
	Significance (2-sided)	.720
Mobile Usage E-Learning	Correlation by Pearson	.065
	Significance (2-sided)	.288
Mobile Usage IM	Correlation by Pearson	.059
	Significance (2-sided)	.255
Mobile Usage Navigation	Correlation by Pearson	-.071
	Significance (2-sided)	.172

**. Correlation p=0.01 (2-sided) significant. /*. Correlation p=0.05 (2-sided) significant

TABLE VI. Correlation Analysis of Email and Online Shopping Usage and Service Data Security Perceptions.

		Fix Usage Email	Mobile Usage Email	Fix Usage Online Shopping	Mobile Usage Online Shopping
Data Security Email	Correlation by Pearson	.105*	.047*	.142**	.011*
Data Security Online Shopping	Correlation by Pearson			.036*	.034*
Data Security Online Banking	Correlation by Pearson			.144**	.023*

**. Correlation p=0.01 (2-sided) significant. /*. Correlation p=0.05 (2-sided) significant

TABLE VII. Correlation Analysis of Mobile Social Media Usage and Service Data Security Perceptions.

		Mobile Usage Social
Data Security Gaming	Correlation by Pearson	**-.185****
	Significance (2-sided)	**.004**
Data Security E-Learning	Correlation by Pearson	**-.158****
	Significance (2-sided)	**.005**

**. Correlation p=0.01 (2-sided) significant. /*. Correlation p=0.05 (2-sided) significant

D. Regression Analyses

The regression analysis follows the same procedure as the correlation analysis. Firstly, the authors consider how the importance and perception of data security of the specific Internet services (independent variables) affect the general perception of data security (dependent variable). Following the application of the least square regression, there is a positively significant regression ($p<0.05$) between the general perception of data security and the evaluation of the data security of email services. Due to a regression coefficient value of 0.299, a higher explanatory rate is reached, which results in a good linear regression (see Table VIII). However, the r-square, which indicates the explanatory rate of the regression, is only 8.2% in this case (see Table VIII).

This value is below the targeted 10% to 20% as found in literature [67], the explanatory power of this regressive connection is quite weak. The Variance Inflation Factor (VIF), which illustrates the rate of multicollinearities, should be below the mark of 3 [64][71][72]. The VIF for this regression is 2.579, which leads to the exclusion of multicollinearities in this case.

The same significantly positively regression ($p<0.05$) can be found between the general data security perception and the importance of data security for email services. Both tests conclude that a better perceived data security for email services lead to a better estimation of the data security at all. These results are supported by the significant ($p<0.05$) regressive connection between the perception of the general data security and the perceived data security of Social Media services. However, the regression coefficient is negative (-0.278) and multicollinearities can be excluded (VIF<3). Nonetheless, the finding that the general perception of data security rises in the case that the perceived data security of the Social Media Accounts decreases, does not lead to a useful relationship between these factors and will not further considered. Considering that the other tests between the named variables also do not lead to significant connections, the authors have to conclude that the perception of data security mostly belongs to the email security. Consequently, the hypothesis H1 can be accepted for the connection with email services only. In general, hypothesis H1 has to be rejected.

The assessment of the interrelation between the password changing behavior, data security and usage of services is not the main target of the authors' analysis, but it would be useful to collect some more information which can be used for further surveys and evaluations. Interestingly, the password changing behavior does not significantly lead to a higher perceived data security ($p>0.05$). Therefore, hypothesis H5 can also be rejected.

This connection implies that the perceived data security bases on different influence factors. Furthermore, the password changing behavior also relies on different customer estimations.

The password changing behavior for emails significantly positive ($p<0.05$) affects the perceived importance of data security of email services. The reached r-square of 3.0% presents a very weak linear regressive connection between these factors. The regression coefficient with 0.174 is also quite weak. Following Petter et al., the reached VIF value of 1 infers an exclusion of multicollinearities [72]. By changing passwords for the email services more regularly, an increased perception of data security could be achieved.

The password changing behavior for social media networks significantly positively ($p<0.05$) affects the perceived importance of data security of social media services. The reached r-square of 2.2% and the regression coefficient of 0.149 illustrates a very weak linear regressive connection between these factors. Following Petter et al., the reached VIF value of 1 infers an exclusion of multicollinearities [72]. By changing passwords for the social media network services more regularly, an increased perception of data security can be reached. A further connection can be found in the positive significant regression of the password changing behavior for Social Media accounts with downloads ($p<0.05$, r-square 0.125, regression coefficient 0.253). Due to the huge volume of information distributed in the social networks, the customers are able to download a lot of materials. This means, if users take care about their personal Social Media accounts, they also use downloads. Nonetheless, the other tests do not lead to significant results and therefore the hypothesis H4 has tu be rejected.

In the comparison of password changing behavior for emails and usage of Internet services, the password changing behavior significantly is affected by the usage of online telephony (fixed, mobile) and video on demand (mobile) in a positive way (fixed-line: r-square=12.1%, $p<0.05$, VIF close to 1; mobile: r-square=15.7%, $p<0.05$, VIF close to 1) (see Table IX). Both considerations are significant and display acceptable explanatory rates. Based on the VIF values close to 1, multicollinearities can be excluded. The more the customers use these both services, more often they change their passwords. Additionally, instant messaging in the mobile Internet usage affects negatively significantly (mobile) the changing behavior for email passwords. Here, the more the customers change their passwords the weaker they will use instant messaging in the mobile consideration (see Table IX). However, there is no reason why there is no connection to the services email or social media.

To test the hypothesis H6, the previous findings have to be analyzed from another perspective, i. e. the authors evaluate the dependence of each single service usage on the password changing behavior of customers (for emails and Social Media accounts). The hypothesis H6 has to be rejected. There are only three weak negatively significantly regressive relations between (a) the password changing behavior for emails and Social Media accounts and the mobile usage of IPTV ($p<0.05$, r-square 2.1%, coefficient -0.197), (b) online shopping ($p<0.05$, r-square 1.1%, coefficient -0.162) and (c) video telephony ($p<0.05$, r-square 1.7%, coefficient -0.161). Based on the low regression coefficients (below 0.500) and the weak values for r-square below the mark of 10%, the regressive connections are quite weak and cannot lead to an agreement of the hypothesis [69][70]. Following Petter et al., the reached VIF-values below of 3 indicate an exclusion of the multicollinearities [72]. Especially, the authors could not find any connection between the consideration of the password changing behaviors and the usage of fixed Internet services.

The consideration of the connection between Internet services usage and perception of data security and importance of data security will be divided in a fixed and mobile perspective. Table X illustrates how each single service usage in the fixed-line infrastructure is affected by the perceptions of data security and data security importance (Dependent variable = specific usage of the respective Internet services; Independent variable = perception of data security and data security importance of the specific service). The consideration indicates that the usage of Internet services with fixed-line infrastructures is not significantly influenced by the general customer perception of data security. However, for different Internet services the authors can find significantly positive regressions between the perception of data security importance of the single services and the usage of services.

As Table X illustrates, the usage of email services, online telephony and online shopping is significantly positively ($p<0.05$) influenced by the perception of data security importance for email services. Therefore, the customers intend to use email services, online telephony and online shopping if they perceive the email services to be secure and indicate a high data security importance. The connection between the usage and perception of data security importance for email services appears naturally. Also, the usage of online telephony and online shopping normally needs an account, which is generally linked to an email account. Following Schöneck and Voß, and Brosius, the r-squares between 8.7% and 10.8% and the regressions coefficients of 0.096 to 0.114 indicate quite weak significant regressions [67][70].

TABLE VIII. Regression Analysis of the General Data Security Perception and the Single Service Data Security Perceptions

Model	Not-standardized Coefficients		Sig.	VIF
	Regression Coefficient B	Standard Deviation		
Constant	3.845	.696	.000	
Password CHR Email	.018	.110	.871	2.736
Password CHR Social Media	.099	.117	.397	2.731
Data Security Email	**.299**	.140	**.034**	**2.579**
Data Security Online Telephony	-.030	.112	.785	2.068
Data Security Social Media	**-.278**	**.137**	**.043**	**2.131**
Data Security Online Shopping	.033	.131	.804	2.215
Data Security Online Banking	-.284	.172	.102	1.938
Data Security Cloud Computing	.081	.105	.441	1.824
Data Security Online Gaming	.011	.088	.902	2.111
Data Security IM	-.009	.137	.950	1.812
Data Security Downloads	-.106	.106	.318	1.665
Data Security E-Learning	.003	.105	.979	2.855
Data Security Administration	-.016	.106	.883	2.606

. a Dependent Variable: Data Security
CHR = Change Rate

Model	R	R-Square	Corrected R-Square
1	.286[a]	.082	.019

TABLE IX. Regression Analysis of the Password Changing Behavior and Usage of Internet Services

Model	R	R-Square	Corrected R-Square	Standard Deviation
1	.347[a]	.121	.031	1.110

a. Dependent Variable: Password Change Rate Email

Model	Not-standardized Coefficients		Sig.	VIF
	Regression Coefficient B	Standard Deviation		
Constant	2.622	.510	.000	
Fix Usage Online Telephony	.831	.398	.039	1.991

Model	R	R-Square	Corrected R-Square	Standard Deviation
1	.396[a]	.157	.071	1.087

a. Dependent Variable: Password Change Rate Email

Model	Not-standardized Coefficients		Sig.	VIF
	Regression Coefficient B	Standard Deviation		
Constant	2.622	.510	.000	
Mobile Usage Online Telephony	.609	.247	.015	1.584
Mobile Usage Video on Demand	.630	.255	.015	1.791
Mobile Usage_ Instant Messaging	-1.017	.431	.020	1.844

Therefore, the linear connection between the usage of these services and the estimation of the data security importance of email services can be assessed as quite weak. The VIF values below the mark of 3 exclude possible multicollinearities between the analyzed variables [64][71][72]. However, the open question is, why the perception of data security importance for emails services just affects the usage of these three named components and does not impact other Internet service usages.

The other two connections in the usage of Internet services in fixed-line infrastructures can be found in (a) the significantly positive influence ($p<0.05$) of the importance of data security on cloud computing on the usage of video on demand, and (b) the significantly positive dependence ($p<0.05$) of importance of data security on online banking and online administration on the usage of instant messaging. Due to r-squares of 10.8% and 9.8% and regression coefficients below 20%, the authors follow the estimated values for regression analyses by Schöneck and Voß and conclude quite weak regressive connections between the analyzed variables [67]. Based on the VIF below the value of 3, multicollinearities can be ruled out [64][71][72].

For case (a), the authors assume that people, who often consume videos on demand, also use clouds to save their videos, pictures and data, which they produce and consume. In the customers' mind, the usage of video on demand is influenced by the perception of data security importance for cloud computing. The only possibility to explain the circumstance would be that the customers need higher data security to consume and produce more videos. In this case, more and more people, who consume videos on demand, will also produce more and more own videos.

For case (b), no useful connection is evident. Generally, administration (e g. employment office) inform their customers with short messages services, which can be linked to the use of instant messages and so a relation to the usage of services can be predicted. Here, it can be assumed that the customers want a secure news exchange, because the information of the administrations are normally personal. Due to the fact, the highest regression coefficient is 0.162, this possible relation should be analyzed by further research. The connection to online banking could be that banks often send authentication codes per short or instant messages. With the authentication codes, the customers are able to do their transactions. Therefore, customers perceive a higher data security importance, because people are taking care that no other third party can enter this communication and can possibly copy critically personal information.

Considering the usage of the Internet services in the mobile infrastructure in Table XI, there is a significant influence ($p<0.05$) between perceived data security and the usage of navigation services. However, the regression coefficient of 0.042 and a r-square of 10.0% indicate a quite weak linear regression (the coefficient value is close to 0 instead of close to 1) between these variables. Following Schöneck and Voß, the r-square for should be higher than 20% (at least 10%) [67]. Following Hagl, and Brosius, the linear regression between the variables is weak [69][70]. Based on a VIF value below 3, multicollinearities can be ruled out [72]. The authors assume that customers use navigation services. However, the most people do not want to be tracked. Therefore, a safer perception of data security could induce higher usage rates. In contrast to the importance of emails in the fixed-line usage of Internet services, the mobile Internet services usage is dominated by the application of instant messaging. For the services, instant messaging, e-learning and social media, the data security importance of instant messaging significantly impacts ($p<0.05$) all three named factors. Based on regression coefficient factors, which are ranging between -0.154 (E-Learning negatively) and 0.101 (social media positively), the linear regression values are also quite weak. The r-squares reach values between 10.0% and 18.9%, which also do not imply good regressive interrelations. Following Petter et al., the VIF values below 3 leads to an exclusion of multicollinearities [72]. The relation between the perception of data security importance and usage of instant messaging is obvious. As mentioned in literature, the perception of the security of one service should influence the usage of this service. So, this connection should follow the natural order. Also, the connection between social media and the perception of data security importance can be deduced by the issue that the most people communicate with instant messaging through social media platforms. Mostly, people demand that their messages are being transferred securely and without interruptions or eavesdropping by a third party. The interrelation with e-learning cannot be explained at this point and needs further research.

The other two connections concerning the usage of Internet services in mobile infrastructures can be found in (a) the significantly negative influence ($p<0.05$) of the importance of data security for email services on the usage of online telephony, and (b) the significantly positive dependence ($p<0.05$) of importance of data security for online gaming on the usage of video on demand. Due to r-squares of 10.2% and 8.6% and regression coefficients below 20%, the authors follow the estimated values for regression analyses by Schöneck and Voß and conclude quite weak regressive relations between the analyzed variables [67]. Based on the VIF below the value of 3, multicollinearities can be ruled out [64][71][72]. Both cases cannot be explained from the current point of view. Normally, a positive relation between online telephony and the importance of data security for email services exists (like in the fixed-line consideration) but, the negative interrelation does not lead to a useful explanation in the current moment. A similar argumentation could be performed for the connection of video demand usage and the importance of data security for online gaming services. The authors cannot identify a meaningful influence of this perception on the usage of video on demand. Therefore, this result will not be considered in this paper. The above mentioned possible negative relations between IM and SM and e-learning and online gaming cannot be supported. Therefore, it can be concluded that the above-mentioned correlations depend on third unknown factors.

Consequently, the authors only find few regressive relationships between perceived data security, perceived importance of data security and the usage of Internet services. In the whole consideration, the authors have to reject the hypotheses H2 and H3.

V. DISCUSSION

The analysis within this paper considers how the test persons evaluate the importance of data security.

As mentioned above, nearly 70% of the interviewed persons have indicated that they do change their password less than once a year. It can be expected that they more or less never change their primary passwords.

From this point of view, the authors conclude: (1) the most people are not aware of the importance of data security and the safety of their personal data or they do not care about the possible risks, or (2) they do not understand the relation between the password changing behavior and the data security. The authors assume that the people (a) do not care about, (b) are not aware of the consequences, or (c) are too lazy to take care about these issues.

The majority of nearly 85% uses anti-virus programs to protect their devices. However, in the most cases (round about 70%) people are not willing to pay money for security of their devices. However, the people do not take care about that normally the free version of an anti-virus program has a smaller program scope and possibly some necessary elements for the protection of the devices are not implemented.

This paper examines the influence of the perception and importance of data security regarding the usage of Internet services, especially mobile Internet services.

The presented findings in the previous chapter indicate that a general interrelation between the perception of data security, data security importance and the usage of Internet services cannot be found. However, in the consideration of single services and their perception and importance of data securities, some positive and negative regressions could be found. But often the natural service data perception does not fit with the usage of the service (see Tables IV and V). The missing connections support the absence of direct relationships between the analyzed variables. Therefore, the authors have to reject all hypotheses in general.

Though, the particular single relations between the usage and the perception/importance of data security of the specific services could induce that a possible relation between these variables exist. The data security of email services seems to be the most important factor for customers. Since the overall data security of the customers is essentially influenced by their assessment of the data security of emails as well as the significance of this data security. These lead to the conclusion that if customers feel a higher email security they will use more Internet services (independent of the infrastructure). This relation is supported by the fact that people on a fixed-line connection often communicate via emails. In contrast to the fixed-line usage, mobile instant messaging takes the same position as the explained email services importance for the fixed-line infrastructures. Based on the fact that a lot of people use instant messengers like WhatsApp, Facebook Messenger, Line and others per mobile phone, obviously the services with highest importance also gain the highest data security importance. Other possible variables and services can also have an influence but further research would be needed.

Hence, the authors do not reject the hypotheses completely. It can be noted that the perceived data security for emails significantly influences the general perception of data security. However, the previous findings indicate that further research is necessary. The comparison of fixed with mobile Internet usage in connection with estimation of data security does not yield useful results.

TABLE X. Regression Analysis of Usage, Data Security and Data Security Importance of Internet Services in the Fixed-Line Network.

Services Fixed-Line Usage	Test of Perceived Security Importance	Test of Perceived Data Security
Usage Email	Dependent Variable: Usage of Email Services Independent Variable: Data Security Importance of Email Services Regression: $p<0.05$ R-square = 8.7% Coefficient = 0.114 VIF<3	No Significance
Usage Online Telephony	Dependent Variable: Usage of Online Telephony Independent Variable: Data Security Importance of Email Services Regression: $p<0.05$ R-square = 10.8% Coefficient = 0.096 VIF<3	No Significance
Usage Video on Demand	Dependent Variable: Usage of Video on Demand Independent Variable: Data Security Importance of Cloud Services Regression: $p<0.05$ R-square = 10.8% Coefficient = 0.062 VIF<3	No Significance
Usage IPTV	No Significance	No Significance
Usage Online Shopping	Dependent Variable: Usage of Online Shopping Independent Variable: Data Security Importance of Email Services Regression: $p<0.05$ R-square = 10.2% Coefficient = 0.103 VIF<3	No Significance
Usage Cloud_ Computing	No Significance	No Significance
Usage Social Media	No Significance	No Significance
Usage E-Learning	No Significance	No Significance
Usage Instant Messaging	Dependent Variable: Usage of Online Telephony Independent Variables: Data Security Importance of Online Banking and E-Government Services Regression: $p<0.05$ R-square = 9.8% Coefficient = 0.162 (Banking) Coefficient = 0.089 (Online Administration) VIF<3	No Significance
Usage Online Gaming	No Significance	No Significance
Usage Navigation	No Significance	No Significance

Therefore, no significant differences in the usage or in the perception of data security can be found. The authors do not find a significant connection between the perception of data security in general and in particular (regarding the specific services). The presented literature, which discloses different significant connections between the perceived trust/perceived risk and the behavioral intention to use mobile payments and mobile banking, show significantly better results. In comparison to these findings, the authors aim to explain how the discrepancy between the own and external results can be comprehended. One possible difference in the results bases on the importance of data security. The different questions for data security importance possibly inhibit the significance of the perception of data security. The results for the perceived security could be therefore affected and overwhelmed by the concept of data security importance. Secondly, the TAM and UTAUT2 normally use the external variables as impact factors for the behavioral intention to use [12][13][14]. The adaptation of the model with a direct influence of perceived security and user behavior can possibly lead to the discrepancies. It must be considered that this relation possibly does not exist. Furthermore, the authors did not include questions to prove the other concepts of the TAM and the UTAUT2 in the questionnaire, which would possibly be able to support the findings of the data security analysis.

Thirdly, the combined consideration of the influence on multiple mobile services, which all have different conditions and customer evaluations in direction of data security, user-friendliness and technical requirements poses the problems of potentially not being able to examine all factors in one analysis.

TABLE XI. Regression Analysis of Usage, Data Security and Data Security Importance of Internet Services in the Mobile Network.

Services Mobile Usage	Test of Perceived Security Importance	Test of Perceived Data Security
Usage Email	No Significance	No Significance
Usage Online Telephony	Dependent Variable: Usage of Online Telephony Independent Variable: Data Security Importance of Email Services Regression: $p<0.05$ R-square = 10.2% Coefficient = -0.136 VIF<3	No Significance
Usage Video on Demand	Dependent Variable: Usage of Video on Demand Independent Variable: Data Security Importance of Online Gaming Services Regression: $p<0.05$ R-square = 8.6% Coefficient = 0.095 VIF<3	No Significance
Usage IPTV	No Significance	No Significance
Usage Online Shopping	No Significance	No Significance
Usage Cloud Computing	No Significance	No Significance
Usage Social Media	Dependent Variable: Usage of Social Media Independent Variable: Data Security Importance of Instant Messaging Services Regression: $p<0.05$ R-square = 13.5% Coefficient = 0.101 VIF<3	No Significance
Usage E-Learning	Dependent Variable: Usage of E-Learning Independent Variables: Data Security Importance of Instant Messaging and Online Gaming Services Regression: $p<0.05$ R-square = 18.9% Coefficient = -0.154 (IM) Coefficient = -0.111 (Gaming) VIF<3	No Significance
Usage Instant Messaging	Dependent Variable: Usage of Instant Messaging Independent Variables: Data Security Importance of Instant Messaging Regression: $p<0.05$ R-square = 10.0% Coefficient = 0.056 VIF<3	No Significance
Usage Online Gaming	No Significance	No Significance
Usage Navigation	No Significance	Dependent Variable: General Data Security Independent Variables: Data Security Importance of Navigation Regression: $p<0.05$ R-square = 10.0% Coefficient = 0.042 VIF<3

The fourth issue could be that the test persons, who are mainly between 20 and 29 years old, are very affine in the usage of mobile services and possibly do not take care very much for data security. Due to their affinity, the people use the services and increase their experience. In connection to the explanations in the literature review, an increased experience can lead to a higher behavioral intention. Furthermore, the overrepresentation of this age group also influences significantly the whole results of the survey. If other age groups would have nearly the same proportion on test persons, the results could be quite different.

Furthermore, more experience will diminish possible uncertainties and risk with usage of the different mobile services. The last issue could be found in the questions of the survey, because some of the questions are not suitable to generate the desired information concerning the presented concepts.

Therefore, the authors have decided to collect all these open issues to improve the own research and to carry out another survey. The shortly explained open issues and different possible improvements for a second survey will be presented in the following section.

VI. IMPROVEMENTS AND FURTHER APPROACH

Generally, the presented results cannot fully describe the influence of data security issues on the usage of specific Internet services. However, the results enable finding a general perception of data security on the usage of specific Internet services. Nevertheless, the perception of data security respective of single services has shown that an influence of data security issues on the usage of specific Internet services can be comprehended.

However, the first survey has to be seen as a pre-test as some questions do not lead to the aimed findings and cannot illustrate possible relationships. To reach better results for the examination of the named concepts, the authors will do a second survey. The second questionnaire will include some improvements to get closer to the perception of perceived credibility, perceived security, initial trust and firms' reputation. Especially the firms' reputation will be important, because researches found out that reputation increases trust in mobile banking [40][44][73][74]. This relation may also fit in the consideration of the usage of other services. These implications can be used for the estimations of the relation between trust and the usage of mobile Internet services.

Based on the findings that (a) the perceived credibility and (b) the initial trust will play a major role if customers decide to use a system or service, the authors will include these two components in the consisting model. In consideration of the presented problem, perceived credibility will cover the questions how the customers estimate and perceive reliability of the fixed and mobile Internet network, services and content providers.

As mentioned above, perceived credibility covers (a) the users' beliefs that the used systems would be free of threats for privacy and security and (b) their according attitudes, which is known to positively influence the behavioral intention to use the systems [17][20]. The authors relate to the perceived credibility with the initial trust, as known through the literature.

Based on this relationship, initial trust indicates how the customers feel their data safe by the providers based on the estimation of the questions to perceived credibility. To support these findings, the concepts of perceived data security and perceived importance of data security will be related with initial trust too. On the base of the literature, the authors adapt the previous model in the way that they relate initial trust directly to the use behavior of an Internet services, instead of the behavioral intention to use.

Besides the analysis of the relationships in the TAM, the improvements are necessary to closer analyze the issues of data security and trust from the perspective of the UTAUT2. The questions need to be tailored to the findings of perceived credibility which shall support the previous findings of perceived security. This approach is needed to prioritize the focus on the consumer perspective instead of an organizational perspective. Nevertheless, the main focus of this work is to examine the influence of data security in general and in relation to the single services. Here, the authors examine the user perception of data security regarding single Internet services. This approach also enables the analysis of the difference between the general and single service perception of data security.

Therefore, the other concepts like perceived ease of use, performance expectancy, social influence, habit, effort expectancy, trust propensity, and structural assurance are not considered in detail [12][13][14]. As described above, the focus of the research and the analysis is on the concepts of perceived credibility, perceived security, initial trust and firms' reputation.

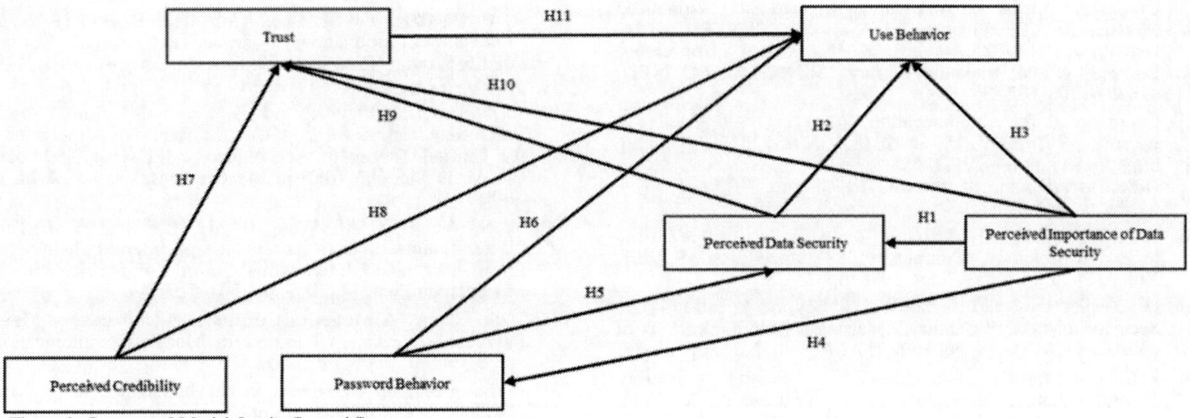

Figure 2. Conceptual Model for the Second Survey

This approach could possibly lead to reduced results and information from the second survey, due to the issue that the authors do not include the other used concepts from the UTAUT2 and the TAM. But the authors try to focus on the assessment of the single influence of data security (regarding trust and credibility) on the customer usage of Internet services.

The authors are aware of the fact that this approach might not lead to the aimed results, due to the small number of considered concepts and the non-observance of moderators.

In contrast to the first survey, the second survey includes the frequency of Internet services usage. Here, the authors share the opinion that this approach gives a better overview of the usage of services and possibly how data security issues impact the frequency of usage.

In order to cover the perceived credibility about the used system, in this paper the fixed and mobile telecommunication networks, the second survey includes questions about how the customers perceive the security of the infrastructure and how the network operators use the gained data from the customer. These questions should also cover how the customers perceive that the infrastructure is free of risks. Furthermore, the customer estimation of the network operators enables a possible assessment of enterprises' trustworthiness and adhere the accepted rules from customer perspective [75]. Consequently, the authors are testing the concepts from TAM and UTAUT2 in combined questions.

Finally, the difference to the previous study will be underlined by the analysis of other impact factors like culture values and traditions. The general idea of this paper should be to examine a relationship between the perception of data security and usage of Internet services, especially of mobile Internet services.

REFERENCES

[1] E. Massarczyk, and P. Winzer, "Influence of the perception of data security on customer usage of internet services," In L. Berntzen, & S. Böhm (Eds.), The Ninth International Conference on Advances in Human oriented and Personalized Mechanisms, Technologies, and Services (CENTRIC 2016, IARIA) [21. - 25. August 2016, Rome]. Conference Proceedings and Thinkmind Library (ISSN: 2308-3492, ISBN: 978-1-61208-502-9).

[2] International Telecommunication Union (ITU), "ICT Facts & Figures – The world in 2015," May 2015, [Online]. https://www.itu.int/en/ITU-D/Statistics/Documents/facts/ICTFactsFigures2015.pdf, retrieved 2016.07.11.

[3] P. W. Dowd and J. T. McHenry, "Network Security: It's Time to Take It Seriously," Computer (1998), vol. 31, issue 9, IEEE Xplore Digital Library, Sept. 1998, pp. 24-28.

[4] D. Desai, "Law and Technology – Beyond Location: Data Security in the 21st Century," Magazine Communications of the ACM (2013), vol. 56, issue 1, ACM, Jan. 2013, pp. 34-36.

[5] F. S. Ferraz and C. A. Guimarães Ferraz, "Smart City Security Issues: Depicting Information Security Issues in the Role of a urban environment," 7th International Conference on Utility and Cloud Computing, IEEE/ACM, 2014, pp. 842-846.

[6] S. Dhawan, K. Singh, and S. Goel, "Impact of Privacy Attitude. Concern and Awareness on Use of Online Social Networking," 5th International Conference - Confluence The Next Generation Information Technology Summit 2013, IEEE Xplore Digital Library, Sept. 2014, pp. 14-17.

[7] D. Malandrino, V. Scarano, and R. Spinelli, "How Increased Awareness Can Impact Attitudes and Behaviors Toward Online Privacy Protection," International Conference on Social Computing (Social Com), IEEE Xplore Digital Library, Sept. 2013, pp. 57-62.

[8] A. N. Joinson. U.-D. Reips, T. Buchanan, and C. B. Paine Schofield, "Privacy, Trust, and Self-Disclosure Online," Human-Computer Interaction, vol. 25, no. 1, 2010, pp. 1-24.

[9] B. Krishnamurthy, K. Naryshkin, and C. Wills, "Privacy Leakage vs. Protection Measures: the Growing Disconnect," in Web 2.0 Security and Privacy Workshop, 2011, pp. 1-10.

[10] D. Nayak, N. Rajendran, D. B. Phatak, and V. P. Gulati, "Security Issues in Mobile Data Networks," Vehicular Technology Conference (VTC 2004), vol. 5, IEEE Xplore Digital Library, Sept. 2004, pp. 3229-3233.

[11] Q. Tan and F. Pivot, "Big Data Privacy: Changing Perception of Privacy, International Conference on Smart City/SocialCom/SustainCom," IEEE Xplore Digital Library, 2015, pp. 860-865.

[12] F. D. Davis, "Perceived Usefulness, Perceived Ease of Use, and User Acceptance of Information Technology," MIS Quarterly, vol. 13, 1989, pp. 318-340.

[13] F. D. Davis, R. P. Bagozzi, and P. R. Warshaw, "User Acceptance of Computer Technology: a Comparison of Two Theoretical Models," Management Science, Vol. 35, 1989, pp. 982-1003.

[14] V. Venkatesh, J. Y. L. Thong, and X. Xin, "Consumer Acceptance and Use of Information Technology: Extending the Unified Theory of Acceptance and Use of Technology," MIS Quarterly, vol. 36, issue 1, 2012, pp. 157-178.

[15] V. Venkatesh, M. G. Morris, G. B. Davis, and F. D. Davis, "User Acceptance of Information Technology: Toward a Unified View," MIS Quarterly, vol. 27, issue 3, 2003, pp. 425-478.

[16] S. A. Brown, and V. Venkatesh, "Model of Adoption of Technology in the Household: A Baseline Model Test and Extension Incorporating Household Life Cycle," MIS Quarterly, vol. 29, issue 4, 2005, pp. 399-426.

[17] F.-T. Lin, H.-Y. Wu, and T. T. Nguyet Nga, "Adoption of Internet Banking: An Empirical Study in Vietnam," 10th International Conference on e-Business Engnineering, IEEE Xplore Digital Library, 2013, pp. 282-287.

[18] R. P. Bagozzi, and K. Lee, "Consumer Resistance to, and Acceptance of Innovations," Advances in Consumer Research, vol. 26, Provo,UT: Association for Consumer Research, 1999, pp. 218–225.

[19] T. Escorbar-Rodriguez, and E. Carvajal-Trujillo, "Online Purchasing Tickets for Low Cost Carriers: An Application of the Unified Theory of Acceptance and Use of Technology (UTAUT) Model," Tourism Management, vol. 43, 2014, pp. 70-88.

[20] Y. S. Wang, Y. M. Wang, H. H. Lin, and T. I. Tang, "Determinants of User Acceptance of Internet Banking: an Empirical Study," International Journal of Service Industry Management, vol. 14, 2003, pp. 501-519.

[21] L.-D. Chen, "A Model of Consumer Acceptance of Mobile Payment," International Journal of Mobile Communications, vol. 6, issue 1, 2008, pp. 32-52.

[22] J. Zhong, A. Dhir, M. Nieminen, M. Hämäläinen, and J. Laine, "Exploring Consumer Adoption of Mobile Payments in China," Academic Mind Trek'13, 2013, pp. 318-325.

[23] R. De Sena Abrahao, S. N. Moriguchi, and D. F. Andrade, "Intention of Adoption of Mobile Payment: An Analysis in the Light of the Unified Theory of Acceptance and Use of

Technology (UTAUT)," Innovation and Management Review, vol. 13, 2016, pp. 221-230.

[24] D. H. McKnight, L. L. Cummings, and N. L. Chervany, "Initial Trust Formation in New Organizational Relationships," Academy of Management Review, vol. 23, 1998, pp. 473-490.

[25] D. H. McKnight, V. Choudhury, and C. Kacmar, "The Impact of Initial Consumer Trust on Intentions to Transact with a Web Site: a Trust Building Model," The Journal of Strategic Information Systems , vol. 11, 2002, pp. 297-323.

[26] T. Zhou, "Understanding Mobile Internet Continuance Usage from the Perspectives of UTAUT and Flow," Information Development vol. 27, 2011, pp. 207-218.

[27] T. Zhou, Y. Lu, and B. Wang, "Integrating TTF and UTAUT to Explain Mobile Banking User Adoption," Computers in Human Behavior, vol. 26, 2010, 760–767.

[28] T. Zhou, "An Empirical Examination of Initial Trust in Mobile Banking," Information Development, vol. 21, issue 5. 2011, pp. 527-540.

[29] A. Y. L., Chong, "Understanding Mobile Commerce Continuance Intentions: An Empirical Analysis of Chinese Consumers," Journal of Computer Information Systems, 2013.

[30] A. Zmijewska, E. Lawrence, R., and R. Steele, "Towards Understanding of Factors Influencing User Acceptance of Mobile Payment Systems," In: Proceedings of the IADIS WWW/Internet, Madrid, Spain, 2004.

[31] T. Dahlberg, and A. Öörni, "Understanding Changes in Consumer Payment Habits - Do Mobile Payments and Electronic Invoices Attract Consumers?," In: 40th Annual Hawaii International Conference on System Sciences (HICSS), 2007, pp. 50.

[32] P. G. Schierz, O. Schilke, and B. W. Wirtz, "Understanding Consumer Acceptance of Mobile Payment Services: An Empirical Analysis," Electronic Commerce Research and Applications, vol. 9, issue 3, 2010, pp. 209-216.

[33] C. Kim, W. Tao, N. Shin, and K. S. Kim, "An Empirical Study of Customers' Perceptions of Security and Trust in E-Payment Systems," Electronic Commerce Research and Applications, vol. 9, issue 1, 2010, pp. 84-95.

[34] K. Yang, "Exploring Factors Affecting the Adoption of Mobile Commerce in Singapore," Telematics and Informatics, vol. 22 issue 3, 2005, pp. 257-277.

[35] J. Cheong, M. Cheol, and J. Hwang, "Mobile Payment Adoption in Korea," In: ITS 15th biennial conference, Berlin, Germany, 2002.

[36] T. Dahlberg, N. Mallat, and A. Öörni, "Consumer Acceptance of Mobile Payment Solutions," In: G.M. Giaglis (ed.), mBusiness 2003 – The Second International Conference on Mobile Business, Vienna, 2003, pp. 211-218.

[37] N. Mallat, "Exploring Consumer Adoption of Mobile Payments – a Qualitative Study," In: Presentation at Helsinki Mobility Roundtable, Helsinki, Finland, 2006.

[38] K. Pousttchi, and M. Zenker, "Current Mobile Payment Procedures on the German Market from the view of Customer Requirements," In: 14th International Workshop on Database and Expert Systems Applications, 2003, pp. 870-874.

[39] Y. Lu, S. Yang, P. Y. K. Chau, and Y. Cao, "Dynamics between the Trust Transfer Process and Intention to Use Mobile Payment Services: A Cross-Environment Perspective," Information & Management, vol. 48, issue 8, 2011, pp. 393-403.

[40] M. A. Mahfuz, L. Khanam, and W. Hu, "The Influence of Culture on M-Banking Technology Adoption: An Integrative Approach of UTAUT2 and ITM," 2016 Proceedings of PICMET'16: Technology Management for Social Innovation, 2016, pp. 70-88.

[41] X. Luo, H. Li, J. Zhang, and J. P. Shim, "Examining Multi-dimensional Trust and Multi-faceted Risk in Initial Acceptance of Emerging Technologies: an Empirical Study of Mobile Banking Services," Decision Support Systems, vol. 49, issue 2, 2010, pp. 222-234.

[42] H.-P. Lu, and P. Y.-J. Su, "Factors Affecting Purchase Intention on Mobile Shopping Websites," Internet Research, vol. 19, issue 4, 2009, pp. 442-458.

[43] G. Kim, B. Shin, and H. G. Lee, "Understanding dynamics between Initial Trust and Usage Intentions of Mobile Banking," Information Systems Journal, vol. 19, issue 3, 2009, pp. 283-311.

[44] Y.-H. Chen, and S. Barnes, S., "Initial trust and online buyer behavior," Industrial Management & Data Systems, vol. 107 issue 1, 2007, pp. 21-36.

[45] Y. Lu, Z. Deng, and B. Wang, "Exploring Factors Affecting Chinese Consumers' Usage of Short Message Service for Personal Communication," Information Systems Journal, vol. 20, issue 2, 2010, pp. 183-208.

[46] Y. M. Shin, S. C. Lee, B. Shin, and H. G. Lee, "Examining Influencing Factors of Post-Adoption Usage of Mobile Internet: Focus on the User Perception of Supplier-Side Attributes," Information Systems Frontier, vol. 12, issue 5, 2010, pp. 595-606.

[47] T. Oliveira, M. Faria, M. A. Thomas, and A. Popovic, "Extending the Understanding of Mobile Banking Adoption: When UTAUT meets TTF and ITM," International Journal of Information Management, vol. 34, 2014, pp. 689-703.

[48] S. S. Kim., and N. K. Malhotra, "A Longitudinal Model of Continued IS Use: An Integrative View of Four Mechanisms Underlying Post-Adoption Phenomena," Management Science vol. 51, issue 5, 2005, pp. 741-755.

[49] P. Gerrard, and J. Barton Cunningham, "The Diffusion of Internet Banking Channels: Young Consumers' View," International Journal of Bank Marketing, vol. 21, 2003, pp. 16-28.

[50] H. Hsin Chang, and S. Wen Chen, "The Impact of Online Store Environment cues on Purchase Intention: Trust and Perceived Risk as a Mediator," Online Information Review, vol. 32, 2008, pp. 818-841.

[51] P. A. Pavlou, and D. Gefen, "Building Effective Online Marketplaces with Institution-based Trust," Information Systems Research, vol. 15, 2004, pp. 37-59.

[52] A. P. Pavlou, and M. Fygenson, "Understanding and Predicting Electronic Commerce Adoption: An Extension of the Theory of Planned Behavior," MIS Quarterly, 2006, pp. 115-143.

[53] P. B. Lowry, A. Vance, G. Moody, B. Beckman, and A. Read, "Explaining and Predicting the Impact of Branding Alliances and Website Quality on Initial Consumer Trust of E-Commerce Websites," Journal of Management Information Systems, vol. 24, issue 4, 2008.

[54] A. Diekmann, "Empirical Social Research,“ [German] "Empirische Sozialforschung,“ Reinbek / Hamburg, Rowohlt-Taschenbuch-Verlag, vol. 5, 2011.

[55] J. Bortz and N. Döring, "Research Methods and Evaluations,“ [German] "Forschungsmethoden und Evaluation: für Human- und Sozialwissenschaftler,“ Heidelberg, Springer-Medizin-Verlag, vol. 4, 2009.

[56] M. Kaya, "Data Collection Procedure“, [German] "Verfahren der Datenerhebung,“ in Albers, S./Klapper, D./Konradt, U./Walter, A./Wolf, J. (Hrsg.): Methodik der empirischen Forschung, Wiesbaden, Gabler, vol. 3, 2013, pp. 49-64.

[57] R. Likert, "A Technique for the Measurement of Attitudes," Archives of Psychology, 1932, pp. 199-224.

[58] Destatis, Statistisches Bundesamt, "Population,“ [German] "Bevölkerung,“ [Online] https://www.destatis.de/DE/ZahlenFakten/GesellschaftStaat/B

evoelkerung/Bevoelkerungsstand/Tabellen_/lrbev01.html, 2015, retrieved 2017.02.11.

[59] Statista, "Internet Users in Germany from 2001 to 2015," [German] "Anteil der Internetnutzer in Deutschland in den Jahren 2001 bis 2015," [Online]http://de.statista.com/statistik/daten/studie/13070/umfrage/entwicklung-der-internetnutzung-in-deutschland-seit-2001/, 2015, retrieved 2017.02.12.

[60] Statista, "Customers without Anti-Virus Protection," [German], "Anteil der Verbraucher ohne aktives Antivirenprogramm in ausgewählten Ländern weltweit," https://de.statista.com/statistik/daten/studie/226942/umfrage/anteil-der-verbraucher-ohne-aktives-antivirenprogramm/, 2017, retrieved 2017.02.12.

[61] L. J. Cronbach, "Coefficient Alpha and the Internal Structure of Tests," Psychometrika, vol. 16, 1951, pp. 297-334.

[62] C. Fornell, and D. Larcker, "Evaluating Structural Equation Models with Unobservable Variables and Measurement Error," Journal of Marketing Research, vol. 18, issue 1, 1981, pp. 39-50.

[63] R. Hossiep, "Cronbachs Alpha," [German] "Cronbachs Alpha," In Wirtz, M. A. (editor): Dorsch – Lexikon der Psychologie, vol. 17. Verlag Hans Huber, Bern, 2014.

[64] J. F. J. Hair, R. E. Anderson, R. L. Tatham, and W. C. Black, "Multivariate Data Analysis," Macmillan, New York, NY, Macmillan, vol. 3, 1995.

[65] S. Fromm, "Data Analysis with SPSS Part 1," [German] "Datenanalyse mit SPSS für Fortgeschrittene," Arbeitsbuch, vol. 2, VS Verlag für Sozialwissenschaften, GWV Fachverlage GmbH, Wiesbaden, 2008.

[66] S. Fromm, "Data Analysis with SPSS Part 2," [German] "Datenanalyse mit SPSS für Fortgeschrittene 2: Multivariate Verfahren für Querschnittsdaten," Lehrbuch, vol. 1, VS Verlag für Sozialwissenschaften, Springer Fachmedien Wiesbaden GmbH, Wiesbaden 2010.

[67] N. M. Schöneck, and W. Voß, "Research Project," [German] "Das Forschungsprojekt – Planung, Durchführung und Auswertung einer quantitativen Studie," vol. 2. Springer Verlag, Wiesbaden, 2013

[68] A. Field, "Discovering Statistics Using SPSS," Sage Publications Ltd., vol. 4, 2013.

[69] S. Hagl, „Fast Entry in SPSS", [German], "Schnelleinstieg Statistik," Rudolf Haufe Verlag, vol. 1, München, 2008.

[70] F. Brosius, "SPSS 8 Professional Statistics in Windows," [German] "SPSS 8 Professionelle Statistik unter Windows," Kapitel 21 Korrelation, International Thomson Publishing, vol. 1, 1998.

[71] D. Lin, D. P. Foster, L. H. Ungar, Lyle, "VIF Regression: A Fast Regression Algorithm for Large Data," Journal of the American Statistical Association, vol. 106, 2011.

[72] S. Petter, D. W. Straub, and A. Rai, "Specifying Formative Constructs in Information Systems Research," MIS Quarterly, vol. 31, issue 4, 2007, pp. 623-656.

[73] C. Flavian, M. Guinaliu, and E. Torres, "The Influence of Corporate Image on Consumer Trust – a Comparative Analysis in Traditional Versus Internet Banking," Internet Research, vol. 15 issue 4, 2005, pp. 447-470.

[74] M. A. Fuller, M. A. Serva, and J. Benamati, "Seeing is Believing: the Transitory Influence of Reputation Information on E-Commerce Trust and Decision Making," Decision Sciences, vol. 38, issue 4, 2007, pp. 675-699.

[75] D. Gefen, and D. David, "Reflections on the Dimensions of Trust and Trustworthiness among Online Consumers," Database for Advances in Information Systems, vol. 33, issue 3, 2002, pp. 38-53

Appendix 1. Adapted UTAUT2 following [14][15][19]

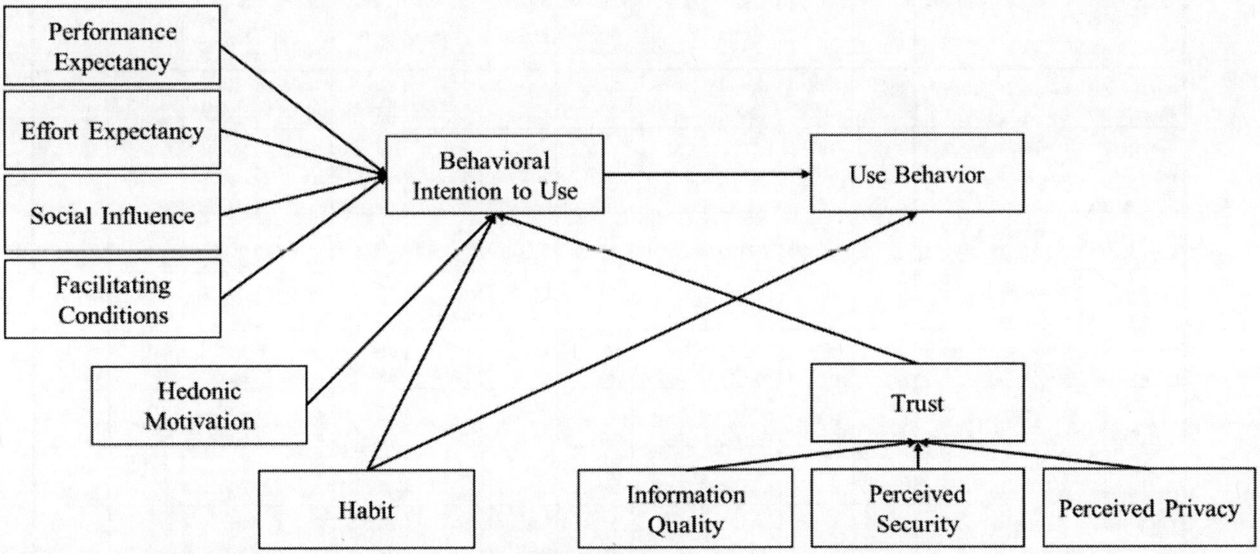

Source: Venkatesh et al., and Escorbar-Rodriguez and Carvajal-Trujillo [14][15][19]

Appendix 2. Correlation Analysis of Data Security Perceptions of all Considered Services.

		Data Security	Data Security Email	Data Security Online Telephony	Data Security Social Media	Data Security Online Shopping	Data Security Online Banking	Data Security Cloud Compu-ting	Data Security Online Gaming	Data Security IM	Data Security Down-loads	Data Security E-Learning	Data Security Admin-istration
Data Security Email	Correlation by Pearson	.025	1	.593**	.435**	.546**	.398**	.427**	.290**	.388**	.365**	.330**	.400**
	Sign. (2-sided)	.607		.000	.000	.000	.000	.000	.000	.000	.000	.000	.000
Data Security Online Telephony	Correlation by Pearson	-.043	.593**	1	.485**	.305**	.191**	.263**	.355**	.504**	.353**	.358**	.385**
	Sign. (2-sided)	.383	.000		.000	.000	.000	.000	.000	.000	.000	.000	.000
Data Security Social Media	Correlation by Pearson	-.072	.435**	.485**	1	.381**	.259**	.390**	.204**	.601**	.412**	.275**	.276**
	Sign. (2-sided)	.163	.000	.000		.000	.000	.000	.001	.000	.000	.000	.000
Data Security Online Shopping	Correlation by Pearson	-.029	.546**	.305**	.381**	1	.521**	.343**	.213**	.197**	.367**	.264**	.369**
	Sign. (2-sided)	.560	.000	.000	.000		.000	.000	.001	.000	.000	.000	.000
Data Security Online Banking	Correlation by Pearson	-.099	.398**	.191**	.259**	.521**	1	.467**	-.004	.130*	.177**	.041	.160**
	Sign. (2-sided)	.054	.000	.000	.000	.000		.000	.947	.014	.001	.462	.005
Data Security Cloud Comp	Correlation by Pearson	.003	.427**	.263**	.390**	.343**	.467**	1	.438**	.249**	.321**	.345**	.400**
	Sign. (2-sided)	.954	.000	.000	.000	.000	.000		.000	.000	.000	.000	.000
Data Security Online Gaming	Correlation by Pearson	.041	.290**	.355**	.204**	.213**	-.004	.438**	1	.244**	.441**	.572**	.486**
	Sign. (2-sided)	.527	.000	.000	.001	.001	.947	.000		.000	.000	.000	.000
Data Security IM	Correlation by Pearson	-.059	.388**	.504**	.601**	.197**	.130*	.249**	.244**	1	.427**	.264**	.287**
	Sign. (2-sided)	.251	.000	.000	.000	.000	.014	.000	.000		.000	.000	.000
Data Security Downloads	Correlation by Pearson	-.072	.365**	.353**	.412**	.367**	.177**	.321**	.441**	.427**	1	.440**	.364**
	Sign. (2-sided)	.155	.000	.000	.000	.000	.001	.000	.000	.000		.000	.000
Data Security E-Learning	Correlation by Pearson	-.016	.330**	.358**	.275**	.264**	.041	.345**	.572**	.264**	.440**	1	.705**
	Sign. (2-sided)	.776	.000	.000	.000	.000	.462	.000	.000	.000	.000		.000
Data Security Administration	Correlation by Pearson	-.020	.400**	.385**	.276**	.369**	.160**	.400**	.486**	.287**	.364**	.705**	1
	Sign. (2-sided)	.726	.000	.000	.000	.000	.005	.000	.000	.000	.000	.000	

**. Correlation p=0.01 (2-sided) significant. /*. Correlation p=0.05 (2-sided) significant.

Appendix 3. Correlation Analysis of Internet Services Usage in Fixed Infrastructures.

		Fix Usage Email	Fix Usage Surf	Fix Usage Online Telephony	Fix Usage Video on Demand	Fix Usage IPTV	Fix Usage Online Shopping	Fix Usage Cloud Compu-ting	Fix Usage Social Media	Fix Usage Video Telephony	Fix Usage E-Learn-ing	Fix Usage IM	Fix Usage Naviga-tion
Fix Usage Email	Correlation by Pearson	1	.705**	.550**	.550**	.222**	.508**	.530**	.538**	.432**	.590**	.201**	.324**
	Sign. (2-sided)		.000	.000	.000	.000	.000	.000	.000	.000	.000	.000	.000
Fix Usage Surf	Correlation by Pearson	.705**	1	.640**	.656**	.320**	.563**	.477**	.557**	.407**	.480**	.195**	.295**
	Sign. (2-sided)	.000		.000	.000	.000	.000	.000	.000	.000	.000	.000	.000
Fix Usage Online Telephony	Correlation by Pearson	.550**	.640**	1	.681**	.457**	.707**	.512**	.458**	.393**	.468**	.136*	.236**
	Sign. (2-sided)	.000	.000		.000	.000	.000	.000	.000	.000	.000	.014	.000
Fix Usage Video on Demand	Correlation by Pearson	.550**	.656**	.681**	1	.526**	.588**	.543**	.557**	.435**	.397**	.187**	.242**
	Sign. (2-sided)	.000	.000	.000		.000	.000	.000	.000	.000	.000	.000	.000
Fix Usage IPTV	Correlation by Pearson	.222**	.320**	.457**	.526**	1	.513**	.324**	.296**	.456**	.252**	.093	.177**
	Sign. (2-sided)	.000	.000	.000	.000		.000	.000	.000	.000	.001	.158	.007
Fix Usage Online Shopping	Correlation by Pearson	.508**	.563**	.707**	.588**	.513**	1	.364**	.480**	.399**	.442**	.186**	.301**
	Sign. (2-sided)	.000	.000	.000	.000	.000		.000	.000	.000	.000	.000	.000
Fix Usage Cloud Computing	Correlation by Pearson	.530**	.477**	.512**	.543**	.324**	.364**	1	.549**	.433**	.512**	.214**	.230**
	Sign. (2-sided)	.000	.000	.000	.000	.000	.000		.000	.000	.000	.000	.000
Fix Usage Social Media	Correlation by Pearson	.538**	.557**	.458**	.557**	.296**	.480**	.549**	1	.486**	.505**	.287**	.394**
	Sign. (2-sided)	.000	.000	.000	.000	.000	.000	.000		.000	.000	.000	.000
Fix Usage Video Telephony	Correlation by Pearson	.432**	.407**	.393**	.435**	.456**	.399**	.433**	.486**	1	.434**	.255**	.295**
	Sign. (2-sided)	.000	.000	.000	.000	.000	.000	.000	.000		.000	.000	.000
Fix Usage E-Learning	Correlation by Pearson	.590**	.480**	.468**	.397**	.252**	.442**	.512**	.505**	.434**	1	.257**	.361**
	Sign. (2-sided)	.000	.000	.000	.000	.001	.000	.000	.000	.000		.000	.000
Fix Usage IM	Correlation by Pearson	.201**	.195**	.136*	.187**	.093	.186**	.214**	.287**	.255**	.257**	1	.373**
	Sign. (2-sided)	.000	.000	.014	.000	.158	.000	.000	.000	.000	.000		.000
Fix Usage Navigation	Correlation by Pearson	.324**	.295**	.236**	.242**	.177**	.301**	.230**	.394**	.295**	.361**	.373**	1
	Sign. (2-sided)	.000	.000	.000	.000	.007	.000	.000	.000	.000	.000	.000	

**. Correlation p=0.01 (2-sided) significant. /*. Correlation p=0.05 (2-sided) significant.

Appendix 4. Correlation Analysis of Internet Services Usage in Mobile Infrastructures.

		Mobile Usage Email	Mobile Usage Surf	Mobile Usage Online Telephony	Mobile Usage Video on Demand	Mobile Usage IPTV	Mobile Usage Online Shopping	Mobile Usage Cloud Compu-ting	Mobile Usage Social Media	Mobile Usage Video Telephony	Mobile Usage E-Learn-ing	Mobile Usage IM	Mobile Usage Naviga-tion
Mobile Usage Email	Correlation by Pearson	1	.552**	.261**	.281**	.085	.361**	.217**	.370**	.272**	.417**	.243**	.444**
	Sign. (2-sided)		.000	.000	.000	.186	.000	.000	.000	.000	.000	.000	.000
Mobile Usage Surf	Correlation by Pearson	.552**	1	.306**	.411**	.154*	.409**	.208**	.371**	.260**	.372**	.217**	.467**
	Sign. (2-sided)	.000		.000	.000	.016	.000	.000	.000	.000	.000	.000	.000
Mobile Usage Online Telephony	Correlation by Pearson	.261**	.306**	1	.420**	.389**	.444**	.330**	.236**	.279**	.295**	.088	.208**
	Sign. (2-sided)	.000	.000		.000	.000	.000	.000	.000	.000	.000	.116	.000
Mobile Usage Video on Demand	Correlation by Pearson	.281**	.411**	.420**	1	.405**	.382**	.331**	.301**	.418**	.364**	.134*	.244**
	Sign. (2-sided)	.000	.000	.000		.000	.000	.000	.000	.000	.000	.012	.000
Mobile Usage IPTV	Correlation by Pearson	.085	.154*	.389**	.405**	1	.362**	.236**	.124	.358**	.177*	.030	.089
	Sign. (2-sided)	.186	.016	.000	.000		.000	.001	.062	.000	.016	649	.178
Mobile Usage Online Shopping	Correlation by Pearson	.361**	.409**	.444**	.382**	.362**	1	.386**	.335**	.398**	.338**	127*	.284**
	Sign. (2-sided)	.000	.000	.000	.000	.000		.000	.000	.000	.000	018	.000
Mobile Usage Cloud Computing	Correlation by Pearson	.217**	.208**	.330**	.331**	.236**	.386**	1	.200**	.352**	.358**	160**	.162**
	Sign. (2-sided)	.000	.000	.000	.000	.001	.000		.001	.000	.000	.008	.008
Mobile Usage Social Media	Correlation by Pearson	.370**	.371**	.236**	.301**	.124	.335**	.200**	1	.282**	.428**	368**	.447**
	Sign. (2-sided)	.000	.000	.000	.000	.062	.000	.001		.000	.000	.000	.000
Mobile Usage Video Telephony	Correlation by Pearson	.272**	.260**	.279**	.418**	.358**	.398**	.352**	.282**	1	.355**	.213**	.219**
	Sign. (2-sided)	.000	.000	.000	.000	.000	.000	.000	.000		.000	.000	.000
Mobile Usage E-Learning	Correlation by Pearson	.417**	.372**	.295**	.364**	.177*	.338**	.358**	.428**	.355**	1	.249**	.323**
	Sign. (2-sided)	.000	.000	.000	.000	.016	.000	.000	.000	.000		.000	.000
Mobile Usage IM	Correlation by Pearson	.243**	.217**	.088	.134*	.030	.127*	.160**	.368**	.213**	.249**	1	.481**
	Sign. (2-sided)	.000	.000	.116	.012	.649	.018	.008	.000	.000	.000		.000
Mobile Usage Navigation	Correlation by Pearson	.444**	.467**	.208**	.244**	.089	.284**	.162**	.447**	.219**	.323**	.481**	1
	Sign. (2-sided)	.000	.000	.000	.000	.178	.000	.008	.000	.000	.000	.000	

**. Correlation p=0.01 (2-sided) significant. /*. Correlation p=0.05 (2-sided) significant.

The CloudFlow Infrastructure for Multi-Vendor Engineering Workflows: Concept and Validation

Håvard Heitlo Holm*, Volkan Gezer†, Setia Hermawati‡, Christian Altenhofen§, and Jon M. Hjelmervik*
*Heterogeneous Computing Group
SINTEF Digital
Oslo, Norway
Emails: havard.heitlo.holm@sintef.no
and jon.m.hjelmervik@sintef.no
†Innovative Factory Systems (IFS)
German Research Center for Artificial Intelligence (DFKI)
Kaiserslautern, Germany
Email: volkan.gezer@dfki.de
‡Human Factors Research Group,
University of Nottingham,
Nottingham, United Kingdom,
Email: setia.hermawati@nottingham.ac.uk
§Interactive Engineering Technologies (IET),
Fraunhofer Institute for Computer Graphics Research IGD,
Darmstadt, Germany,
Email: christian.altenhofen@igd.fraunhofer.de

***Abstract*—In this paper, we present the CloudFlow Infrastructure, which aims to provide an independent platform for engineering workflows, leveraging both cloud and high performance computing. Each workflow can combine software from different vendors, promoting interoperability through open standards, and easy access to data and compute resources. Here, we focus on the technological uniqueness of the infrastructure, and how end users within the manufacturing industries have validated it for real world applications. We also describe how high performance computing and remote desktop applications easily are integrated in cloud-enabled workflows. The infrastructure provides an easy-to-use platform for software providers to offer their software in the cloud and get access to a new distribution channel. At the same time, small businesses get pay-as-you-go access to advanced multi-vendor software solutions that will improve their products.**

Keywords–Workflows; Cloud computing; HPC; Semantic descriptions; One-stop-shop.

I. Introduction

Cloud computing is currently becoming a natural part of the daily life, both for professionals and consumers. Users are already expecting to have access to all their data independent of which computer they are using, and they will soon expect the same behavior for advanced engineering tools. An ideal engineering workflow consists of software from different vendors, operating on the same data. A cloud platform that provides efficient and user-friendly workflows by combining different tools, is therefore needed to meet these expectations.

In manufacturing industries, different software suites are used across the lifetime of their products, including design, numerical analysis, quality assurance and maintenance. Furthermore, engineering software solutions are often computationally demanding and designed for parallel execution in a high performance computing (HPC) environment. Small and medium-sized enterprises (SMEs) in this market often find it too expensive to install the different solutions locally, due to hardware costs, installation overhead and license costs. This may cause loss in quality in their products due to insufficient analysis, and increased time to market and overly expensive design phases due to inefficient work procedures. For such companies, having access to a cloud solution that spans over different clouds and software providers, all integrated in tailored workflows, will not only save time and cost, but also improve their final products.

In this paper, we present the CloudFlow Infrastructure [1], [2], which is a cloud-based solution where users can execute workflows consisting of software from one or multiple vendors, providing ubiquitous access to compute resources, software and data. Workflow orchestration is made available through a workflow design tool, using semantic information associated to available software and its input and output data. Workflow execution is then automatically managed and monitored by a workflow execution tool, which acts upon these semantic descriptions. Data is passed automatically between the stages of the workflows, providing a seamless user experience. Through the use of open standards and cloud interfaces, interoperability between software from different vendors is obtained. The workflow is ignorant of the underlying operating systems, and whether simulations are executed in a cloud or HPC environment. The CloudFlow Infrastructure is not only attractive for end users, but also allows software vendors to reach new customers through a pay-per-use distribution channel for their existing or new software solutions.

In contrast to other approaches, the aim here is to integrate existing software solutions into one common platform, combining them to work together as multi-vendor workflows. Furthermore, the proposed solution supports installation in private clouds, as well as access to multiple cloud and HPC providers through one common web portal. To facilitate a broad selection of existing software solutions, the CloudFlow Infrastructure target cloud providers offering Infrastructure as a Service (IaaS), where software providers can install their own operating systems and fully control the virtual machines.

The private cloud option allows for deployment in environments without network communication to the outside world. This also opens up for companies that for security reasons require that data is stored within their computing facilities, can take advantage of the user-friendly multi-vendor workflows.

The CloudFlow Infrastructure has been continuously tested and evaluated by SME end-users in the manufacturing industries. The evaluation results have been used to improve the usability of the infrastructure, as well as the workflows developed by the software vendors. The validation has shown that the infrastructure is particularly useful for *engineering apps*. An engineering app is a design centric workflow that is applied to concrete artefacts such as pumps, structures, wings, etc., and is easily employed by end-users without domain knowledge nor experience with dedicated software tools. These apps makes it feasible for the involved manufacturing end-users to use more advanced technology than today, reducing design cost as well as time-to-marked. The involved software vendors and consultancy companies are given an opportunity to gain economic benefit through a partnership with an SME start-up that will offer engineering apps as a service. The technology behind the CloudFlow Infrastructure is not restricted to manufacturing industries, and can be applied to any other computationally intensive domain.

This paper is an extension and improvement of [1] with respect to end user validation of the infrastructure and its deployed software solutions; support for more advanced flow control in the workflows; and workflow integrated remote access to desktop applications executing in the cloud environment.

The paper is organized as follows: An overview of related work is given in Section II. The CloudFlow Infrastructure is then presented in Section III, where the focus is on the aspects and infrastructure components related to workflow orchestration and execution, resource monitoring, authentication, data storage, utilization of HPC clusters, and remote access to desktop applications. Section IV describes the methods for end user validation and discusses the validation results. A detailed example of a workflow running in the CloudFlow Infrastructure is given in Section V, before Section VI gives some concluding remarks and discusses the future of the infrastructure.

II. Related Work

Several providers currently deliver cloud-based engineering and computing solutions. One dedicated software vendor delivering such a solution is SimScale [3], offering simulators for computational fluid dynamics, finite element analysis and thermodynamics in the cloud. Based on these simulation tools and web-based visual pre- and post-processing, SimScale targets end users only. Combining their cloud solution with software developed by other vendors is therefore not straightforward.

The cloudSME project [4], [5] combines a business model targeting both end users and software vendors. Software vendors are offered a Platform as a Service (PaaS) solution, where they offer Software as a Service for their existing and new end users. This approach also makes it possible for end users to combine software from different software vendors to perform more complex engineering tasks. CloudSME does however not use any semantic information to orchestrate or combine the different software, and it lacks the use of HPC.

The Fortissimo and Fortissimo2 projects [6], [7] also offer a platform that supports business models for both end users and software vendors. They do however not target the cloud aspect, and mainly offer a platform where independent software vendors provide HPC simulations to end users. Similar to CloudSME, Fortissimo does not orchestrate combinations of different software based on semantic information.

There are several initiatives to simplify the process of deploying software in the Cloud. Ferry et al. [8] propose a modelling approach, where the cloud deployment is described by a vendor independent language CloudML. Deployment models are implemented in this language and can include descriptions of virtual machines, definitions of network communication, and instructions for service deployments. In addition to simplifying deployment of interconnected software, the language aims at helping their users avoid vendor lock-in.

Multiple approaches exist to gain remote access to software deployed in the Cloud. The platform-independent Virtual Network Computing (VNC) [9] and Microsoft's Remote Desktop Protocol (RDP) [10] are widely used to share applications across a local network or the internet. Both transmit images of the remotely running software or the remote machine's entire desktop, and receive the user's mouse and keyboard input for interaction. Network bandwidth and latency are crucial factors for a good user experience when using these technologies. Other techniques for remote visualization are, e.g., the Tinia framework [11] for interactive 3D data, or the Rixels approach for visualizing simulation results [12].

Stahl et al. [2] proposed the initial work and the main concepts of the CloudFlow Infrastructure. Among the newly introduced concepts are a unified way to access HPC resources, functionality to use external cloud providers, resource monitoring, and a graphical tool to define workflows.

Semantic Markup for Web Services (OWL-S) and *Business Process Execution Language* (BPEL) are two technologies that allow web service execution as processes. BPEL is a language for executing business processes with web services, as stated by Grolinger [13]. According to its specifications, BPEL executes web services defined using Web Service Description Language (WSDL). It supports orchestration of actions within such services, by structuring them as sequences and supporting branches and loops. The structure is described using a syntax based on Extensible Markup Language (XML). OWL-S is a markup that is built on top of Web Ontology Language (OWL) and describes web services semantically introducing an XML-based syntax. It also supports orchestration and due to semantic technologies, structuring the sequences using OWL-S is both machine and human understandable. OWL-S and WSDL are usually used to describe services based on the Simple Object Access Protocol (SOAP) specification. It allows web services to send requests in a predefined structure encoded in a XML format.

BPEL is similar to OWL-S in terms of orchestration and XML-based syntax, but it lacks utilizing semantic technologies. Therefore, making web services machine-understandable and automating them without user interaction is a non-trivial task using BPEL [14].

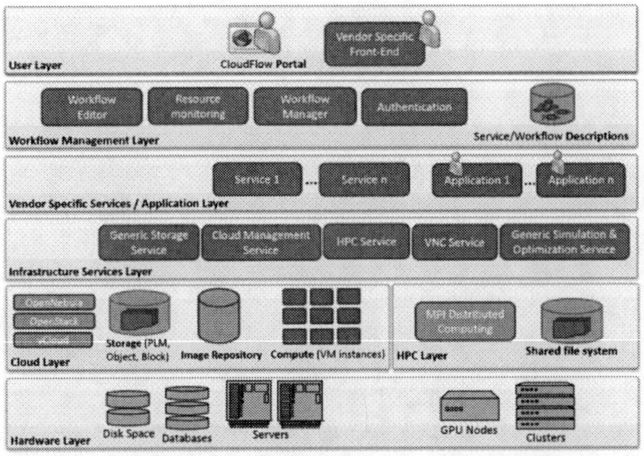

Figure 1. Simplified diagram of the system layers with their main components.

The process execution is usually performed by designing an execution order and monitoring it with an execution engine. There are several execution engines designed for this purpose. Execution engines, or managers, introduce an editor or a syntax to specify the order and then track the progress. Depending on the implementations, they can also provide user interface.

One of the available execution engines for BPEL is Process Manager by Oracle. It provides a graphical interface to manage cross-application business processes in a service oriented architecture (SOA) [15]. It also allows designing workflow steps and connecting external systems into the workflow. However, lack of semantic technologies inside BPEL prevents automation of these design steps. Involving semantic technologies will therefore increase the productivity by reducing the time needed to design the task steps, and is hence quite important.

To achieve the goal of CloudFlow, a manager that can facilitate semantic technologies, integrate web services from different providers and locations, and provide automation during the design and execution phase was necessary.

III. Architecture Overview

This section presents key components and concepts of the CloudFlow Infrastructure. The infrastructure can be described as a layered architecture, as shown in Figure 1. The layers represent different abstraction levels, and communication between layers is most often initiated in a downwards or sideways direction. In general, each layer consists of several loosely coupled components, where communication between the components is done through web services.

The *User Layer* is the user interface towards the CloudFlow Infrastructure, and is what the end user sees. This is typically the CloudFlow Portal, but can in principle be any application (e.g., web, mobile, desktop, etc.) that communicates with the components in the *Workflow Management Layer*. The workflow layer consists of components that are strictly needed for running any workflows in the infrastructure, and these components handle workflow management (Section III-A), resource monitoring (Section III-B), and authentication (Section III-C). The *Vendor Specific Services/Application Layer* contains all services that are executed as part of a workflow. Software provided and integrated into CloudFlow by independent software vendors belongs to this layer, and these services can only be accessed through the Workflow Manager. Components in the *Infrastructure Layer* are generic services that expose central functionality in the infrastructure. Some of the components can be used by services in the vendor specific service/application layer to access resources, such as cloud storage through the Generic Storage Services described in Section III-D. Other services can be used as individual workflow steps, such as the HPC and VNC Services described in Section III-E and Section III-F, respectively. All services mentioned above are deployed in the *Cloud Layer*, and the *HPC Layer* is available for executing computationally intensive applications. These layers yet again rely on the hardware found in the *Hardware Layer*.

A. Workflow Management

A workflow is an orchestrated and repeatable pattern of several activities enabled by the systematic organization of resources into processes that transform materials, provide services, or process information. Workflows may be as trivial as browsing a file structure and visualizing a Computer-Aided Design (CAD) model, or they can be more complex, including describing the full set of operations used to design, analyse and prepare a product for manufacturing. Semantic technologies, such as OWL-S, make it possible to design and automatically execute workflows.

As described in Section I, one of the main goals of CloudFlow is to host software from different software providers and chain appropriate parts of them to perform end user tasks in workflows within one common platform. In the following, we will describe how web services are integrated into the CloudFlow Infrastructure, and how workflows are designed and executed.

1) Services: A set of complementary reusable functionalities that are provided by a software for different purposes is called "service." More particularly, a web service is a software system designed to support interoperable machine-to-machine interaction over a network [16]. A web service invocation consists of a single request/response pair and is expected to execute in a short time.

The CloudFlow Infrastructure defines Application Programming Interfaces (APIs) that services have to follow in order to be integrated into the infrastructure and used within workflows. The services have to be exposed through a SOAP interface and defined by WSDL files. The simplest web services that follow those requirements are called *synchronous services*, and are used when their operations only take up to a few seconds to complete. In contrast, *asynchronous services* do not have any restrictions when it comes to execution times, and are suitable for long-running software executions without user interaction. For this kind of services, progress information is expected to be passed to the user through their service interface during the execution. Common for these two service types are that they represent operations that take predefined input parameters and generates output parameters without user interaction. Software designed for user interaction are made available as *applications*. Examples of applications are 3D CAD visualization software, web forms where users provide input parameters, and web interfaces to navigate in the cloud storage. Throughout this paper, the term *CloudFlow service* denotes services and applications compatible with the CloudFlow API.

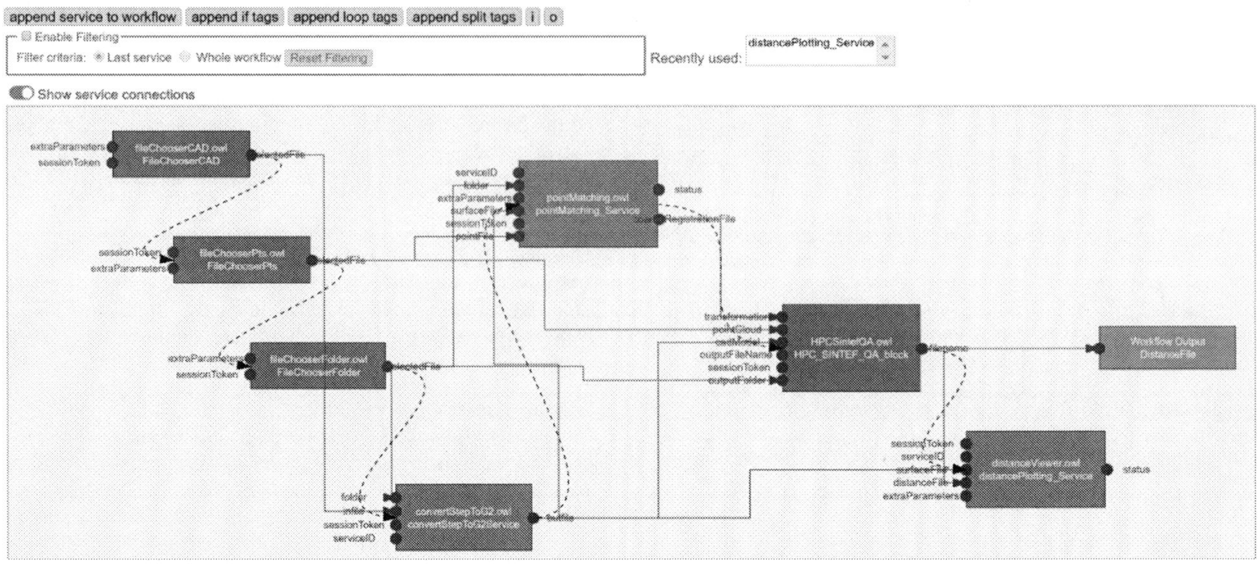

Figure 2. The graphical user interface of Workflow Editor displays buttons to append services and to add code snippets for conditional branches, loops, parallel service execution (split), etc., as well as options for service filtering. It also lets users add inputs and outputs to the workflow with appropriate buttons shown as I and O. The workflow is shown as a directed graph, where blue boxes represent single CloudFlow services, and dark green boxes are sub-workflows. The execution order is represented by the dotted arrows, while data flow is visualized by solid lines, which connect output parameters from services to be input parameters of others.

2) Workflow Definition: In order to transform a web service into a CloudFlow service, and then to create workflows from a chain of CloudFlow services, the web services need to be integrated into the CloudFlow Infrastructure. This integration is done using a tool named *Workflow Editor*.

Workflow Editor is a workflow modelling tool provided through both a graphical and textual interface [17] within the CloudFlow platform. It is based on XML, SOAP, and WSDL standards. In order to integrate web services into the CloudFlow Infrastructure, service providers submit the WSDL endpoints into a web form in Workflow Editor, and semantic descriptions are created, describing the services themselves and their input and output parameters. This information is then added to a semantic database, and the services can finally be used within workflow.

Workflows are created and edited through the textual and graphical editors of Workflow Editor. The data flow between services is defined by connecting outputs of services with inputs of others, using drag and drop functionality. The execution order is represented using dotted arrows and the data flow is visualized using solid lines, as shown in Figure 2. Based on the semantic description of a service, it is possible to find other services whose input parameters are semantically compatible with its output parameters. Semi-automatic orchestration of workflows is made available by letting the system suggest such compatible services to workflow designers.

All content in the graphical editor is also shown in an XML-based meta-formatted textual editor. The XML-based representation is sent to the Workflow Editor back-end, and contains all information required to save a workflow. This format is also sometimes preferred by experienced users. The textual and graphical editors are synchronized, so that each change made on a workflow in one of them is immediately reflected in the other.

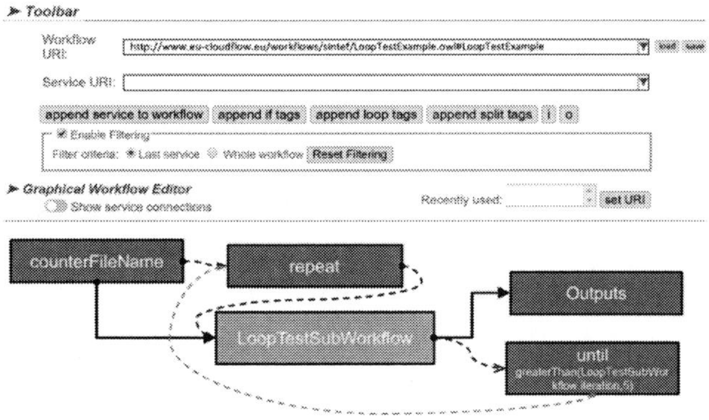

Figure 3. A simple example workflow for loop usage. The condition is modified by double clicking on the *until* block.

In earlier versions of the CloudFlow Infrastructure, all workflows were executed in a linear and sequential order [1]. However, it is sometimes desirable to design more complex workflows, where certain services are repeated, and different execution paths are triggered based on previous states. As non-sequential workflow execution was required by end users and software providers, support for conditional branches and loops have been added in the infrastructure. These functionalities are represented in the workflow design by the *If-Then-Else* and *Repeat-Until* OWL-S statements, respectively. In Workflow Editor, these expressions are adapted for simplification and compatibility with both the graphical and textual editor. The control of these expressions are handled via logical conditions such as *greaterThan*, *greaterOrEqual*, *equalTo*, etc., and they can be set by double clicking on the *if* or *repeat* blocks in Workflow Editor. Figure 3 shows a very simple workflow consisting of a loop which iteratively execute a sub-workflow.

In some cases, workflows contain services whose parameters do not depend on each other, allowing them to be executed in parallel. It is possible to design and execute workflows containing parallel execution of different services, by using the *split* statement of OWL-S. A current limitation, however, is that the user can only interact with one of the parallel branches, meaning that the parallel section can only have one branch which requires user interaction in the form of applications.

Even though each CloudFlow service typically represents an individual operation with dedicated input and output parameters, some services naturally belong together. Instead of having to connect the same sequence of services repeatedly for multiple different workflows, such services can be modelled as smaller workflows of their own, called *sub-workflows*. Sub-workflows can be added as a single component into any other workflows, similar to a regular CloudFlow service. The changes made within a sub-workflow are applied to all workflows using it, reducing time and effort for the workflow designer through avoiding a repetitive task.

3) Workflow Manager: The semantic descriptions created by Workflow Editor contain meta-data and describe how the data is bound. The component *Workflow Manager* is an execution tool acting on the semantic descriptions. It executes and monitors all services in a workflow providing the input parameters, as defined in Workflow Editor, either as constant values or outputs from previous services. The status of each asynchronous service is checked at regular intervals in order to determine if it is finished, and to present the service's status to the user. The Workflow Manager itself consists of a back-end, which is working in a Java Virtual Machine, and a web service front-end, with which the Portal communicates. A simplified communication diagram of the components in the Workflow Management Layer is shown in Figure 4.

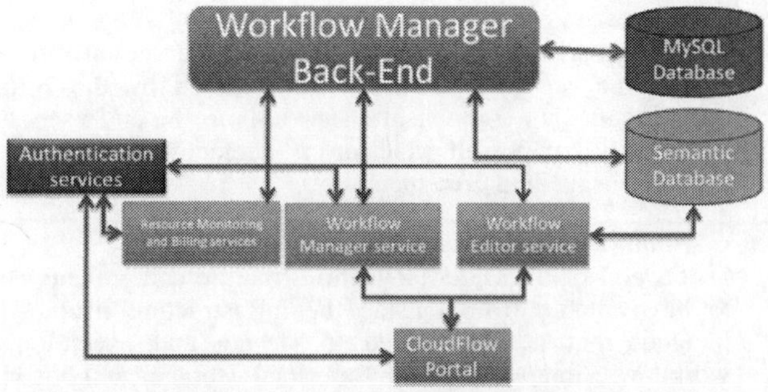

Figure 4. Simplified interaction between the components in the Workflow Management Layer in the CloudFlow Infrastructure.

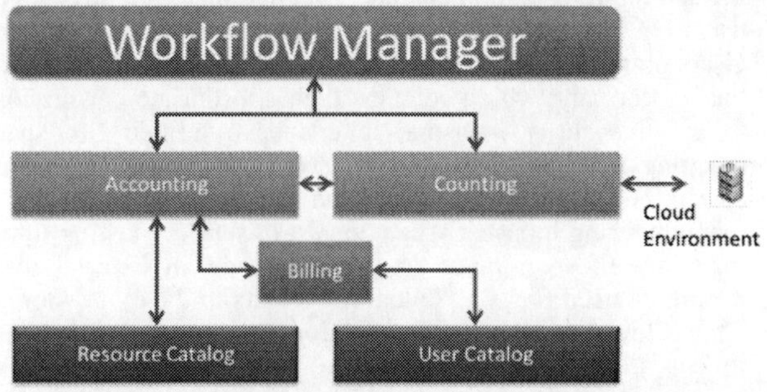

Figure 5. Communication between components related to billing and resource monitoring inside the CloudFlow Infrastructure. All components make additional calls to the Authentication services, which are not depicted.

The main access point for starting, monitoring and interacting with workflows, is through the CloudFlow Portal. The workflow execution, however, is independent from the Portal, and non-interactive CloudFlow services are automatically executed by the Workflow Manager back-end, even if the user leaves the client that initiated the workflow. If a workflow reaches an application, Workflow Manager waits for user interaction before continuing to the next service. Since workflow execution is independent from the Portal, users can also re-login on any device and still have access to all running workflows, continuing from their current stage. Workflow results are stored in a MySQL database by the Workflow Manager back-end, and are accessible for the users at any time.

In order to have access to a workflow, the end user needs to have valid licenses for all services within that workflow. Before every workflow execution, license validation is done by Workflow Manager towards the billing services. Workflow Manager also tracks execution times by utilizing resource monitoring components.

B. Resource Monitoring and Billing

To facilitate that CloudFlow becomes a one-stop-shop where software vendors integrate and offer their software for new customers, functionality to monitor the resource usage by each workflow and service is needed. Based on different requirements, the software vendors are able to use different business models, such as offering their software as pay-per-use, or for a fixed monthly or annual fee. For computationally intensive software requiring exclusive access to hardware resources, it is also natural to charge the end users based on the number of central processing unit (CPU) hours spent.

Each service within CloudFlow belongs to a *software package*. All license costs related to the software package are described in the *Resource Catalog* component, as either a time based license requirement, runtime cost, or a combination of both. The Resource Catalog also holds information about hardware costs and the vendors who will get paid from the revenue. Figure 5 illustrates how the different components are connected.

As a workflow is executed, the resources consumed through this workflow is gathered, and the related cost for running the workflow is calculated. Collection of this information and cost calculation is performed within the resource monitoring and billing components of the CloudFlow Infrastructure. When an end user starts a workflow, Workflow Manager lists all software packages within the workflow and checks with the *Accounting* service whether the user has the required licenses to run them. Later, if the user is allowed to execute the workflow, the *Counting* service is used to track the execution times delivered by Workflow Manager. This service passes these data back to the Accounting service to calculate the bill for CPU usage, as well as the software costs within the workflow.

The Resource Catalog holds a list of software and hardware/data centers, whereas the *User Catalog* keeps a list of organizations or users. The calculations and usage information at the end of each workflow are gathered by the *Billing* component. This component issues bills to the end users and is the only component which users interact with in order to get their usage and cost reports.

C. Authentication and Multi-Cloud

Several of the CloudFlow Infrastructure components need to be available from outside the infrastructure itself. This includes, but is not limited to, design and execution of workflows, interaction with the cloud storage, and viewing how much resources a user has spent. Since only registered users should be allowed to issue such requests, and since users should only have access to their own files and resource usage information, all web services within the CloudFlow Infrastructure need an authentication parameter identifying the user. For this, a token-based authentication system is used. Users obtain a token at login which represents them throughout the session, and which contains their appropriate permissions.

As a security measure, tokens have limited life spans, meaning that requests containing old tokens will be unsuccessful. However, workflows (and perhaps especially within manufacturing industries) can consist of services lasting longer than any lifespan given to tokens. Since an expired token cannot be used for, e.g., uploading results to the cloud storage, CloudFlow needs an authentication scheme that invalidates tokens after a certain time while allowing workflows of arbitrary lengths to have access to all required infrastructure components.

In order to support these requirements, the *Authentication services* are introduced to CloudFlow. These services build on top of OpenStack's Keystone component [18], and extend it with functionality to handle the challenge related to long lasting workflows. In addition, vendor lock-in towards OpenStack is avoided through these services. Changing the communication with Keystone, or replacing Keystone itself, will require changes in the implementation of the Authentication services only, while its API, and all components relying on the authentication, are kept unchanged.

The problem consisting of tokens expiring during workflow executions is solved by issuing and storing special *workflow tokens* in the Authentication services. Each time a workflow is started, such a token is created by combining the regular token with the ID of the workflow execution. This workflow token is stored in a database, along with other relevant information, and is passed to all services within the workflow. During validation, the regular token is checked first, but if it has expired, the workflow token is checked with the database. As long as the combination of the regular token and the execution ID is found and recognized by the database, the token is still marked as valid. A new regular and valid token, holding the same permissions as the original token, can then be generated based on the database entry. When the workflow later is finished or aborted, the special workflow token is deleted from the database, and thus invalidated.

As CloudFlow is not tied to any one cloud, it is possible to use multiple clouds for hosting CloudFlow services. One reason for doing this might be that customers are physically too far away from the main CloudFlow cloud, making a local cloud more attractive in terms of network costs and delays. Other reasons might be that alternative clouds might be cheaper, or equipped with hardware not available in the CloudFlow cloud, for example by offering more powerful processing resources.

The main challenge related to such solutions is authentication across the different clouds. The external clouds have their own authentication methods, and they are not necessarily compatible with those used in CloudFlow. Services that are written for multi-cloud settings should therefore be implemented with an additional external token parameter. The semantic information can then describe which cloud the external token should be authenticated against, and external authentication services can be added to such workflows. Such a service will provide a web form where the user can login to the external cloud, and where the external token is passed to the next steps in the workflow. The external token can also be stored in a cookie in the browser, so that if a valid token is already present, this token will be used and the users are spared from typing their username and password more often than necessary.

D. Cloud Storage

In order to follow the loosely coupled layered architecture design of the CloudFlow Infrastructure (see Figure 1), the interaction with the cloud storage is designed to be vendor independent. CloudFlow supports various storage solutions and different cloud storage solutions have different APIs. Therefore, a set of services exposing a unified API for all storage solutions available in CloudFlow is required. Further, in order to avoid unnecessary network cost and to avoid potential security issues, files need to be transferred directly between the cloud storage and the client, and not via an intermediate server. To support these requirements, the *Generic Storage Services* (GSS) have been developed.

The GSS exposes an API consisting of both SOAP and REpresentational State Transfer (REST) web services, and offers functionality for interacting with all cloud storage solutions available in CloudFlow. In contrast to SOAP, RESTful web services come with a smaller overhead and are better suited for transferring large amounts of data. All file transfers are therefore done through RESTful services. Each available storage solution is added as a back-end to GSS, and SOAP services provide information in the form of a pre-defined recipe, on how to use the native REST interfaces. The client then follows this recipe to transfer files directly to and from the cloud storage, with no additional overhead. Through this design, GSS acts like a lookup service providing information on how to make requests toward the different back-ends, where each back-end is treated as an object storage. Beside transferring files, other functionality such as listing folder content, checking existence of files, creating folders, etc., are made directly through the SOAP API.

Unique references to files are obtained by assigning file IDs to them. A file ID includes a prefix indicating which storage back-end the files belongs to, and the location of the file within the native storage. The file ID and a valid authentication token is sufficient for downloading any file. As long as all CloudFlow services are implemented using this API, interoperability and vendor independent file access is obtained within CloudFlow workflows. Further, any cloud storage solution with a RESTful API can be made available in CloudFlow by adding an additional back-end in GSS. Existing services can then immediately use the new cloud storage solution without making any changes to their implementation. A cloud storage can also use external authentication solutions,

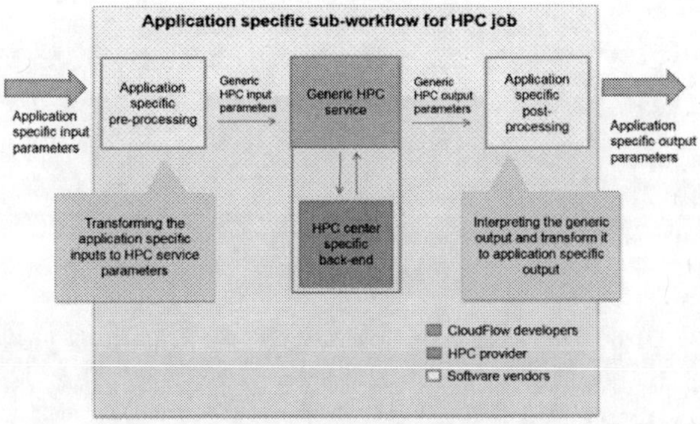

Figure 6. The encapsulation of a HPC job within an application specific HPC sub-workflow.

even though it is not a requirement when the authentication token used towards the cloud storage is a valid CloudFlow token.

A web-based file browser application is available for all workflows. It is configurable through Workflow Editor to tailor its behavior for each workflow, and has a user-friendly interface with a context dependent right-click menu. Here, end users can upload and download files between their computers and the cloud.

Since the CloudFlow services have SOAP interfaces, their parameters should consist of short messages rather than entire files. Because of this, the file browser gives the file ID of the chosen files as output instead of the content of it. This rule illustrate best practice and applies to all CloudFlow services.

Currently, four cloud storage solutions are made available in the CloudFlow Infrastructure through GSS. There are two OpenStack Swift installations (one internal and one external), a product lifecycle management (PLM) system, and a native storage at one of CloudFlow's HPC providers.

E. HPC Access

Computationally intensive tasks that benefit from running on HPC clusters are common in many engineering workflows. To support this, the CloudFlow Infrastructure facilitates seamless and secure integration of job scheduling, making it easy for software vendors to offer their applications on an HPC cluster as part of a CloudFlow workflow. This is supported through the design and concept of *HPC application sub-workflows*, with the generic *HPC service* as the central component.

An HPC application sub-workflow is built from three CloudFlow services as shown in Figure 6; an application specific pre-processing service, the generic HPC service, and an application specific post-processing service. The HPC service is designed to be generic with respect to both the application and the type of job scheduling system used by the HPC provider. Through this design, the HPC providers can make changes to their queuing systems, or CloudFlow can be expanded to more HPC centers, without requiring the software vendors to make changes to their services or workflows.

In order to make the service independent from details specific to the HPC center, the HPC service communicates internally with an HPC back-end through a pre-defined API. Since user credentials defined in CloudFlow are not necessarily compatible with the user definitions at the HPC center, the back-end may perform a mapping between the two sets of user definitions through a method seen fit by the HPC provider. The two existing HPC providers within CloudFlow currently use different approaches to solve this challenge:

- The HPC provider assigns a one-to-one mapping between the two types of users, providing each unique CloudFlow user with a dedicated user in their HPC infrastructure.
- The HPC provider has a set up pool of HPC users reserved for CloudFlow. Each execution of the HPC service is then assigned an arbitrary available user from the pool, and that user is then reserved until the execution is completed. To avoid that users can access other users' data, the home directory of each such HPC user is deleted between each job.

The first approach is particularly suitable to private cloud installations of CloudFlow, where the same system administrators control both the cloud and compute cluster environments.

The input and output parameters for the HPC service are designed to be highly generic, and should support the vast majority of applications that will be run on the compute cluster. The most important input parameter is the *HPC command lines*, which is the set of command lines to be executed through the HPC job. This typically includes loading required modules in the HPC system, downloading input files from the cloud storage, executing the application with the appropriate arguments, and uploading result files back to the cloud storage. Since the set of command lines is different for every HPC application, this parameter is expected to be created in an application specific pre-processing service. The idea is that this service has the same input parameters as the application, and generates a string as output that can be connected with the input parameter of the generic HPC service. Besides the HPC command lines parameter, the HPC service has input parameters such as number of nodes and cores to be used by the job, license required by the user to be allowed to submit the job, and maximum execution time used to limit costs and handle non-converging simulations.

In order to provide good user experience, the HPC service allows the application to provide HTML based progress information to the user. The progress reports provided by currently integrated services range from simple progress bars to complete web pages, including embedded 3D rendered models and plots illustrating the convergence of the computation. The latter example execute unmodified software, and generate the HTML based on the log files from an ongoing simulation. The HPC service continuously monitors a pre-defined status file within the application's working directory, and the content of this file is displayed to the user through the browser. It is up to the application provider to fill this file with meaningful content.

When the application is finished, it uploads any output files to the cloud storage. The name of the output files, however, and other output parameters needed by services later in the workflow, are reported back to the HPC Service, and given as service output parameters. Since a HPC job can have any number of output parameters, outputs are supported through a similar design as input parameters. When a job is finished, the HPC service reads a pre-defined result file in the job's working directory. The content of this file is passed as output from the HPC service as a single string. It is then up to the application provider to first write all output parameters to this file at the end of the job execution, and then provide an application specific post-processing service. The post-processing service should take the output from the HPC service as input, and parse it to separate the different output parameters. The application specific output parameters can then be given semantic information and be passed to any other subsequent service.

The application specific pre- and post-processing services are naturally related to each other, and they only make sense together with the generic HPC service. By modelling these three services as a sub-workflow, the HPC job can be added to any other workflow as a single block with input and output parameters natural to the application. The HPC specific parameters (number of nodes, number of cores, maximum execution time) can either be hardcoded within the HPC application sub-workflow, dynamically defined in the pre-processing service, or user defined through an application consisting of a web form. If they are defined in any other way than by the user, the user experience for a HPC job will be similar to a simulation running in the cloud environment through a regular asynchronous service.

Slow data transfers can potentially introduce performance bottlenecks for HPC jobs. Since each application downloads input data from the cloud storage, and since GSS (Section III-D) is used to handle the file transfers, the software vendors and HPC centers cannot provide restrictions on which cloud storage the users are using. In order to maximize performance, it is recommended that the users make use of the storage solution that is closest to the HPC centers hosting their HPC job. Currently, both of the existing HPC centers in CloudFlow have available cloud storage solutions that are connected to their HPC cluster with high-speed network. Since one of the centers is the host of a private CloudFlow installation, their cloud storage is the only storage available for their users. For the HPC center in the public CloudFlow installation, the closest cloud storage is also the default storage solution for all users. In the current installations, the cost of file transfers to the HPC cluster is similar to the transfer cost between virtual machines in the cloud and the cloud storages. Therefore, data transfers between the cloud and HPC environment do not impose a bottleneck for the users of CloudFlow.

Even though the HPC service is generic, the application that is executed through it will be the part of a software package (as mentioned in Section III-B). The name of the software package that it is part of will therefore be hardcoded as input to the HPC service within the application sub-workflow. This information is then used by the service to check with the Resource Monitoring component that the user has a license to run the application, and to ensure that the software vendor receives the correct license fees. Other resource management tasks, such as reporting CPU hours spent on the computation, are also reported from within the generic HPC service.

To conclude this section, the HPC service facilitates that computationally demanding applications can be executed within a HPC environment, with an interface consisting of semantically described input and output parameters, allowing it to be part of a larger workflow. The service also supports application specific progress reports to be presented to the user during execution, opening for a well informed user experience.

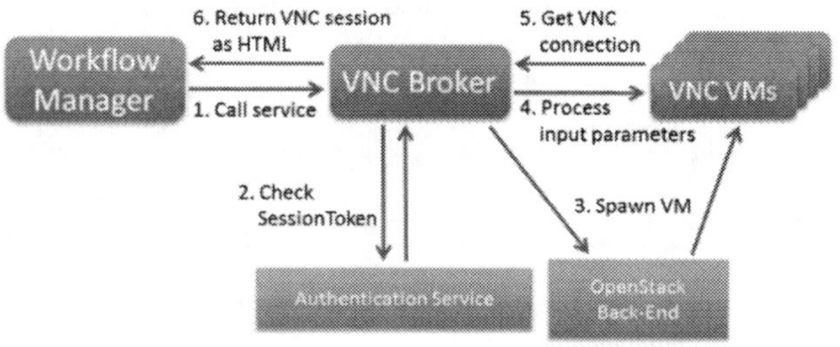

Figure 7. The design of the CloudFlow VNC Service. The VNC Broker handles the requests from the Workflow Manager and manages a set of virtual machines on which the actual desktop applications and the VNC servers run. Input and output parameters are forwarded between the Workflow Manager and the individual VMs.

F. Remote Desktop Applications

Existing engineering desktop applications have typically been developed over several years, and offer their functionality through complex graphical user interfaces. Providing such an application as a CloudFlow web application by re-implementing its complete user interface in a web-based manner, would take a lot of effort and would not be reasonable. Therefore, the CloudFlow Infrastructure offers the possibility to integrate such software directly through a remote desktop concept realized by using the VNC technology [9]. This integration is made through the *VNC Service*. The VNC Service can be used in a workflow as a building block to grant remote access to complex desktop applications. Instead of re-implementing the application's user interface with HTML/JavaScript, the application can be hosted as-is on a virtual machine (VM) inside the cloud environment and can be accessed through a VNC connection. The software providers only have to prepare dedicated VM images for their individual applications.

The CloudFlow VNC Service consists of two parts:

1) A VNC management service, the so-called *VNC Broker*, as part of the core infrastructure.
2) The individual virtual machines that host the actual software and are spawned and despawned by the VNC Broker on demand.

The VNC Broker is a CloudFlow service that interacts with Workflow Manager and manages all incoming VNC requests. Upon request, it spawns a new VM from a prepared image via CloudFlow's OpenStack back-end, and establishes a VNC connection to it. This VNC connection is then converted into an HTML canvas and forwarded to Workflow Manager to be shown in the CloudFlow Portal. When the connection is set up and the user receives the VNC content through the Portal, all communication is done directly between the user's client machine and the VM hosting the desktop application. No intermediate stages are involved. The back-end is realized with an installation of Guacamole [19]. A Guacamole VNC server is installed and configured on the VNC Broker and connects to every individual VNC VM. The mapping of the IP address and port number is done dynamically for each new VM based on the parameters returned from OpenStack. Authentication is handled using the CloudFlow session token passed along with the request from Workflow Manager. The overall architecture of the VNC Service is shown in Figure 7.

The VNC Broker also handles input and output parameters to and from the VNC session. In contrast to standard CloudFlow services, the VNC Service suffers from a similar problem as the HPC integration, as input and output parameters have not only to be passed from the workflow to the service, but all the way through the VNC Broker into the individual virtual machines. To solve this problem, the VMs are equipped with an additional custom SOAP service that is called by the VNC Broker to pass these parameters. If there are more than one input parameter, all inputs have to be serialized into one and deserialized again inside the VM, similarly as for the HPC pre-processing service. Most common input and output parameters however, will be files or folders defined by their GSS file IDs. Therefore, the service on the VM includes the functionality to download files or folders via GSS, and upload results to a dedicated folder in the cloud storage via GSS as well. Once this pre-processing is completed, the service launches the desktop application with optionally provided command line parameters. As the CloudFlow VNC Service is a generic service, billing has to be done individually, depending on which VM image that has been spawned. The total uptime of the VM, as well as usage and license costs of the desktop application, will be taken into account and assigned correctly to the associated software provider.

As mentioned in Section II, network bandwidth and latency are the key factors when operating a VNC session. To reduce latency as much as possible within the infrastructure, we use a direct communication between the virtual machine and the end user. However, in the current setup, spawning the virtual machine upon request is the biggest performance bottleneck. Detailed performance measurements, as well as an in-depth analysis of the additional overhead induced by using an HTML solution instead of a dedicated VNC client application, will be looked into at a later stage.

IV. Validation

The development of the CloudFlow Infrastructure is organized to meet the requirements from end users in manufacturing industries and their software providers. This has given us the opportunity to arrange validations where the end users test the platform and the deployed software against these requirements.

A. Validation methods

To facilitate development and validation, three *waves of experiments* have been set up. In the first wave of experiments, all workflows were tailored towards the needs of one end user in hydropower engineering. Software from six different independent software vendors were integrated with the infrastructure and accessible through the cloud solution, and validated with one common end user. For the second and third wave, European software vendors and end users were invited to test the infrastructure and develop new workflows based on the needs of the end user. In total 14 new experiments were selected, each with one new end user.

At the beginning of each wave of experiments, user requirements analysis was conducted. The user requirements were gathered from the end user, software vendor, and HPC provider, each being a stakeholder of the experiment. Initially, the experiment description provided by each experiment was analyzed, filtered and transformed into a first set of user requirements. Then, during group discussion sessions, experiment stakeholders were invited to confirm, add or remove, and prioritize their user requirements. They were also encouraged to provide success criteria and methods for measuring the success that contributed to experiments validation criteria. In parallel, a discussion related to which services to design and to combine to workflows in order to address the requirements for all of the experiments was also performed. In addition to this, the software vendor in each experiment developed business plans for how to realize the economical potential benefiting both the end user and software vendors. This way, not only the theoretical potential of the software platform is verified, but also that the final solution can sustain as an attractive option.

Formative and summative evaluations were conducted for each experiment. The formative evaluation, which was done remotely, was aimed to fine-tune the development of experiment applications to ensure that the final experiment applications met user requirements. Two activities were performed as part of formative evaluation, i.e., 1) heuristic evaluation by Human-Computer Interactions (HCI) experts to analyze the usability of experiment applications, and 2) assessment of how user requirements were met by the current state of experiment applications. Summative evaluation, which was conducted at end users sites, was aimed to provide final assessment of experiment applications. Four activities were performed as part of summative evaluation, i.e., 1) usability evaluation by end users, 2) recommendation by HCI experts to improve the usability of experiment applications, 3) assessment of how the user requirements were met by the final version of experiment applications, and 4) interview with end users on various aspects of CloudFlow Infrastructure and experiment applications. As part of usability evaluation by end users, they were required to provide complex engineering problems to solve in order to test the extent of experiment application and CloudFlow Infrastructure technical capabilities. The two stages of evaluation meant that the success of both CloudFlow Infrastructure and experiments were validated.

B. Validation results

The results of user requirements revealed that the motivation to use the CloudFlow Infrastructure from end users' point of view varies among the experiments, including attracting new customers, reducing license cost, reducing time spent to create a new product and improving the design of new products. On the other hand, it was also found that there was an overall common goal between software vendors and HPC providers, i.e., to enhance availability of easy to use software and computational resources through

- user friendly interfaces, and
- easy access to advanced computing resources.

For end-users, the user requirements were then extracted to identify metrics that can be used to measure and evaluate the performance of the CloudFlow Infrastructure, e.g., speed, accuracy and usability.

The assessment of how user requirements were met from the 13 already finished and seven ongoing experiments have been processed and shows that the main goals of all experiments have been reached. More importantly, the results showed that end user requirements in each wave were successfully achieved. For instance, in the second wave of experiments, which was composed of seven experiments and involved seven different end users, 30 of 32 (94%) of end user requirements were met, as shown in the left image of Figure 8. The remaining of the user requirements were partially met, and

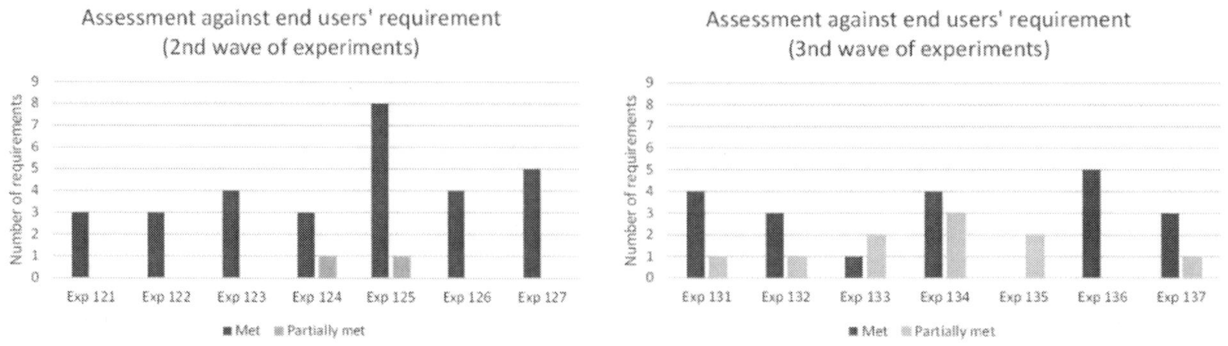

Figure 8. Assessments of end users' requirements for the second wave experiments (left) and third wave experiments (right).

did not represent any critical weaknesses in the infrastructure. Meanwhile, in the third wave of experiments, which was also composed of seven experiments and involved eight different end users, 66.7% of end user requirements were met, as shown in the right image of Figure 8. While this figure was much lower compared to the second wave experiments, on a closer observation, this was due to the fact that the assessment of how user requirements were met is still an ongoing process.

Furthermore, the results of interviews with the end users showed that they would benefit economically from using more computing resources than today, and that the CloudFlow Infrastructure can make it economically feasible. For instance, in the first wave of experiments, by using the experiment applications provided on the CloudFlow Infrastructure, the end user (a hydropower manufacturing SME) has achieved, among others, the following:

- A substantial reduction of time spent (89% faster) on quality check of sub-assembly parts.
- An improvement of the accuracy of the calculated results.

Other examples of economic benefits by end users from the second and third waves can be found in more details on CloudFlow project website [20].

To summarize, the validation results revealed that the concept is functional and makes it more attractive to use cloud computing for various stakeholders. The biggest benefits were found where computationally intensive workflows are presented as engineering apps, that models the expert knowledge for the very concrete artefacts within a unified web-based user interface. These apps allow end users to perform operations that would otherwise require computational resources and human specialists that they do not have access to in-house.

V. Example - Quality Assurance in the Cloud

This section presents a workflow designed to span the functionalities of the CloudFlow Infrastructure. The workflow was originally a first wave experiment, and has been expanded throughout the development of the platform. The requirements are provided by the original end user, who also evaluated the workflow. The workflow is used to align and compare a 3D scan of a model to its original CAD model. Here, the model is a turbine blade used in a hydro power plant. The goal is to confirm that the turbine blade is manufactured according to its design within given tolerances, and later to control wear on the blade after it has been in production for some time.

Before the development of the quality assurance workflow took place, the end user put forward the following five requirements to the workflow:

1) The remote rendering of CAD models and point clouds needs to be provided with low latency, and with at least a frame rate of 15 frames per second.
2) The workflow and services within it must be easy to use.
3) Both experts and non-experts needs to be able to run the workflow. Complex functionality should therefore be hidden, but still accessible for expert users.
4) Improve the engineering process by providing new information not accessible for the end user prior to CloudFlow.
5) Time reduction for the quality assurance process.

Prior to the CloudFlow quality assurance workflow, the end user aligned the CAD model and point cloud manually. This process was prone to error and the result was subject to quality variations.

The quality assurance process consists mainly of three steps, where each step contains one or several CloudFlow services. The main challenge is to align properly the 3D scan data to the CAD model, which usually is a tedious manual process. A fully automated alignment is not necessarily feasible, especially if the CAD model has symmetries. The first step is therefore a coarse manual alignment, which is performed before an automated alignment process, where an optimization process iterates to make the point cloud fit as close as possible to the surfaces of the CAD model. Thereafter, the result of the alignment is reported to the user in an informative and user-friendly manner. The entire workflow, and the four software packages within it, is shown in Figure 9.

A. File selection and conversion

The workflow starts by letting the user choose the CAD model, 3D point cloud, and location for where to store the results from the alignment and distance computations. This functionality is covered by the File Browser, mentioned in Section III-D.

Since CAD models can be stored in different file formats, and since the services later in the workflow expect a predefined file format, a file conversion might be needed at this point. The branching functionality of Workflow Manager described in Section III-A is used at this point, and a conversion service is triggered if the chosen file is not on the

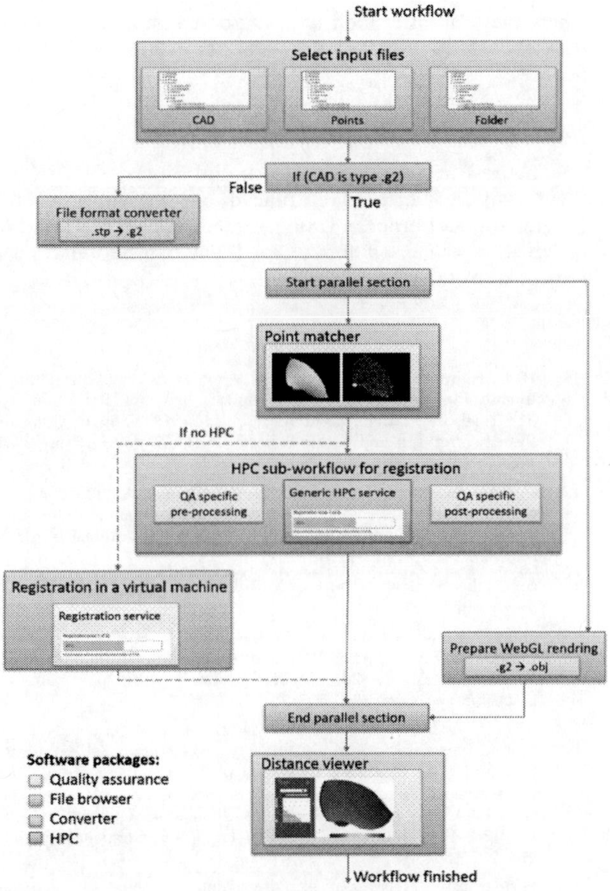

Figure 9. A workflow for quality assurance where a 3D scan of a produced product is compared with the initial CAD model.

pre-defined file format. If triggered, the conversion service accesses a dedicate virtual machine in the cloud which runs the conversion. The conversion service is not guaranteed to finish within a HTTP time out, and is therefore implemented as an asynchronous service. The service launches the conversion as a background process, and Workflow Manager polls on the service to check if the process is finished or not. Before the conversion finishes, it provides a progress bar along with a text describing the current status. Note that this conversion requires no interaction from the user, allowing Workflow Manager to proceed automatically to the next step of the workflow after the conversion is completed.

B. Coarse alignment

The manual alignment step, where the starting point for the automatic alignment is made, is a web application. Here, the CAD model and the point cloud are shown in separate canvases and the user selects corresponding points from the two models. Since the models can be quite large, and to meet the first requirement set by the end user, a hybrid rendering is done through the Tinia framework [11]. The models are rendered server side, generating 3D images that are sent to the web client. The user can freely interact with the local model for an interactive experience, without transferring the CAD model. A drop-down menu is available for expert users to choose rendering configuration manually, according to requirement number 3. Using these configurations can improve the rendering quality, but is not required for a good user experience. Similarly to the file browser, Workflow Manager awaits a message from the client to proceed in the workflow, and this signal is sent when the user has completed the coarse alignment.

C. Automatic alignment

The automatic alignment is computationally intensive and to get the best performance, it executes in the HPC environment through the HPC service described in Section III-E. An application specific pre-processing service is implemented to generate the set of command lines required to run the alignment based on the file IDs obtained in the file chooser applications, converter and coarse alignment application. A post-processing service for the alignment is also implemented in order to enable semantic descriptions to the result from the HPC service. In this case, it will be the file ID holding the aligned point cloud together with the pointwise distance to the CAD model. These three services are then stored as an automatic alignment sub-workflow, hiding any complexities from the HPC service.

The automatic alignment has also been implemented as a single asynchronous service, where the alignment is run in the cloud environment instead of on the HPC cluster. Since the alignment HPC sub-workflow has application specific inputs and outputs, the sub-workflow can be exchanged with the single cloud service directly. This can be useful as a cheaper alternative for users who do not prioritize performance. The service or the HPC block could potentially also be chosen dynamically, using the branching functionality in Workflow Manager. It would even be possible to send the computation to another cloud / HPC provider if the chosen one has limited capacity.

D. Distance visualization

The results after the alignment process are visualized by a WebGL application showing both the CAD model and the aligned point cloud in the same view. Since the browser has limited capabilities, it does not receive the CAD model itself, but rather an approximation more suitable for web rendering. Since the approximation task is independent of all other steps of the workflow, it can be executed in a parallel background service, significantly reducing the start-up time for the post-processing service.

The distance between the models is illustrated both trough statistical information and color-coding of the point cloud. Through the quality assurance approach prior to CloudFlow, the end user had no access to statistical information on the difference between the CAD and the point cloud. This statistical information is therefore provided to meet end user requirement number 4. The user will typically view and inspect these results and take screenshots for documentation before exiting the application. As there are no more next steps, the workflow is completed with a list of workflow output parameters. This list can be accessed later through the user's list of finished workflows.

E. Validation of the quality assurance workflow

The validation showed that all five requirements listed in the beginning of this section was met.

1) Rendering of CAD models was achieved with low latency and acceptable frame rate through hybrid rendering with Tinia, and WebGL.
2) The user interaction was limited to selecting files and destination folder for workflow results, making the coarse manual alignment, and inspecting the result. All these steps provide good user experience, and end users can easily use the quality assurance workflow without any guidance. The workflow is therefore considered user friendly and easy to use.
3) Optional menus for improving rendering quality is available for expert users.
4) Enhanced statistical information was provided to the end user.
5) Following the use of quality assurance application, the end user reported that the quality assurance application reduced the processing time for the alignment from 3 hours to less than 20 minutes.

The quality of the alignment was also improved by at least 10% when compared to the end user's existing approach, which involved many manual steps.

VI. Conclusion and Future Work

In this paper, we have presented the CloudFlow Infrastructure where software packages from different vendors can combined into seamless workflows that are offered to engineering end users. It supports, and has the ability to combine, different HPC and cloud providers, and takes a generic/unified approach to cloud storage solutions and authentication to ensure interoperability. The generic HPC Service allows computationally intensive software to take advantage of HPC resources, while still being an integrated part of workflows and providing good user experience. Similarly, a generic service is presented for providing access to remote desktop applications, through the VNC Service. Complex workflow design is supported through the workflow editor, where conditional branches, loops and parallel service execution can be modelled. The functionality to track and monitor resource consumption by end users, enables that the workflows offered in the infrastructure can be commercialized and open up new business models for the companies involved.

The next steps for the CloudFlow Infrastructure will be to validate the newest additions of the infrastructure. This includes validation of the VNC Service, and the more advanced flow control for workflows. The successful validation shows that the infrastructure is viable, and it is therefore natural to extend CloudFlow to support more cloud providers and HPC centers, and increase the amount and complexity of provided workflows. Another interesting future extension is to combine data streams directly from the factory floors into CloudFlow services, according to Industry 4.0.

We have demonstrated that the CloudFlow Infrastructure can open up the world of advanced multi-vendor software solutions for engineering SMEs, who can not afford to host a computing infrastructure in-house. The use of generic solutions for handling data and utilizing HPC resources, shows the flexibility of our approach, and makes it easy for software vendors to integrate their software in a cloud environment. CloudFlow provides a new distribution channel for the software vendors where they can offer their software based on new cloud-based business models, either as a pay-per-use license, or by periodic licenses.

Acknowledgement

This research was conducted in the context of the CloudFlow project, which is co-funded by the 7th Framework Program of the European Union, project number 609100. More information and news about CloudFlow can be found on the project website at http://eu-cloudflow.eu/.

References

[1] H. H. Holm, J. M. Hjelmervik, and V. Gezer, "CloudFlow - an infrastructure for engineering workflows in the cloud," in UBICOMM 2016: The Tenth International Conference on Mobile Ubiquitous Computing, Systems, Services and Technologies. IARIA, October 2016, pp. 158–165.

[2] C. Stahl, E. Bellos, C. Altenhofen, and J. Hjelmervik, "Flexible integration of cloud-based engineering services using semantic technologies," in Industrial Technology (ICIT), 2015 IEEE International Conference on, March 2015, pp. 1520–1525.

[3] SimScale. Website, retrieved: 2017-05-29. [Online]. Available: https://www.simscale.com/ (2017)

[4] cloudSME, simulation for manufacturing & engineering. Seventh Framework Programme (FP7) under grant agreement number 608886. Website, retrieved: 2017-05-29. [Online]. Available: http://www.cloudsme-apps.com/ (2017)

[5] S. J. E. Taylor, T. Kiss, G. Terstyanszky, P. Kacsuk, and N. Fantini, "Cloud computing for simulation in manufacturing and engineering: Introducing the cloudsme simulation platform," in Proceedings of the 2014 Annual Simulation Symposium, ser. ANSS '14. San Diego, CA, USA: Society for Computer Simulation International, 2014, pp. 12:1–12:8. [Online]. Available: http://dl.acm.org/citation.cfm?id=2664292.2664304

[6] Fortissimo factories of the future resources, technology, infrastructure and services for simulation and modelling. Seventh Framework Programme (FP7) under grant agreement number 609029. Website, retrieved: 2017-05-29. [Online]. Available: https://www.fortissimo-project.eu/ (2017)

[7] B. Koller, N. Struckmann, J. Buchholz, and M. Gienger, "Towards an environment to deliver high performance computing to small and medium enterprises," in Sustained Simulation Performance 2015. Springer International Publishing, 2015, pp. 41–50.

[8] N. Ferry, H. Song, A. Rossini, F. Chauvel, and A. Solberg, "CloudMF: Applying MDE to Tame the Complexity of Managing Multi-Cloud Applications," in UCC 2014: 7th IEEE/ACM International Conference on Utility and Cloud Computing, R. Bilof, Ed. IEEE Computer Society, 2014, pp. 269–277.

[9] T. Richardson, Q. Stafford-Fraser, K. R. Wood, and A. Hopper, "Virtual network computing," IEEE Internet Computing, vol. 2, no. 1, 1998, pp. 33–38.

[10] Microsoft. Remote desktop protocol. Website, retrieved 2017-02-15. [Online]. Available: https://msdn.microsoft.com/en-us/library/aa383015(VS.85).aspx (2017)

[11] C. Dyken, K. O. Lye, J. Seland, E. W. Bjønnes, J. M. Hjelmervik, J. O. Nygaard, and T. R. Hagen, "A framework for opengl client-server rendering," in 4th IEEE International Conference on Cloud Computing Technology and Science Proceedings, CloudCom 2012, Taipei, Taiwan. IEEE Computer Society, 2012, pp. 729–734. [Online]. Available: http://dx.doi.org/10.1109/CloudCom.2012.6427506

[12] C. Altenhofen, A. Dietrich, A. Stork, and D. Fellner, "Rixels: Towards secure interactive 3d graphics in engineering clouds," Transactions on Internet Research (TIR), vol. 12, no. 1, Jan. 2016, pp. 31–38.

[13] K. Grolinger, M. A. M. Capretz, A. Cunha, and S. Tazi, "Integration of business process modeling and web services: a survey," Service Oriented Computing and Applications, vol. 8, no. 2, 2014, pp. 105–128. [Online]. Available: http://dx.doi.org/10.1007/s11761-013-0138-2

[14] M. A. Aslam, S. Auer, J. Shen, and M. Hermann, "Expressing business process model as owl-s ontologies," in Proceedings of the 2nd International Workshop on Grid and Peer-to-Peer based Workflows (GPWW 2006), 2006, 4th International Conference on Business Process Management (BPM 2006), Vienna, Austria, September 2006.

[15] Oracle, "Oracle BPEL process manager datasheet," 2009, [retrieved: 2017-05-29]. [Online]. Available: http://www.oracle.com/technetwork/middleware/bpel/overview/ds-bpel-11gr1-1-134826.pdf

[16] R. Cyganiak, D. Wood, and M. Lanthaler, "Web Services Architecture," W3C Working Group Note, 2004, [retrieved: 2017-05-29]. [Online]. Available: https://www.w3.org/TR/2004/NOTE-ws-arch-20040211/

[17] V. Gezer and S. Bergweiler, "Service and workflow engineering based on semantic web technologies," in UBICOMM 2016: The Tenth International Conference on Mobile Ubiquitous Computing, Systems, Services and Technologies. IARIA, October 2016, pp. 152–157.

[18] Openstack Keystone. Website, retrieved: 2017-05-29. [Online]. Available: http://docs.openstack.org/developer/keystone/ (2017)

[19] The Apache Software Foundation (ASF). Guacamole VNC. Website, retrieved 2017-05-29. [Online]. Available: http://guacamole.incubator.apache.org/ (2017)

[20] CloudFlow: Computational cloud services and workflows for agile engineering. Seventh Framework Programme (FP7) under grant agreement number 609100. Website, retrieved: 2017-05-29. [Online]. Available: http://eu-cloudflow.eu/ (2017)

Cloud-based Infrastructure for Workflow and Service Engineering Using Semantic Web Technologies

Volkan Gezer and Simon Bergweiler

German Research Center for Artificial Intelligence (DFKI)
Innovative Factory Systems
Kaiserslautern, Germany
Email: firstname.lastname@dfki.de

***Abstract*—This paper presents the concept and implementation of a cloud-based infrastructure platform and tailored tools for graphical support for user-driven experiments. The focus lies on the creation of a platform that allows multiple users to integrate their expertise via Web service interfaces and combine them to compose workflows for their experiments in the engineering domain. The platform employs Semantic Web technologies, which increase interoperability of the services and assist during workflow design by suggesting compatible services. The implemented tools give users the possibility to utilize the platform using a standard Web browser, without any knowledge of service engineering and the underlying complex technologies. An experiment is described as a workflow and consists of orchestrated services from several software vendors that encapsulate specific tasks for improving product development. One advantage of this approach is the automatic execution of the services and data flow among them. The cloud-based platform can also be combined with high-performance computing when services require complex calculations. The created platform offers optimal conditions to involve independent specialists and conduct short or long-running experiments, depending on the complexity of the task. This results in tremendous time savings and allows experts to carry out more experiments with products, which were omitted due to the complexity and the limited computing power, until now. The possibility to conduct these experiments improves the productive know-how of the companies and enhances the products they are selling.**

Keywords–Cloud infrastructure; semantic workflow description; Semantic Web services; graphical workflow editing; workflow execution.

I. INTRODUCTION

In this paper, we present the concept and implementation of a flexible cloud-based platform for the vendor-independent integration of Semantic Web services and their execution in the engineering domain. This platform is provided as Infrastructure as a Service (IaaS), and is able to integrate, combine and orchestrate Web services [1]. Cloud-based solutions are part of the daily life, and their usage is increasing day by day. The advantage of access to data from a cloud solution from anywhere allows increased mobility of people and their applications, and changes also behavior and attitude of responsible persons in the engineering domain [2].

Involving Semantic Web technologies inside a cloud-based solution significantly improves usability by structuring the data in a standardized way. These standardized data structures can be understood by machines and humans and utilized to create interoperable and vendor-independent applications. With this approach vendor lock-in problems can be avoided [3].

The platform enables experts from various application domains to independently plan, design, and execute their individual experiments for the analysis and optimization of their products. Each experiment is described as a workflow that uses the functionality of different products of different software vendors in any combination. With the help of this platform, several independent specialists act as software vendors and offer their expertise, e.g., strong calculation procedures or routines for the comparison of 3D models, wrapped by Web service interfaces in a system-wide infrastructure. These advanced analytical capabilities, which are accessible via the platform, can be used to enhance the products, identify weaknesses and subsequently improve the positive effects of the products.

Thanks to this distributed architecture, the platform offers optimal conditions for both short and long-running experiments [4]. To provide an added value and according to customer requirements, the developed platform is able to pass the execution of dedicated services to a cluster of high-performance computers (HPC). These HPC clusters are to perform calculation of complex tasks and are spread across different virtualization solutions. This design of the platform allows experts to carry out more experiments with products because of enormous time savings. The developed tailored tools of this cloud-based platform, described below as core backend components, allow engineering companies and software solution vendors to integrate their Software as a Service (SaaS). Services are orchestrated in specific workflows, seamlessly supported by graphical user interfaces. They do not even require specific skills or knowledge of the underlying Semantic Web technologies. The developed solution uses standardized Internet technologies and all workflows can be executed using a standard Web browser, requiring no additional software download and installation. The provided platform wraps all complexity of the technologies and provides Application Programming Interfaces (API) for communication.

Section II introduces used technologies and describes the topics under consideration. For a better understanding, Section III describes a concrete application scenario and the requirements in the engineering domain. This leads over to Section IV, where the methodology and concept of the developed approach is discussed. Section V describes the architecture and the interaction of the developed core backend components. The paper ends with a conclusion and an outlook on future work and extensions.

II. BACKGROUND

A set of complementary reusable functionalities that are provided for various purposes by software are called "services". If a service is offered via World Wide Web using Web technologies, such as the Hypertext Transfer Protocol (HTTP), the service is labeled as Web service. Web services are designed to support machine-to-machine interaction over a network and allow interoperable communication [5]. With the help of description languages, which will be discussed in the upcoming sections, Web services create communication between peer-platforms, prevent vendor dependency and increase reusability.

A. Web Services Description Language

The Web Service Description Language (WSDL) is a language and platform-independent XML-based interface definition language, designed with the aim to create a standardized mechanism for the description of Web services. It describes SOAP-based Web services in detail, their technical input and output parameters, ports, data types, and how services must be invoked. With this machine-readable description language, the automatic detection and execution of Web services is possible. A ready-revised language draft was submitted to the World Wide Web Consortium (W3C) [6], but only version 2.0 was standardized and proclaimed as W3C recommendation [7]. Unfortunately, WSDL is a lower level interface description language that addresses the technical mechanisms and aspects of Web services, and it does not reflect the functionality of a service. Furthermore, it is difficult to create and understand for humans. In this approach, WSDL is used for the technical description of Web services, their input and output parameters, and the SOAP messaging mechanism.

B. Technologies of the Semantic Web

The development of the current Web to the "Semantic Web" is pervasive. Efforts are aiming to add annotations to things and objects of daily life. Through the help of annotations, the vision of the Semantic Web allows better cooperation between people and computers; well-defined meanings are attached to information [8]. The Resource Description Framework (RDF) is one of the most important data formats that has been developed to implement this vision. The Semantic Web combines technologies that deal with the description of information and knowledge sources, such as ontologies, RDF triple stores, and Semantic Web services [9][10]. Ontologies allow the definition of a vocabulary of a dedicated application domain and define for this purpose concepts and properties. These concepts can in turn be connected by relations, which promise a significant value, when conclusions are drawn about these structures. In that field, the W3C defines its recommendations as an open standard like RDF(S) [9][11] and the Web Ontology Language (OWL) [12].

In contrast to a complex and comprehensive infrastructure that tries to solve all problems of the interaction and communication of distributed applications, the Semantic Web Technology Stack, depicted in Figure 1, is a family of modular standards mostly standardized by the W3C. Each of these standards aims at another part of problem or another sub-problem.

This stack of Semantic Web technologies describes the vision of the W3C to create a Web of linked data. The idea of open data stores on the Web, the ability to build vocabularies, and write rules for handling data based on these empowered technologies, such as RDF, OWL, and the SPARQL Protocol And RDF Query Language (SPARQL) [13].

In the following, the individual layers and the associated standards will be briefly explained. Starting at the lowest level with the Unicode standard and Uniform Resource Identifiers (URI). The Unicode standard allows an unambiguous name

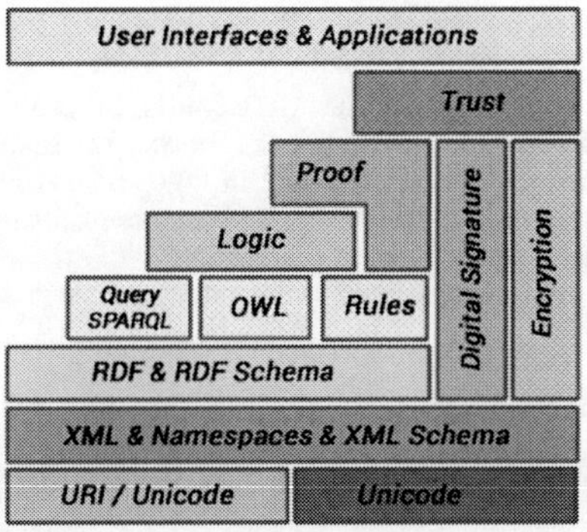

Figure 1. Semantic Web technology stack.

of the resources in any language. This makes the approach multilingual and forces the exchange of messages. In order to identify resources on the Web, it is necessary to have URIs and to use them for the concrete description of specific resources. URIs are used to describe a specific resource uniquely. XML forms the central core technology and is added to the second level of this architecture or hierarchy. XML is used for the storage and universal exchange of data. The technologies on the upper layers rely on it. The third layer of the Semantic Web technology stack is probably the most important layer of all. RDF makes it possible to create metadata in machine-readable form. Here, a sentence structure in the form of triples (subject, predicate, and object) is used. The layers three and four are important pillars of the Semantic Web, they host RDF, RDF Schema, ontologies, and their vocabulary. They serve the communication of different, mutually independent domains at the semantic level. The uppermost layers of the architecture are logic, proof and trust. The Logic level provides technologies to allow computers to recognize specific patterns by the help of dedicated rules. By modifying this rule structures and patterns, new knowledge is inferred and exploited. The Proof level should make it possible to distinguish the trustworthiness of resources. Together with the Digital Signature layer it is possible that computers are able to cope trusting tasks without human intervention.

C. Semantic Web Services

In the recent years, the tendency towards Semantic Web technologies increased the research in the domain, results in an elevated number of available ontologies as well as standards recommended by the W3C. To widen the scope of applicability, one of the submitted ontologies to W3C was the Web Ontology Language for Web Services (OWL-S), which allowed services on the Web to be found, executed, and monitored. The OWL-S ontology is designed on top of OWL with extensions to make service discovery, invocation, composition, and monitoring possible. The provided structure also allowed these operations to be performed autonomously, when desired [14]. Based on the previously described technologies, domain models must be created to form an important conceptual basis. Therefore, parts of the dedicated knowledge domain are categorized and structured in a machine readable form. OWL-S [14] extends this base to a set of constructs that relate to properties, specialties and dependencies of the Web service level and is also machine readable and processable.

A concrete service description in OWL-S is separated in several parts. Figure 2 shows the main concepts and relations of a service model in OWL-S: service profile, service model, service grounding, and important for our approach, the processes.

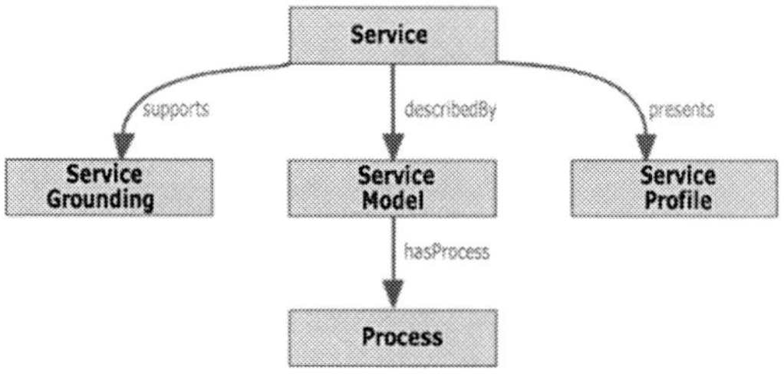

Figure 2. Main Web service concepts in OWL-S.

OWL-S API provides its own native engine to execute Web services described only in WSDL 1.2 and consequently, SOAP interface. Any Web services provided with a WSDL description and SOAP interface can be integrated into the infrastructure and converted into semantic Web service descriptions as long as they satisfy the requirements. For a Web service that is converted into a Semantic Web service with the help of an upper ontology, the following required types of the OWL-S Submission [14] are created:

- The *Service Profile* provides information to describe a service to a requester. The profile provides three types of information: the service creator, the service functionality, and the service characteristics [14]. It is also is used for service discovery and describes the functionality of the service and contains information about the service provider. Furthermore, this profile reflects the overall functionality of a service with its precondition, input and output types, features, and benefits.
- The *Service Model* is a mandatory type for the description how a Web service works. The model describes the inputs, outputs, preconditions and effects. It also specifies the *Process* concepts and their execution order. The process description consists of simple atomic processes or complex composite processes that are sometimes abstract and not executable. Each function provided by the service is considered as an *Atomic Process*, whereas combined multiple services are named as *Composite Service*.
- The *Service Grounding* stores the detailed technical communication information on protocols and formats. This concept provides the physical location to the technical description realized in WSDL. This WSDL-file is called when the service is executed, as well as during conversion process to retrieve the technical inputs and outputs of the service.

The described core concepts are shown in detail in Figure 3 with their subtypes and processes. The listed types provide the basis for OWL-S to create and use relations, which are utilized for improved interoperability.

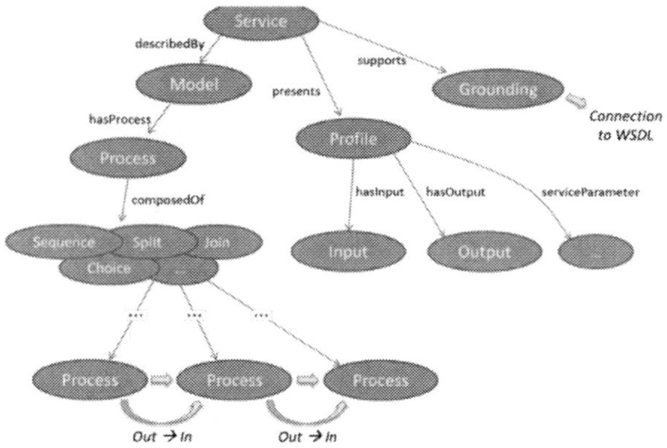

Figure 3. Upper service ontology for OWL-S.

However, the relations generated using only OWL-S ontology form the minimal relationship for services, enough to be operated. If the usage scenario requires involvement of additional relations, these must be defined creating a *service and workflow ontology* and including it inside a Semantic Repository [15]. This ontology can contain more contextual information with relations to enhance the interoperability [16].

D. Triple Stores

Computational tasks often require collection and storage of the results for further usage. Storage of information without a structured form increases the complexity and the time to access the data, and reducing the flexibility for further modifications and enhancements [17] causing fragmentation problems. To address this issue, databases play the role as containers, which collect and organize the data for swift future access [18].

Semantic repositories are similar to the database management systems (DBMS) in terms of providing functionality for organization, storage, and querying the data, but differ from them in terms of the type of organization and data representation. Unlike DBMS, semantic repositories use schemata to structure the data, but are also able to establish relationships between stored values. Regarding to data representations, semantic repositories work with flexible and generic physical data models, which allow merging other ontologies "on the fly" and relate the data among merged schemata [19]. As OWL-S is based on OWL, which is built on top of RDF, see Section II-B, the data operations are performed using the same RDF structure. This structure provides descriptions to query the data, and allows optimal extension of relations allowing multiple use. The Sesame framework [20] is one RDF storage solution, which can be used in this context. It allows creation, processing, editing, storing, and querying RDF data, therefore, it is chosen to serve as a storage solution in this approach.

E. Business Process Execution Language and OWL-S

The Business Process Execution Language (BPEL) is a language for describing and executing business processes in general. It provides an XML-based syntax and allows data manipulation for data processing and data flow. It also allows orchestration of services, after specifying the service set and the service execution order [21]. Numerous platforms (such as Oracle BPEL Process Manager, IBM WebSphere Application Server Enterprise, IBM WebSphere Studio Application Developer Integration Edition, and Microsoft BizTalk Server 2004) support the execution of BPEL processes. Some of these platforms also provide graphical editing tools.

For the languages OWL-S and BPEL, there exist tools for the automated execution of Web services described in WSDL. They also permit implementations in any programming languages as long as they provide valid WSDL descriptions. Different from BPEL, OWL-S facilitates Semantic Web technologies, which make the structure meaningful for human and machines and allow automated design and orchestration of services, whereas BPEL does not [22].

The execution order of services is usually defined using a design tool (textual or graphical), which is then executed and monitored using an engine. For BPEL, Apache BPEL Designer and JBoss Tools BPEL Editor can be given as examples to design tools, whereas Oracle BPEL Process Manager, Apache ODE, IBM WebSphere Process Server, and Microsoft BizTalk Server can be listed as examples for execution and monitoring.

Using OWL-S increases the interoperability and enables automatic orchestration between the services, but it requires a deep knowledge in the domain. Hence, there are few editors available for OWL-S. Additionally, to create complex workflows, Protégé OWL-S Editor [23], which is a plug-in for Protégé, can be utilized. Nevertheless, the usage of this plug-in also requires advanced knowledge in the domain. All of these tools must be locally installed to be used. To convert Web services into Semantic Web services, a design tool and an execution engine are necessary.

In another approach, created in the context of the THESEUS funding program, a framework for the discovery, integration, processing, and fusion of Semantic Web services is described [24]. According to a user request, the framework identifies and assembles matching services for problem solving and creates a plan for the composition and execution order. The focus is on the matching of heterogeneous services and the fusion of all gathered information in real time. The harmonizing and mapping of knowledge is carried out based on ontologies.

The advantage of our approach is the continuous integration of services in an cloud-based infrastructure. The user is guided from the provided Web user interface to a graphical editor, where individual services could be integrated, experiments could be designed by orchestrating these services and stored as specific workflows that could also be executed within the framework in a further step. This execution of workflows could be initiated by the creator of the workflow or by another authorized user who is allowed to get the results. Within the developed infrastructure, specific services can be deployed and assigned to simple or complex workflows graphically. Each provided tool can be used and executed without detailed knowledge of the underlying Semantic Web technologies. All functionality of the cloud-based infrastructure platform can be accessed using a simple Web browser without installation of additional software applications.

III. Scenario

In the engineering domain, a conventional practice for quality assurance of the manufactured final product are comparison checks against the virtual designed product model. This accuracy check is performed by comparing two 3D models. First a scanning process creates and transfers accurate points, and in this way a virtual 3D model is created. The entire model consists of millions of 3D points, which must be matched and compared with the designed product model to find out the discrepancies by calculating the distances of points in both, the designed model and the virtual clone of the final product [25][26].

The manufacturer of these big turbine blades uses different tools to perform this comparison task and these supplementary tools generate additional license and training costs. The handling of different software solutions requires many hours of work. By using the workflow and service infrastructure and the distributed HPC solution described here, the comparison time is significantly reduced. These advantages allow the company to focus on quality measurement and also increase the capacity of the company for initiating new projects. Figure 4 shows a complete Kaplan turbine (a), one blade that is to be evaluated (b) and the scanned and virtualized 3D model with color-coded comparison results (c) [26]. The virtual model is created by an open-source tool for rendering and visualization [27].

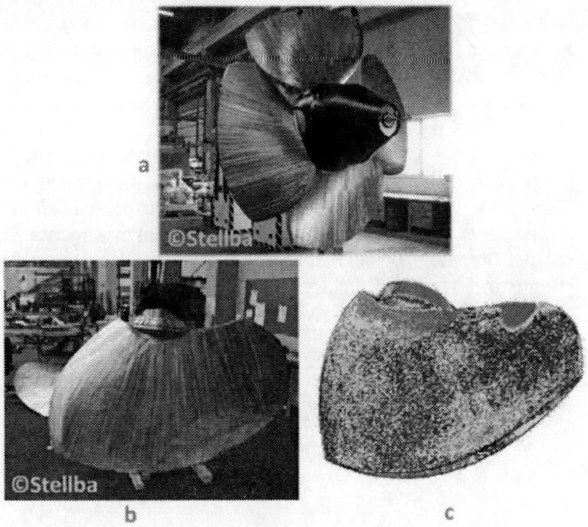

Figure 4. A complete manufactured Kaplan turbine (a), its single turbine blade (b) and the color-coded comparison of its scan and design (c).

The workflow described in this scenario consists of several orchestrated services. In the first step a service is included, which allows to load files as input for the experiment. In this scenario two files, a Computer-Aided Design (CAD) model and a laser scanned point file are chosen. With the help of another service that provides an user interface an initial coarse alignment of both models can be made manually. Finally, the automated comparison of the models is performed in the next service that uses the HPC cluster. This is helpful, in order to shorten the comparative process by increasing the computing power. The result of this calculation is displayed in a dedicated application, the distance viewer. The details on this scenario can be found in the work done by Holm et al. [4].

IV. Concept

This approach follows the idea of offering individual functionality by services via standardized interfaces. These can be easily integrated, offered and consumed via a cloud-based infrastructure platform. Unfortunately, conventional service descriptions do not provide enough self-description capabilities. Therefore, in the concept of this approach, a language has to be chosen, which allows semantic descriptions to add more contextual information to the services. There are a number of semantic technologies that provide machine and human readable descriptions, such as OWL-S, Web Service Modeling Ontology (WSMO), Web Service Modeling Language (WSML), and the Semantic Web Services Framework (SWSF) [28]. The most recently updated language to describe Semantic Web services, OWL-S, is used to provide descriptions that are machine readable and processable.

In this approach OWL-S satisfies the requirements and is chosen to describe the services and their orchestrations, describes further on as workflows. In addition to the description of the technical parameters, each service must also provide the information on the provided functionality, e.g., analyzing methods and calculation models such as the finite element method or the visualization and comparison of 3D-models.

The used ontology, which follows the OWL-S standard, is shown in Figure 3. Based on this upper-level ontology, a Service and Workflow Ontology (SWO) is created to store domain-specific information for interoperability of services and workflows. This SWO with its concepts, instances, and the relationships between them, is shown in Figure 5. The defined SWO makes it possible to differentiate the service categories from each other via *CFServiceType* class. It also introduces *User* and *UserGroup* for permission control, which is one requirement to separate users in multi-user environments. Based on the described *InputParameter* and *OutputParameter* classes suggestions for technically matching services can be made, during the process of the creation of an individual experiment.

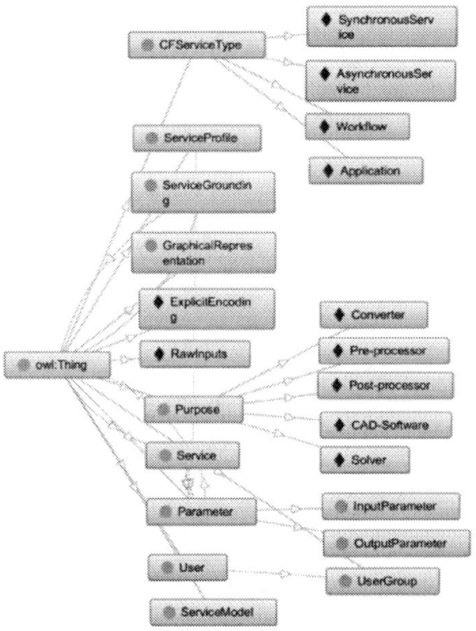

Figure 5. This ontology stores context-specific service and workflow information.

Due to the complexity of OWL-S and the necessary embedding into the application domain, all available technical Web service interfaces need to be described using standards, such as WSDL. The semantic service description is generated out of these WSDL descriptions. All necessary additional information is offered to the user by forms within the Web portal and transferred to the description. Based on this technical description with its functions, input, and output types, a Semantic Web service model, described in OWL-S, is generated and integrated into the Semantic Repository. This transformation and conversion is automatically performed by provided converter library, Semantic Web Service Creator, shown in Figure 6. As depicted, the creator retrieves the URL of the WSDL file, the service type and user provided semantic information for the concrete data types of service inputs and outputs in addition to the data types parsed from WSDL. In a next step, it converts the service into a specific instantiated Semantic Web service description in OWL-S that is stored in the Semantic Repository.

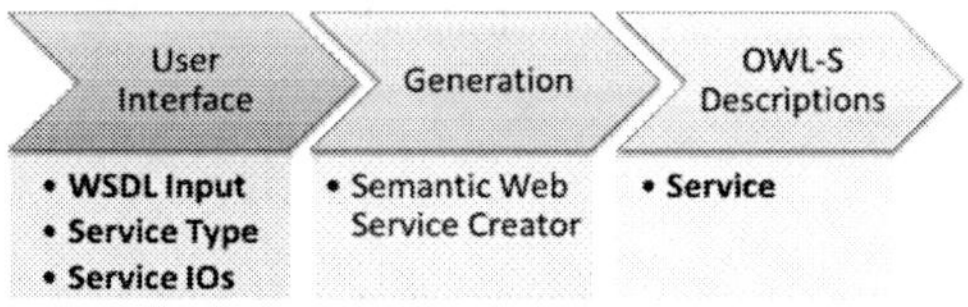

Figure 6. Generation of services in OWL-S.

In principle, according to the different design of the experiments, two service categories are differentiated. On the one hand, services that have a role to play in delivering data within a specified period of time, and on the other hand, those long-lasting services that do not matter that the data quickly land at the addressee. In this approach, we used these services types in three different application categories:

- Synchronous Service
- Asynchronous Service
- Asynchronous Web Application

These application categories are disjoint, i.e., each Web service can only be assigned to exactly one category and stored in the Semantic Repository. Standard Web services belong to the *Synchronous Service* category. Whenever a request is made, they must respond within 60 seconds, which is defined as default timeout limit in HTTP. Every service, which does not require an interaction with the user, is part of this category. An *Asynchronous Service* is a special category that the services within return information whenever the calling component checks the status. Unlike the previous category, asynchronous services can display feedback messages and these services can last days or even weeks to complete. A response to the calling component reports the status by telling either the service is completed or still ongoing. Lastly, the *Asynchronous Web Application* category contains Web services, which are similar to asynchronous services, but without a status check. This type of service is used to provide interactive user interfaces on Web pages within the Web portal. Since the completion of the tasks for this service type depend on user interaction, a trigger must be sent to the called for reporting.

Services provide functionality for special tasks, but complex tasks in the engineering domain usually consist of multiple steps. Therefore, one service is not sufficient and an orchestration of services is needed. The cloud-based infrastructure allows users to create experiments and orchestrate services individually, formalized by a workflow. Depending on the application domain, a workflow can have multiple definitions, but in the context of this paper, a workflow will be considered as a set and ordered list of chained up Web services provided with a service description in WSDL and with SOAP-based APIs to involve, deploy and perform each specific task with or without user interaction. According to the different requirements of the experiments to the editing and execution environment, four different constructs were defined in order to be able to model corresponding workflows, as depicted in Figure 7.

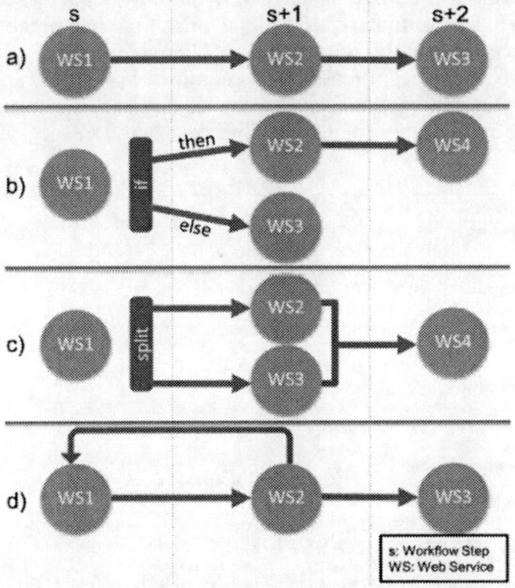

Figure 7. Possible workflow design and execution types.

A workflow of an experiment can of course be designed with a combination of these and consist of one or more of the listed types. The following workflow design and execution types are possible using the OWL-S:

(a) A linear, sequential execution of several Web services, which often fits for many situations. The services within the workflow will be executed one after another, one at each workflow step.
(b) Branching the workflow with *if-then-else*, which follows one of the two possible branches after evaluating the inserted condition. This is mostly useful for evaluation of a simulation and performing additional tasks in case the results are not satisfactory.
(c) Parallel execution of two branches simultaneously via *split*, in case their inputs and outputs do not depend on each other. This type of workflow is generally useful if a sequential execution of multiple services would take long time and a separate execution of independent services would reduce this.
(d) Looping back to a specific step using *repeat-until*, until a condition is fulfilled. This type is useful to iterate specific step(s) until the result is the acceptable value.

As shown in Figure 8, a user interacts with the Web portal of cloud-based infrastructure platform via standard Web browser. A part of the portal is the graphical user interface for the creation and editing process of workflows. Each workflow describes an experiment and consists of several orchestrated services. Within this concept, the workflow editing component stores these individual experiments in an storage solution with attached annotations, the Semantic Repository, when the editing task is finished. Furthermore, independent of the editing step, the user can initiate the execution of stored workflows of the respective experiments. The result of each conducted experiment is delivered to the Web portal by the execution component of the workflow management and execution component.

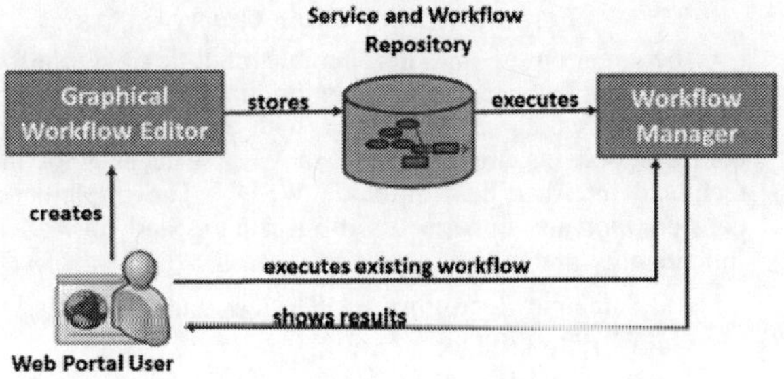

Figure 8. User creates a workflow of an experiment and initiates the execution.

This suggested kind of service categorization and interaction make it possible to support users and their specific needs to complete their tasks with synchronous or asynchronous processes executed in the background. A service orchestration is performed by using a component for workflow editing to create a semantic workflow description. First, the workflows are created or edited and the services are arranged in the correct order, in which they have to be executed. In the process chain, the output of a service is passed to the input of the next service. This can be done by an supported graphical editing tool. The use of a tool has the advantage that the complexity remains hidden from the user. The user must not have a detailed knowledge of OWL-S to describe their workflow. The graphically sketched sequence of services is formalized in a workflow and stored in an XML-based meta-format that serves as input for the conversion into OWL-S. The automatic conversion of these inputs into workflows is also performed by the aforementioned Semantic Web Service Creator. Figure 9 shows the process of the generation of workflow descriptions for different experiments. Both processes in Figure 6 and Figure 9 use the same library for conversion. However, the inputs and outputs of the converter shown in bold text are different depending on the purpose. The former is for Semantic Web service creation whereas the latter is for workflow creation.

The service domain is structured by an upper model for the generic description and vocabulary of services and workflows in OWL-S. It defines how services must be described and specified, using annotations and technical descriptions. The knowledge of different application domains is represented by several domain ontologies that describe application functionalities in detail. The SWO provides properties to define several additional relations. The next section describes the special tooling to design individual workflows, where each step in the workflow

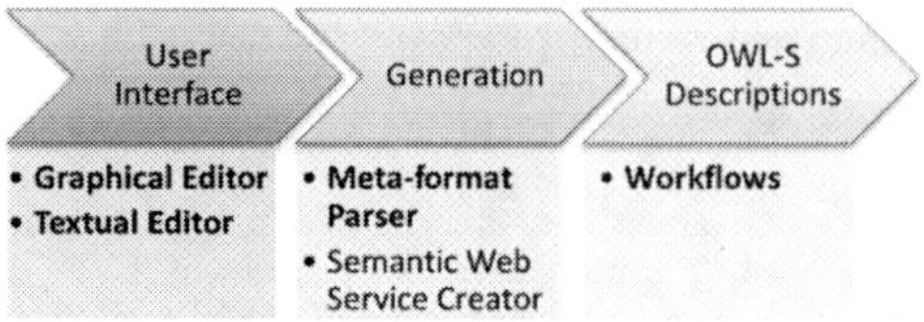

Figure 9. Generation of workflows in OWL-S.

must be assigned to a service.

V. Interaction of Core Components

The creation of an interoperable and flexible platform provided as IaaS requires an embodiment of several core components which are compatible with each other [4]. These core components are presented as Web services with their technical interface description in WSDL. The implemented core components to form the infrastructure and host all the functionality are:

- Semantic Repository for Services and Workflows
- Workflow Editor
- Semantic Web Service Creator
- Workflow Manager

Generic platform services are utilities which can be used for generic purposes such as loading data structures with different formats, e.g., Computer-Aided Engineering (CAE) and Computer-Aided Design (CAD) data. On the other hand, vendor-provided Web services introduce and wrap functionality for specific software components of different complexity levels. The services can encapsulate complex calculations and comparison operators or even provide the interface to third-party systems to perform complex calculations in HPC clusters. *Semantic Repository for Services and Workflows* component hosts the OWL-S descriptions of these services as well as workflows in triple store format. As a requirement by the project, a Web-based solution for easy integration of new services was necessary. Tools which works with OWL-S did not provide either a Web interface or were too complex for new users. Therefore, a wrapper and interface for easy conversion between WSDL and OWL-S is implemented. New services can be integrated with the help of a graphical user interface starting with a technical description of the service in WSDL. Using this description and additional information added to forms, the services are automatically converted into Semantic Web services, without requiring specific knowledge of used complex Semantic Web technologies, such as OWL and OWL-S. The service providers are able to deploy the WSDL description of their Web services via the *Workflow Editor (WFE)* component using the Web portal. This component assists in the integration of Web services in the Semantic Repository and creation of workflows. Unlike existing tools that available for different technologies as mentioned by Grolinger et. al. [28], the implemented WFE performs all tasks without installation of any software on the end-user side and targets all users with different knowledge in the domain. The *Semantic Web Service Creator* uses the absolute URL to the WSDL description of the service to generate the Semantic Web service descriptions in OWL-S. Then it stores and registers them in the Semantic Repository, including the inputs and outputs of the services. In another context, this component creates semantic workflow descriptions in OWL-S, based on the XML meta-format introduced by the WFE and stores the creator of the workflow along with their user group. A partial and incomplete example of this meta-format is given in Figure 10. The basic requirement for all saved services and workflows are unique names which are created automatically and a unique identifier of the user to set the ownership of a workflow. This identifier, a session token, is retrieved using an external identity service, OpenStack Keystone, therefore, no usernames or passwords are stored in the semantic repository [29]. The Semantic Repository is based on a central domain model, formalized as an OWL ontology, that describes the input and output types for the matchmaking process of the services. Finally, the *Workflow Manager (WFM)* component starts, manages, orchestrates, monitors workflows, and checks permissions of the users for the execution. This component is also responsible for passing the data between services.

```
<workflow URI="namespace/Workflow.owl#Name">
  <input ID="input1"
      URI="namespace/workflows/Workflow#extraParameters"
      x="-6" y="527"/>
  <input ID="input2" URI="namespace/workflows/Workflow#file"
      x="53" y="623"/>
  <input ID="input3"
      URI="namespace/workflows/Workflow#sessionToken"
      x="55" y="721"/>
  <output ID="output1"
      URI="namespace/workflows/Workflow#DistanceFile"
      x="1535" y="783"/>
  <services>
    <sequence>
      <service URI="namespace#CADFileService" x="387" y="43">
        <input URI="namespace#buttonText"/>
        <input URI="namespace#desc" value="Select"/>
        <input URI="namespace#filter" value="pts"/>
        <input ID="input3" URI="namespace#sessionToken"/>
        <input ID="input1" URI="namespace#extraParameters"/>
        <input URI="namespace#gssToken"/>
        <input URI="namespace#header_base64"/>
        <input URI="namespace#serviceID"/>
        <output ID="p1_output1" URI="namespace#fileSelected"/>
        <output ID="p1_output2" URI="namespace#status_base64"/>
      </service>
      <service>
        ...
      </service>
    </sequence>
  </services>
</workflow>
```

Figure 10. Workflow description in the XML meta format.

An overview of the interaction of the core components of the developed platform is given in Figure 11. The main user interface of the developed platform is a Web portal, and it translates user actions into core component specific requests, e.g., during workflow design, workflow and service execution, service monitoring, and result management. The communication between the Web portal and the components are performed using SOAP messages therefore these requests are converted into this format according to the API. With the graphical interface of the WFE, the user gets access to the services stored in the Semantic Repository. Here, services dedicated to experiments can be chained up to create dedicated workflows, such as for the comparison of 3D models. Each created workflow is also stored in the Semantic Repository and can be found easily by simple properties. Determined by the complexity, multiple workflows can be necessary to finalize and perform the tasks needed for the whole experiment. In this case, semantic descriptions can use workflows similar to a Semantic Web service as "sub-workflows". Similar to workflows, sub-workflows are also stored in semantic repositories. Both of them are comparable to Semantic Web services, and reusable. Moreover, their descriptions are updated without causing any fragmentation.

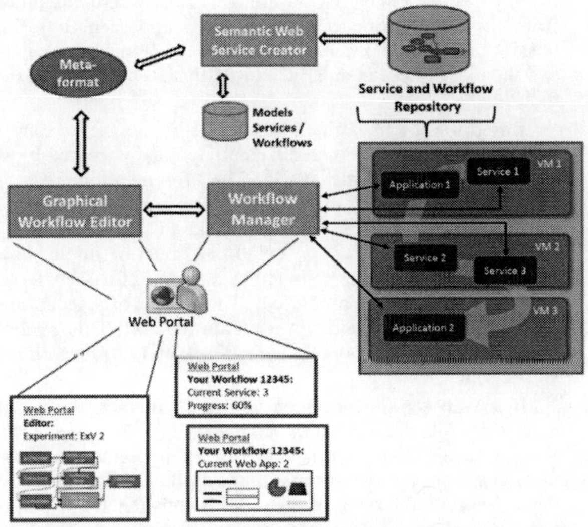

Figure 11. Overview of the interactions of the core components.

To store the experiments, the graphical contents of the related workflows are transferred into a XML-based meta-format. This format serves as input for the Semantic Web Service Creator that generates the workflow descriptions in OWL-S. The WFE is provided as a Web service which is described in WSDL. Additionally, all methods that available in its description are accessible through its graphical implementation. The graphical implementation of the WFE is currently developed using PHP and JavaScript, but can completely be written using another programming language. To allow that and prevent language lock-in, the workflows can also be defined using the defined meta-format. This format is also easy to understand and sometimes preferable by experts for fine-tunings. The purpose of graphical interface of the WFE is to provide a full-featured yet simple user interface to translate visual actions into this meta-format and then to prepare SOAP messages. These messages are later sent to the service implementation of the WFE.

The WFM component is used for the management and execution of individual predetermined workflows. In the execution task, the component processes the individual workflows and accordingly queries the listed services in the defined order. If the service execution is completed and the answer of a service is received, the next step in the workflow is activated. The results of respective services are unified and added to a single representation structure, which is passed at the end of all processing steps back to the UI of the Web portal.

The WFM can execute the workflows designed following any of the depicted types in Figure 7. For the cases b and d, the next step is determined by a logical expression. These logical expressions are defined during the workflow design. For user friendliness, these expressions are adapted and simplified, and can be one of *greaterThan*, *greaterOrEqual*, *equalTo*, *lessThan*, or *lessOrEqual*.

An example of a graphical workflow is shown in Figure 12. Using the toolbar, one can append the services into the workflow choosing a service to add and using *append service to workflow* button. They can also add snippets for branching (if-then-else), iteration (repeat-until), or parallel execution (split) using the corresponding buttons.

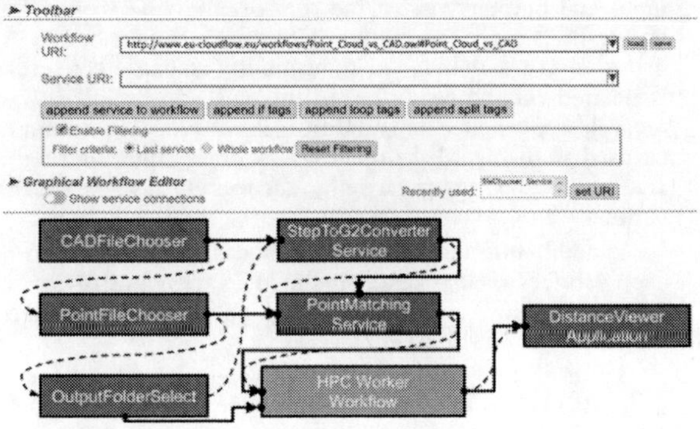

Figure 12. The graphical workflow editor UI shows the scenario workflow.

The more the list of available services within the Semantic Repository grows, the more difficult the user finds it to choose the appropriate service for the workflow. To prevent this, the WFE introduces different filtering mechanisms. The service list has auto-complete functionality which allows searching as the user types. Although this helps to find the service that the user is looking for, it does not, however, provide the information about the compatibility of this service. To solve this, the WFE offers optional filtering method using the semantic information of the services. During service integration into the Semantic Repository, the users provide the acceptable types or file formats for the inputs and outputs of the service. During workflow design, when a service is appended into the workflow, the service list is updated containing only the compatible ones. This filtering has two modes which may suit for different situations. *Last service* mode considers only the last service appended into workflow and lists the services that are only compatible with this one. This is an aggressive mode which is useful if there are too many services registered in the Semantic Repository and only fully compatible services are desired. *Whole workflow* mode provides rather a moderate filter which also takes the previously appended services into consideration during filtering. To illustrate both modes, one can assume that there are several services denoted as S registered in the Semantic Repository R as:

$$\forall S \in R = \{A, B, C, D, E, F\} \tag{1}$$

where each S in R is compatible with the services written in their indices listed in a compatibility list L:

$$L = \{A_{B,C}, B_D, C_{D,E,F}, D_{A,B}, E_F, F_{B,D}\} \tag{2}$$

According to L, for example, $A_{B,C}$ is an integrated service that is compatible with services B and C. If $A_{B,C}$ is appended into the workflow as the first service, with the *Last service* mode enabled, the list will be updated to display only B_D and $C_{D,E,F}$. With this mode still on, when B_D is appended, the list will only display $D_{A,B}$ since this is the only compatible service with B_D. On the other hand, if *Whole workflow* mode is active and $A_{B,C}$ is appended, similarly, B_D and $C_{D,E,F}$ will be listed. When B_D is chosen from these two, the list will contain $D_{A,B}$ as well as B_D and $C_{D,E,F}$ since B_D and $C_{D,E,F}$ were compatible with $A_{B,C}$ which is an existing service inside the workflow. To increase the compatibility of the services, the input and output types of the services must be well defined during the service integration. However, it might be the case that a service with untested compatibility among other services is desired for the next step. In this case, to list all services regardless of their compatibilities, *Reset Filtering* button can be used to disregard the relations. Similarly, the filtering can also be disabled temporarily by unchecking *Enable Filtering* button.

In addition to this two filtering modes, a history of recently used services is also kept. This reduces the work of the user during workflow creation by listing all used services during the active session for quick access.

The execution order in WFE is represented by dashed arrows inside WFE and the blue blocks are the individual workflow steps. If a service is selected to be executed on HPC by the user in the editing process, an HPC sub-workflow is used. In the graphical editor interface this is marked as a green block. This means that the WFM initiates the service execution in a dedicated HPC server environment.

The structure of an HPC sub-workflow in turn consists of a sequence of three tasks:

1) *pre-processing task* to generate the command to be executed by HPC process,
2) *HPC command task*, which receives the command by user interface and gives feedback to the user, and
3) *post-processing task*, which converts the output from the HPC process into application specific output.

If the workflow is complex and consists of more services, the service connections can be shown or hidden using the *Show service connections* toggle.

For each workflow, the manager initiates execution procedures and tracks the progress individually. As the user, who created the workflow, and their group are stored in the semantic repository during workflow creation, it is possible to prepare a list of allowed users for the workflow execution. Therefore, before starting a workflow, the WFM checks whether the user or group has permission to run it to prevent unauthorized execution. It also provides a monitoring functionality, which allows users to leave the workflow anytime and return at later stage to continue where they left off. This maximizes the benefits of such a cloud-based platform, supporting access anytime and from any desktop or mobile device with Internet access. If the workflow does not need user input, the WFM is even able to complete it automatically and display its results to the user at a later time. The usability can be extended by including reusable utility services such as an e-mail service which notifies the user who ran the workflow at any step.

As explained in the previous sections, services of different vendors can be used that are implemented by different programming techniques and run within the cloud on different application servers. Nevertheless, during the lifetime of a workflow, the user does not need to know, where the services are stored and how the data is forwarded to the next service. The manager component retrieves the service descriptions and performs the tasks without user notification and the complexity of all associated services within a workflow remains hidden from the user. Using the cloud-based approach, it is also possible to include a service within a workflow which could execute the services in an HPC cluster that reduces computation times.

Based on their defined service types, synchronous or asynchronous, services are differentiated and executed by the execution engine of the WFM. The aforementioned service for the pre- and post-processing tasks are implemented as *Synchronous Services*, because they take just a few seconds to execute. However, HPC command task must be implemented as *Asynchronous Service*, since the duration of a Web service execution cannot be predicted. The status of execution is monitored and provided via a status method. This result is provided to the user as HTML feedback and displayed on the Web portal.

If a Web service provides an UI to interact, the service must be implemented as an *Asynchronous Web Application*. Services that belong to this category are implemented similar to *Asynchronous Services*, but contrarily do not need to deliver their status. This service type explicitly tells the WFM that the task is completed. After receiving this notification, the WFM performs the next step and gives feedback on the Web portal.

VI. Conclusion and Future Work

This paper explained the concept and realization of a flexible cloud-based infrastructure platform, which involves Semantic Web technologies and tailored tools for the creation, execution, and management of workflows and conducted services by graphical user interface. The realized platform allows a seamless integration and combination of engineering services, and a controlled execution and monitoring of used resources. It satisfies the requirements for the development and execution of user-driven experiments defined as workflows, without requiring detailed knowledge on High Performance Computing or other underlying technologies.

The platform offers a Web portal that can be accessed via standard Web browser, without the need of installing additional software. New services can be integrated and orchestrated to workflows with the help of graphical user interfaces. Starting with a technical description of the service in WSDL and using additional information added to forms, services are automatically converted into Semantic Web services, without requiring specific knowledge of used complex Semantic Web technologies, such as OWL and OWL-S. With another graphical user interface, the Workflow Editor, these integrated services can be orchestrated within the meaning of the experiment and stored as workflow descriptions in an platform-wide accessible Semantic Repository. The component assists the user by allowing search and filtering incompatible services during workflow design. Another core component of the created solution, the Workflow Manager, is used to execute, orchestrate, and monitor the created workflows of the experiments. The result of each conducted experiment is in turn delivered to the user via the Web portal of the cloud-based infrastructure platform.

Another advantage of this approach is the combination of the created platform with high-performance servers. Complex tasks can be outsourced to these servers and this results in enormous time savings and allows the experts to carry out more experiments with products, which was omitted due to the complexity and the required computing power until now. Of course, the possibility to conduct these experiments leads to an enormous increase in expert knowledge.

In future, the Workflow Editor will be able to perform automated dynamic workflow design. A dynamic workflow formalizes an orchestration of services, supported by an automated matchmaking process that provides adequate services ordered by their confidence values, which is only possible using Semantic Web technologies. Furthermore, the Workflow Editor will be able to insert converter services into the workflow automatically, just for adjustment of input and output types, e.g., convert units of measurement and file formats.

Acknowledgments

This research has received funding in part by the European Union's Horizon 2020 research and innovation program under grant agreement No 680448 (CAxMan). And this work is also based on preparatory work, which was funded in part by the 7th Framework Program of the European Union, project number 609100 (project CloudFlow). The responsibility for this publication lies with the authors.

References

[1] V. Gezer and S. Bergweiler, "Service and Workflow Engineering based on Semantic Web Technologies," in Tenth International Conference on Mobile Ubiquitous Computing, Systems, Services and Technologies (UBICOMM 2016), International Academy, Research, and Industry Association (IARIA). IARIA, 10 2016, pp. 152–157.

[2] T. Barton, "Cloud Computing," in E-Business mit Cloud Computing. Springer Fachmedien Wiesbaden, 2014, pp. 41–52.

[3] A. Ranabahu and A. Sheth, "Semantics Centric Solutions for Application and Data Portability in Cloud Computing," in Cloud Computing Technology and Science (CloudCom), 2010 IEEE Second International Conference on, 2010, pp. 234–241.

[4] H. H. Holm, J. M. Hjelmervik, and V. Gezer, "CloudFlow - An Infrastructure for Engineering Workflows in the Cloud," in Tenth International Conference on Mobile Ubiquitous Computing, Systems, Services and Technologies (UBICOMM 2016), International Academy, Research, and Industry Association (IARIA). IARIA, 10 2016, pp. 158–165.

[5] R. Cyganiak, D. Wood, and M. Lanthaler, "Web Services Architecture," W3C Working Group Note, 2004, [retrieved: March 2017]. [Online]. Available: https://www.w3.org/TR/2004/NOTE-ws-arch-20040211/

[6] E. Christensen, F. Curbera, G. Meredith, and S. Weerawarana, "Web Services Description Language (WSDL) 1.1," W3C, W3C Note, March 2001, [retrieved: March 2017]. [Online]. Available: http://www.w3.org/TR/wsdl

[7] R. Chinnici, J.-J. Moreau, A. Ryman, and S. Weerawarana, "Web Services Description Language (WSDL) Version 2.0 Part 1: Core Language," W3C Recommendation, 2007, [retrieved: March 2017]. [Online]. Available: https://www.w3.org/TR/wsdl20/

[8] T. Berners-Lee, J. Hendler, and O. Lassila, "The Semantic Web," Scientific American, 2001, [retrieved: March 2017]. [Online]. Available: http://www.jeckle.de/files/tblSW.pdf

[9] G. Klyne and J. J. Carroll, "Resource Description Framework (RDF): Concepts and Abstract Syntax," W3C Recommendation, 2004, [retrieved: March 2017]. [Online]. Available: http://www.w3.org/TR/2004/REC-rdf-concepts-20040210/

[10] P. Hitzler, M. Krötzsch, and S. Rudolph, Foundations of Semantic Web Technologies. Chapman & Hall/CRC, 2009.

[11] R. Cyganiak, D. Wood, and M. Lanthaler, "RDF 1.1 Concepts and Abstract Syntax," W3C Recommendation, 2004, [retrieved: March 2017]. [Online]. Available: http://www.w3.org/TR/2014/REC-rdf11-concepts-20140225/

[12] P. F. Patel-Schneider, P. Hayes, and I. Horrocks, "OWL Web Ontology Language Semantics and Abstract Syntax," Feb. 2004, [retrieved: March 2017]. [Online]. Available: http://www.w3.org/TR/2004/REC-owl-semantics-20040210/

[13] I. Horrocks, B. Parsia, P. Patel-Schneider, and J. Hendler, "Semantic Web Architecture: Stack or Two Towers?" in Principles and Practice of Semantic Web Reasoning, Third International Workshop, PPSWR 2005, Dagstuhl Castle, Germany, F. Fages and S. Soliman, Eds. Berlin, Heidelberg: Springer Berlin Heidelberg, 2005, pp. 37–41.

[14] D. Martin et al., "OWL-S: Semantic Markup for Web Services," 2004, [retrieved: March 2017]. [Online]. Available: http://www.w3.org/Submission/2004/SUBM-OWL-S-20041122/

[15] S. Bergweiler, "A Flexible Framework for Adaptive Knowledge Retrieval and Fusion for Kiosk Systems and Mobile Clients," in Eighth International Conference on Mobile Ubiquitous Computing, Systems, Services and Technologies (UBICOMM 2014), International Academy, Research, and Industry Association (IARIA). IARIA, 8 2014, pp. 164–171.

[16] M. Loskyll, I. Heck, J. Schlick, and M. Schwarz, "Context-based orchestration for control of resource-efficient manufacturing processes," Future Internet, vol. 4, no. 3, 2012, pp. 737–761.

[17] C. Casanave, "Designing a Semantic Repository - Integrating architectures for reuse and integration," 2007, [retrieved: March 2017]. [Online]. Available: https://www.w3.org/2007/06/eGov-dc/papers/SemanticRepository.pdf

[18] "Webster Database Definition," [retrieved: March 2017]. [Online]. Available: http://www.merriam-webster.com/dictionary/database

[19] Ontotext, "GraphDB - Semantic Repository," [retrieved: March 2017]. [Online]. Available: http://ontotext.com/knowledgehub/fundamentals/semantic-repository

[20] Sesame Framework Contributors, "Sesame Java Framework," [retrieved: March 2017]. [Online]. Available: http://archive.rdf4j.org/users/ch01.html

[21] "Web Services Business Process Execution Language Version 2.0," OASIS Web Services Business Process Execution Language (WSBPEL) Technical Commitee, 2007, [retrieved: March 2017]. [Online]. Available: http://docs.oasis-open.org/wsbpel/2.0/OS/wsbpel-v2.0-OS.html

[22] S. Bansal, A. Bansal, G. Gupta, and M. B. Blake, "Generalized semantic Web service composition," Service Oriented Computing and Applications, vol. 10, no. 2, 2016, pp. 111–133.

[23] D. Elenius et al., "The OWL-S editor - a development tool for semantic web services," in ESWC, 2005, pp. 78–92.

[24] S. Bergweiler, "Interactive service composition and query," in Towards the Internet of Services: The Theseus Program. Springer Berlin Heidelberg, 2014, pp. 169–184.

[25] C. Stahl, E. Bellos, C. Altenhofen, and J. Hjelmervik, "Flexible Integration of Cloud-based Engineering Services using Semantic Technologies," in Industrial Technology (ICIT), 2015 IEEE International Conference on, 2015, pp. 1520–1525.

[26] Stellba, "Comparing CAD Models with 3D Scanned Manufactured Parts on the Cloud," [retrieved: March 2017]. [Online]. Available: {http://eu-cloudflow.eu/experiments/first-wave/experiment_6.html}

[27] C. Dyken et al., "A framework for OpenGL client-server rendering," in Cloud Computing Technology and Science (CloudCom), 2012 IEEE 4th International Conference, 2012, pp. 729–734.

[28] K. Grolinger, M. A. M. Capretz, A. Cunha, and S. Tazi, "Integration of business process modeling and web services: a survey," Service Oriented Computing and Applications, vol. 8, no. 2, 2014, pp. 105–128. [Online]. Available: http://dx.doi.org/10.1007/s11761-013-0138-2

[29] H. H. Holm, J. M. Hjelmervik, and V. Gezer, "CloudFlow - an infrastructure for engineering workflows in the cloud," in UBICOMM 2016: The Tenth International Conference on Mobile Ubiquitous Computing, Systems, Services and Technologies. IARIA, October 2016, pp. 158–165.

Advanced Device Authentication for the Industrial Internet of Things

Rainer Falk and Steffen Fries
Corporate Technology
Siemens AG
Munich, Germany
e-mail: {rainer.falk|steffen.fries}@siemens.com

***Abstract*—Device authentication is an essential security feature to ensure the reliable operation of cyber physical systems and the industrial Internet of Things. Solutions have to be both robust and practical to use. After giving an overview on device authentication options, several proposals for advanced device authentication means are presented to increase the attack robustness of device authentication. A well-known cryptographic device authentication using a symmetric cryptographic key or a digital certificate with a corresponding private key for device authentication can be extended with additional validations to check the device identity. Ideas from advanced human user authentication means like multi-factor authentication, continuous authentication, and secret sharing are applied to enhance device authentication.**

Keywords–device authentication; Internet of Things; embedded security; cyber security.

I. INTRODUCTION

The need for technical information technology (IT) security measures increases rapidly to protect products and solutions from manipulation and reverse engineering [1][2]. The scope of the security considerations is further broadened to also include operational technology (OT) environments, in which IT technology is applied to industrial control systems. Cryptographic IT security mechanisms have been known for many years, and are applied in smart devices (Internet of Things, Cyber Physical Systems, industrial and energy automation systems, operation technology) [3]. Such mechanisms target authentication, system and communication integrity, and confidentiality of data in transit or at rest. Security standards have been developed that define security processes, security requirements, and security solutions [3]. The standard IEC 62443 addresses general industrial and automation control systems and can be applied to different vertical automation systems like factory automation, process automation, or building automation. Also, several security standards and guidelines have been defined specifically for particular vertical application domains [4][5][6]. Examples are ISO/IEC 62351 [4] defining security for energy automation systems, and ISO 15118 [7] that defines security for the charging of electric vehicles.

A central security mechanism is authentication that is required for human users, devices, and for software processes: By authentication, a claimed identity is proven. Authentication of a human user can be performed by verifying something the person knows (e.g., a password), something the person possesses (e.g., a physical authentication token, smart card, or a passport), or something the person is (biometric property, e.g., a fingerprint, voice, iris, or behavior).

Advanced authentication techniques make use of multiple authentication factors, and performing authentication checks continuously during an ongoing, authenticated session. With multi-factor authentication, several independent authentication factors are verified, e.g., a password and an authentication token. This increases the security level of the authentication process as multiple independent authentication factors are verified. With continuous authentication, also called active authentication, the behavior of a user during an authenticated session is monitored to determine if the authenticated user is still the one using the session. This increases the security level of a session after a user has been authenticated. It also helps to improve the user friendliness of a security solution as continuous user authentication is not intrusive to the user as repeated explicit re-authentications would be.

While advanced authentication techniques like multi-factor authentication and continuous authentication are known for human users, it seems that these technologies have not yet been applied for device authentication neither in research work nor in real world deployments.

With ubiquitous machine-oriented communication, e.g., the Internet of Things (IoT) and interconnected cyber physical systems, devices have to be authenticated in a secure way. This paper presents and investigates several approaches for advanced device authentication, being an extended version of [1]. The different approaches can be applied independently or in combination to increase the security level for device authentication. While authentication alone does not ensure a secure overall solution, it is an essential building block to realize secure, robust security architectures for industrial Internet of Things and for automation and control systems in general.

An overview on industrial security resp. secure industrial IoT is given in Section II. After describing single device authentication means in Section III, the combination of authentications is covered in Section IV. The advantages of enhanced device authentication factors to increase the security level of Internet of Things systems and Cyber Physical Systems is investigated in Section V. Section VI summarizes related work. Section VII concludes with a summary and an outlook. Note that the paper investigates different options for providing enhance authentication from a conceptual point of view. The options are discussed in the context of system design and require an implementation as the consequent next step.

II. Industrial Security

Industrial automation control systems (IACS) monitor, and control automation systems in different automation domains, e.g., energy automation, railway automation, or process automation [8]. The main functionality can be summarized on a high level to performing control operations in the physical world using actuators, based on physical measurements obtained by sensors. Automation control systems are using open communication protocols like Ethernet, IP, TCP/UDP, or serial internally, and for communication with external systems (e.g., for monitoring, diagnosis, configuration), realizing an industrial Internet of Things (IoT), or the Web of systems. The term Internet of Things commonly refers to a set of technologies supporting the connection of hitherto stand-alone devices to an IP-based network. These technologies are important enablers for the convergence of today's automation architectures with service-oriented approaches while meeting industry-grade safety, security, reliability, and real-time requirements. As networked automation control systems are exposed to external systems, they have to be protected against attacks to prevent manipulation of control operations.

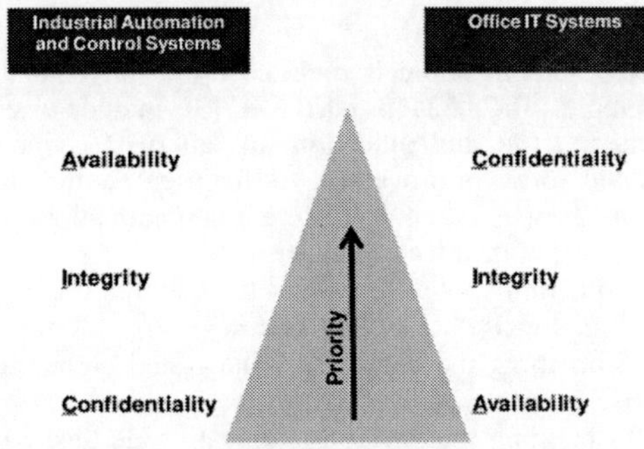

Figure 1. The CIA Pyramid [8]

The three basic security requirements are confidentiality, integrity, and availability. They are also named "CIA" requirements. Fig.1 shows that in common information technology (IT) systems, the priority is "CIA". However, in automation systems or industrial IT, the priorities are commonly just the other way round: Availability has typically the highest priority, followed by integrity. Confidentiality is often no strong requirement for control communication. Shown graphically, the CIA pyramid is inverted (turned upside down) in many automation systems.

Specific requirements and side conditions of industrial automation systems like high availability, planned configuration (engineering info), long life cycles, unattended operation, real-time operation, and communication, as well as safety requirements have to be considered when designing a security solution. The security requirements, for instance defined in IEC 62443, can be mapped to different automation domains, including energy automation, railway automation, building automation, process automation.

The security standard IEC 62443 [3] defines security for industrial automation control systems. Several parts have been finalized, or are currently in the process of being defined. The different parts cover common definitions, and metrics, requirements on setup of a security organization, and processes, defining technical requirements on a secure system, and to secure system components.

A complex automation system is structured into zones that are connected by so-called "conduits". For each zone, the targeted security level (SL) is derived from a threat and risk analysis. The threat and risk analysis evaluates the exposure of a zone to attacks as well as the criticality of assets of a zone. While IEC 62443-3-2 defines security levels, and zones for the secure system design, IEC 62443-3-3 describes the requirements to comply with a dedicated security level in an abstract way, not prescribing the actual implementation.

Four security levels have been defined, targeting different categories of attacks:

SL1: Protection against casual, or coincidental violation

SL2: Protection against intentional violation using simple means, low resources, generic skills, low motivation

SL3: Protection against intentional violation using sophisticated means, moderate resources, IACS specific skills, moderate motivation

SL4: Protection against intentional violation using sophisticated means, extended resources, IACS specific skills, high motivation

For each security level, IEC 62443 part 3-3 defines a set of requirements. Seven foundational requirements group specific requirements of a certain category:

- FR 1 Identification and authentication control
- FR 2 Use control
- FR 3 System integrity
- FR 4 Data confidentiality
- FR 5 Restricted data flow
- FR 6 Timely response to events
- FR 7 Resource availability

The security standard IEC62443 part 3.3 states several requirements affecting device authentication under the group FR1 "identification and authentication control" (see Figure 2 below). The requirements being most relevant for device authentication are summarized here:

- SR1.1 Human user identification and authentication: The capability to identify and authenticate all human users is required. While for SL1, a group based authentication is possible, a unique identification of human users is required for SL2. A multi-factor authentication is required for human users when accessing from an untrusted network in SL3, while SL4 requires support for a multifactor authentication of human users for all networks.

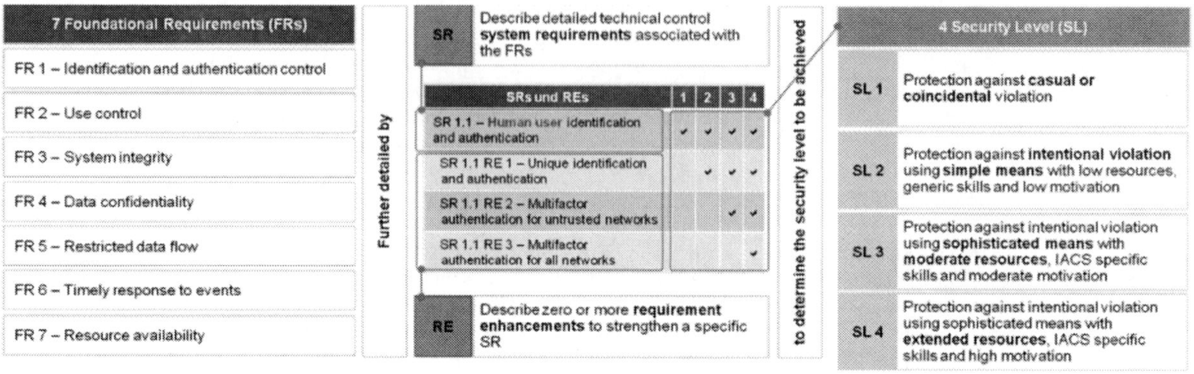

Figure 2. The interrelation of foundational requirements, security requirements, and security levels in IEC 62443

- SR1.2 Software process and device identification and authentication: All devices, and software processes shall be possible to be identified, and authenticated. This requirement is relevant from security level SL2, and higher. While in SL2, group- or role-based identification, and authentication is permitted, for SL3, and SL4, a unique identification, and authentication of devices is required.
- SR1.5 Authenticator management: Authenticators are credentials used to authenticate users, devices, or software processes. They have to be initialized, and refreshed. Initial authenticators shall be possible to be changed. The requirement is relevant for SL2, SL3, and SL4. For SL3, and SL4, a hardware mechanism is required to protect authenticators.
- SR 1.7 Strength of password-based authentication: The required password strength has to be configurable based on minimum length and variety of character types. For SL3, a password history and lifetime restrictions has to be supported for human user passwords. For SL4, the password lifetime has to be restricted for all users, including devices and software processes.
- SR1.8 Public key infrastructure (PKI) certificates: When a PKI is used, it shall be operated according to commonly accepted best practices, or public key certificates shall be obtained from an existing PKI. The requirement is relevant for SL2, SL3, and SL4.
- SR1.9 Strength of public key authentication: When digital certificates are used, the certificate, the certificate path, and the certificate revocation status have to be checked. In SL3, and SL4, private keys have to be protected using a hardware-based mechanism.
- SR1.10 Authenticator feedback: The feedback of authentication information during the authentication process shall be possible to obscure.
- SR 1.11 Unsuccessful login attempts: The number of consecutive, unsuccessful login attempts during a given time period shall be possible to be limited for all users, i.e., human users, devices, and for software processes.

The importance that is given to authentication to protect an industrial automation and control system can be seen from this list of security requirements. These requirements have to be fulfilled while respecting side-conditions on high availability, and keeping safety-critical control networks closed. These imply that a control system should continue to operate locally, independently from any backend systems, or backend connectivity. Local emergency actions, as well as essential control functions shall not be hampered with by security mechanisms.

III. Device Authentication Methods

Device authentication is required by security standards. For example, IEC 62443 part 3-3 [3] includes security requirements for authentication of all users, including devices and software processes. As for users, authentication of a device can be based on different authentication factors, similar to user authentication means [14]:

- Something the device knows: credential (device key, e.g., a secret key or a private key)
- Something the device has (integrated authentication IC, authentication dongle)
- Something the device is (logical properties, e.g., the device type, configuration data, firmware version; physical properties: physical unclonable function (PUF), radio fingerprint)

Besides these well-established authentication factors, more unconventional authentication factors can also be used:

- Something the device does (behavior, functionality, e.g., automation control protocol)
- Something the device knows about its environment (sensors)
- Something the device can (functional capability, actuators)
- The context of the device (neighbors, location, connected periphery)

Different usages in IoT systems apply device authentication:

- Identity Authentication toward a remote system (access control, communication security). May be a supervisory system, or a peer device.
- Network access security (IEEE 802.1X [9], mobile network access authentication [10]).
- Original device authentication
- Attestation of device integrity
- Attestation of device configuration

The remainder of this section provides an overview about device authentication means. The authentication would typically be performed by an authentication server that, after successful authentication, may allow access to further system specific data directly or issues a temporal token (e.g., SAML assertion [11], OAUTH token [12], short-term X.509 certificate [13]).

A. Cryptographic Device Authentication

The authentication of a device allows a reliable identification. For authentication, a challenge value is sent to the object to be authenticated. This object calculates a corresponding response value, which is returned to the requestor and verified. The response can be calculated using a cryptographic authentication mechanism, or by using a PUF [2].

For cryptographic authentication, different mechanisms may be used. Examples are keyed hash functions like HMAC-SHA256 or symmetric ciphers in cipher block chaining (CBC-MAC) mode, or symmetric ciphers in Galois counter mode (GMAC) up to digital signatures (e.g., RSA or ECDSA). For the symmetric ciphers, AES would be a suitable candidate. Common to keyed hashes or symmetric key based cryptographic authentication approaches is the existence of a specific secret or private key, which is only available to the object to be authenticated and the verifier. One resulting requirement from this fact is obviously the need for robust protection of the applied secret key. Also, asymmetric cryptography can be used for component authentication. A suitable procedure based on elliptic curves has been described in [30]. Also in this use case, the secret key has to be protected on the authenticating component.

The device is authenticated as only an original device can determine the correct response value corresponding to a given challenge. The verifier sends a random challenge to the component that determines and sends back the corresponding response. The verifier checks the response. Depending on the result, the component is accepted as genuine/authenticated or it is rejected.

Various approaches are available to realize a cryptographic device authentication:

- Software credential: Credentials are hidden in software, configuration information, or the system registry. Be aware that practices of storing cryptographic credentials in firmware or cleartext configurations are weak [17][18]. However, techniques for whitebox cryptography are available that hide keys in software [19].
- Central processing unit (CPU) and microcontroller integrated circuits (IC) with internal key store: Some modern CPUs and microcontrollers include battery-backed SRAM or non-volatile memory, e.g., security fuses, that can be used to store cryptographic keys on the IC [20]. Also, an internal hardware security module (HSM) or secure execution environment can be included (e.g., Infineon Aurix with integrated HSM [21], or ARM TrustZone [22]).
- Separate authentication ICs can be integrated (e.g., Atmel CryptoAuthentication ECC508A [23] , Infineon Optiga Trust E [24]).
- Crypto controller (e.g., Infineon SLE97 [25]).
- Trusted platform module (TPM 1.2 [26], TPM 2.0 [27], TPM automotive thin profile [40]).

B. Device Authentication based on Intrinsic Device Properties

Physical and logical properties of a device can be verified as part of a device authentication. For this purpose, information about the device properties can be provided in a cryptographically protected way. In particular, an attestation, a digitally signed information confirming properties of a device, can be created by a protected component of the device.

Properties of the device can be logical information (software version, device configuration, serial number of components of the device) or physical properties of the device that can be determined by sensors or a PUF [15].

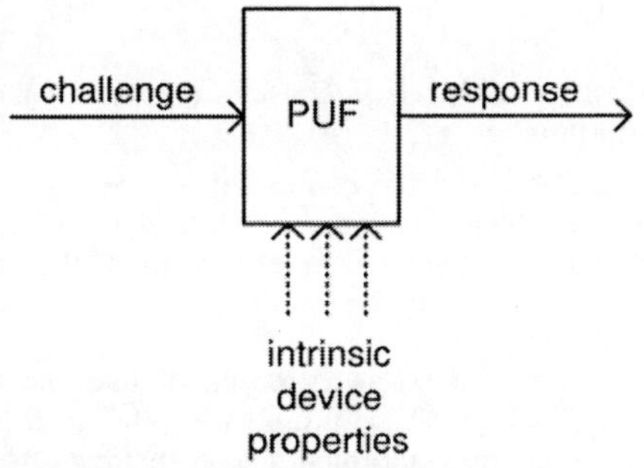

Figure 3. Challenge-Response-PUF [2]

Fig. 3 shows the basic concept of a PUF [2]. A PUF performs a computation to determine a response value depending on a given challenge value. Intrinsic device properties influence the PUF calculation so that the calculation of the response is different on different devices, but reproducible – with some bit errors – on the same device.

A PUF is used here for device authentication in a different way: It is by itself not a strong authentication. Instead, a cryptographically protected attestation can be used to attest physical properties of a device that are measured using a PUF. So, a PUF is not used directly for authentication, but indirectly as integrated device sensor to measure physical properties of the device. It can be considered as a "two-factor device authentication" where the PUF is used as second authentication factor.

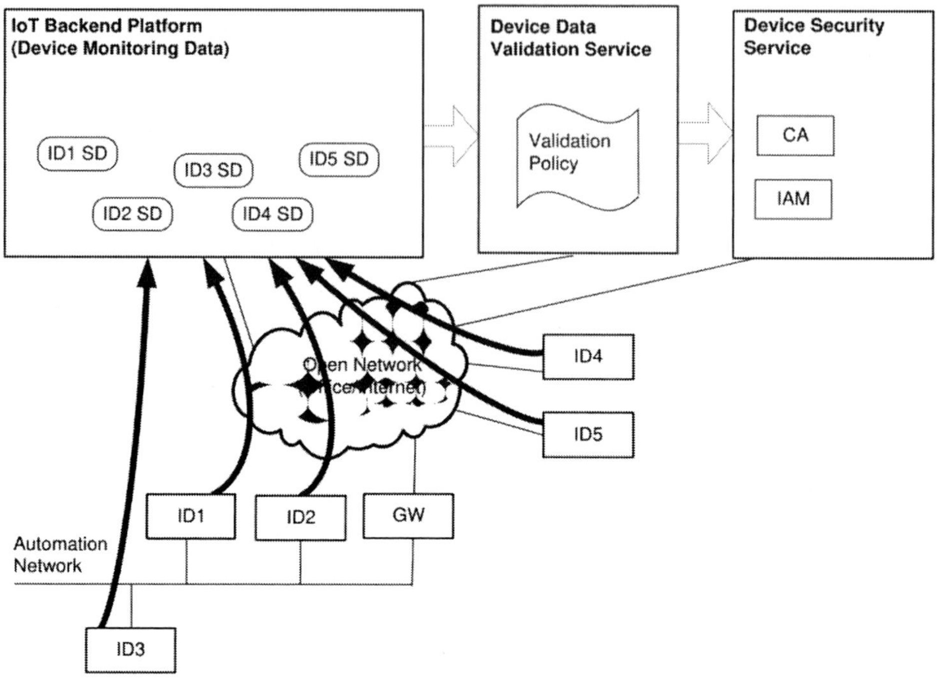

Figure 4. Validation of Device Monitoring Data

C. *Authentication based on Device Context and Monitoring Information*

Information about the context of a device can be used, e.g., the device location, or information about the environment of neighbor devices, the network reachability under a certain network address, or over a certain communication path.

The device context is determined and checked. The context information can be provided by the device itself, or the device's context information can be requested from a context server. One example from industrial environments is the system and device engineering, which basically provides information about the type and functionality of connected devices. Hence, it can be used to retrieve information about the devices deployment environment. The device location can be obtained using known localization technologies, e.g., global navigation satellite systems (GNSS) as GPS, GALILEO, BEIDOU, GLONASS, or localization using base stations (WLAN, cellular, broadcast) and beacons [28].

Furthermore, the device operation can be monitored: The behavior of the main, regular functionality of the device can be monitored and checked for plausibility.

Fig. 4 above shows an example for an IoT system with IoT devices (ID1, ID2, etc.) that communicate with an IoT backend platform. The devices provide current monitoring information about their status, measurements, etc. to the backend platform (e.g., for predictive maintenance). The backend platform maintains supervisory data (SD) data for the IoT devices (ID1 SD, ID2 SD, etc.) as "digital twin". Furthermore, context information about the environment of a device can be provided by the device itself using its sensors, or by neighboring devices.

The devices authenticate, e.g., using a device certificate, towards a device security service that maintains information about registered devices and their permissions. Furthermore, the device security service can issue and revoke device credentials (e.g., device certificate, authentication tokens).

In addition, a device data validation service can ensure that the device operation can be monitored, supporting also a continuous verification of the devices purpose. The validation service requests information about the IoT device supervisory data of supervised devices and checks it for validity using a configurable validation policy. Hence, the behavior of the main, regular functionality of the device can be monitored and checked for plausibility. Additionally, some arbitrary dummy functionality can be realized for monitoring purposes (e.g., predictable, pseudo-random virtual sensor measurement).

If a policy violation is detected, a corrective action is triggered: provide alarm message for display on a dash board (the alarm message can be injected in the device supervisory data set of the affected device maintained by the IoT backend platform). Furthermore, an alarm message can be sent to the IoT backend platform to terminate the communication session of the affected IoT device. Moreover, the device security service can be informed so that it can revoke the devices access permissions, or revoke the device authentication credential.

D. Authentication based on Device Capability

The authenticity of an automation device, e.g., for industrial automation and control systems or industrial IoT, can be verified by checking that a device can in fact perform a certain operation. The device is given an instruction to perform a certain test operation. It is checked that the device can perform a certain computation on provided test data: The device is given a set of input parameters (test data) and has to provide the correct result that is a valid result of the computation. The computational function could be a cryptographic puzzle involving a secret. The functionality can be realized by software/firmware on the control device, by a programmable hardware (FPGA), or by a periphery device (e.g., separate signal processor or IO device). Furthermore, it can be verified that a device can act on the expected physical environment (proofing that it has control on a certain effect in the physical world). The effect is observed by a separate sensor device. In an embodiment, the separate sensor device may provide an assertion.

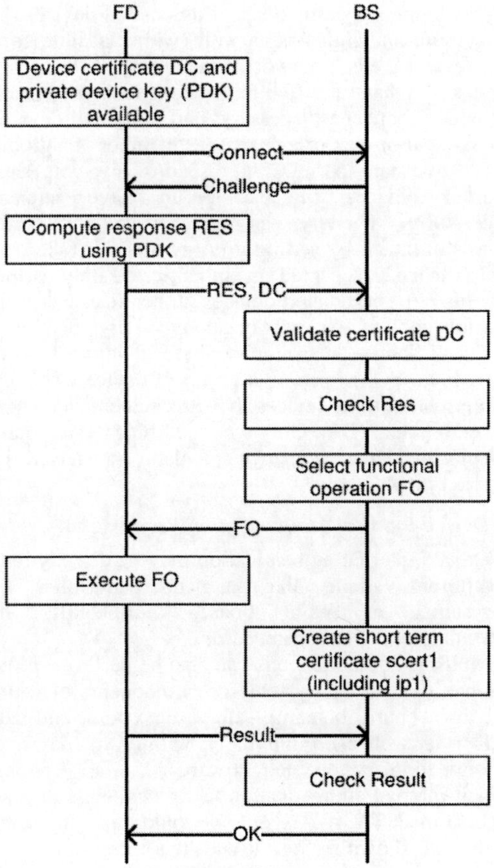

Figure 5. Verification of Device Capability

Fig. 5 shows a possible message exchange. The functional capability check is performed over a cryptographically authenticated communication link (e.g., transport layer security (TLS) protocol [31]). A device passes the authentication if both its cryptographic authentication is valid and its functional operation (FO) is verified successfully. For a successful attack, where a fake device is to be accepted, it is not sufficient that the attacker has access to the used cryptographic key. In addition, the attacker has to realize the expected functionality of the real device.

An example for combining authentication and the property to control a specific environment can be given by the recently established letsencrypt [45] infrastructure. Here, a (web)server applies for an X.509 certificate to be used for authentication in the context of https connections made to the web server. The certificate will be issued once the server can prove that it controls the domain it is requesting a certificate for. The proof is provided by putting dedicated information onto a random address in the applying servers address space. If this information can be retrieved externally, the proof of control is provided.

IV. COMBINED DEVICE AUTHENTICATIONS

This section describes various advanced options for device authentication where multiple device authentications are combined.

A. Multi-Factor Device Authentication

A device can support multiple independent authentications. These authentication options may be performed iteratively.

In particular, an initial cryptographic device authentication can be used to setup an authenticated communication session with an authentication server. Additional checks can be performed to complete the device authentication, e.g., in the scope of a specific application.

B. Separate Re-authentication Connection

In communication security, a secure session is established by an authentication and key agreement protocol (e.g., IKEv2, TLS authentication and key agreement). The authentication is typically performed for each communication session.

It is proposed that a single device has to set-up multiple authenticated communication sessions. The device has to re-authenticate regularly towards a backend system respectively a separate authentication server using a first communication session. If this is not done, the second communication session is terminated or blocked by the backend system. This realizes a form of continuous device authentication where a device is continuously re-authenticated during a communication session, but without degrading the main communication link, for which delays and interruptions shall be avoided.

Figure 6 shows an example message exchange where a separate communication session is established for performing a regular re-authentication. A second communication session is setup for control communication that may have specific requirements on real-time behavior, interruptions, delay, and jitter. This second communication session is terminated if the re-authentication on the first session is not performed as expected.

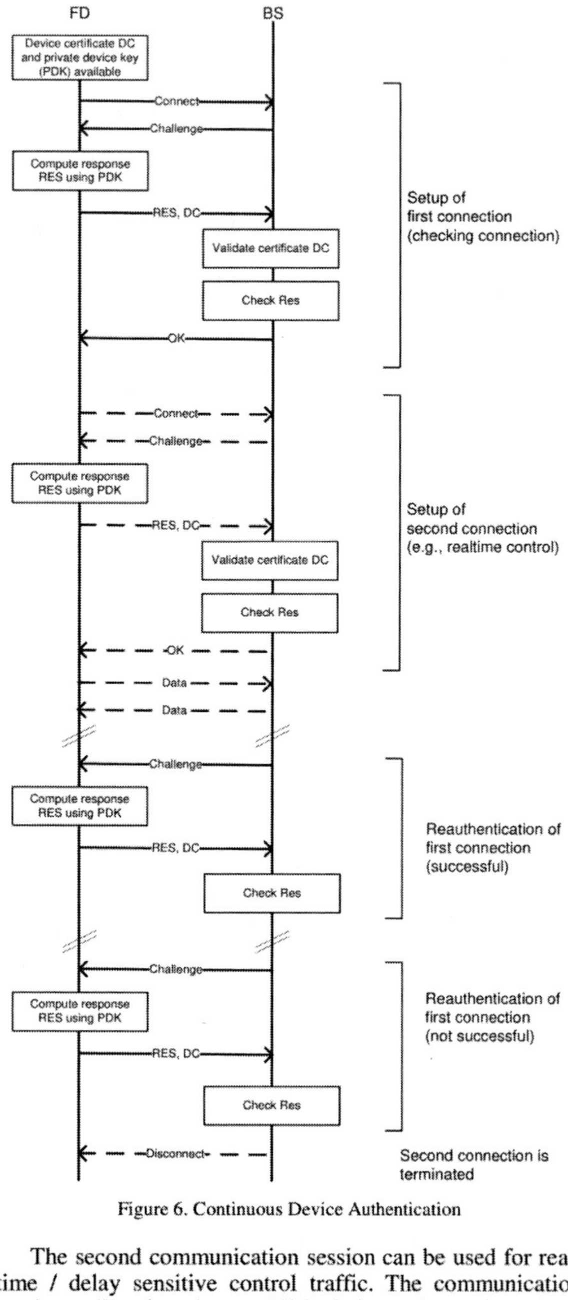

Figure 6. Continuous Device Authentication

The second communication session can be used for real-time / delay sensitive control traffic. The communication session will often be established for a long time (e.g., months). The re-authentication of the device can be performed independently using a second communication session without interfering with the first communication session (interruptions, delays during re-authentication). Note that the different communication sessions may terminate at different points in the backend systems. Hence, besides the multiple authentication sessions from the device, there needs to by a synchronization of the authentication sessions in the backend.

Also, the re-authentication of the first connection may be used to create a dynamic cryptographic binding with a further (separate) security session. This property can be used, to ensure that the entities involved in a separate security session know that there is a persistent first session with either the same entity or a different entity. This approach may be used for instance in publish/subscribe use cases to ensure that there is a persistent connection with the publish/subscribe server, while actually having an end-to-end communication session between the clients.

C. *System Authentication*

In industrial control systems and the Internet of Things, often a set of field devices will be used to realize a system. It is proposed to check the authentication of a set of devices (system authentication) that have to authenticate towards a backend system. A single device is accepted as authenticated only as long as a defined set of associated devices, forming the system, authenticates as well (with plausible context of the devices, e.g., network connectivity, location). The devices may have a different criticality assigned to enable a distinction between necessary and optional devices. The communication link of a device (as member of a group) is set to an active state (permission to send/receive data) only if all required devices of the group have authenticated successfully. Thereby, an attacker cannot perform a successful attack by setting up only a single fake device. A single device is accepted as authenticated only as long as a defined set of associated devices authenticates as well (with plausible context, e.g., network connectivity, location).

Fig. 7 shows an example where all three field devices (FD1, FD2, FD3) forming a group of devices, i.e., a system of interrelated field devices, have to authenticate against the backend system (BS). Only when all three devices have been authenticated, the exchange of data transfer with these devices is enabled.

D. *Device-internal Authentication Verification*

Device internal authentication may be directly integrated in different variants, like on a microcontroller, a safety subsystem, a main board, peripherals, housing authentication, or extension cards.

Multiple authentications can also be performed internally within a device. Subsystems or components of a device – e.g., main board, housing, safety subsystem, and extension cards – are checked internally within the device before authentication is enabled toward external systems. An explicit internal authentication using challenge response can be performed. The message flow would look almost identical for the one shown in Fig. 7, with the exception that device-internal components are authenticated instead of field devices of a device group.

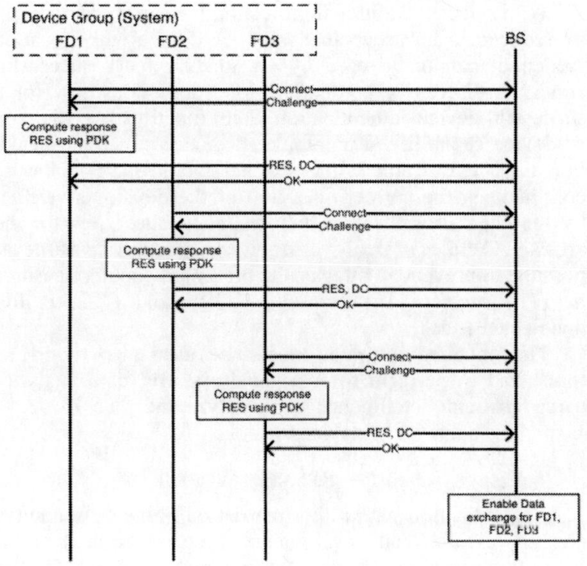

Figure 7. System Authentication

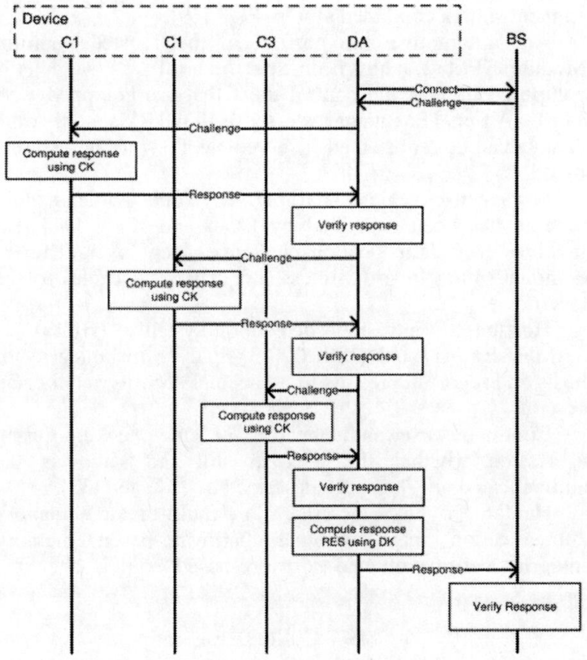

Figure 8. Device-internal Authentication

Fig. 8 shows an example where a device is authenticated by a backend system (BS). The device authenticates extranally using its device authentication functionality (DA). Before DA computes the response using the device key DK and providing the response to BS, it authenticates the device-internal components C1, C2, C3. Each component is authenticated using a device-internal challenge-response authentication.

Alternatively, a cryptographic secret sharing scheme can be used where a cryptographic operation can be performed only when all the required shares, i.e., partial computations that are performed independently, are available. For a device authentication, typically a public/private key pair is used. The public key is contained in an X.509 certificate and is associated to the devices by containing information about the device identity (e.g., serial number, MAC address). The private key – the secret – is supposed to never leave the device. Multiple parts of the device can be involved to access the private key needed to perform certain cryptographic operations (e.g., a digital signature, device authentication).

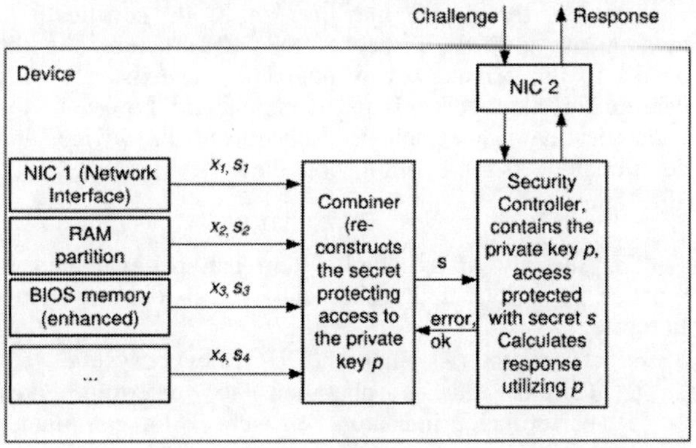

Figure 9. Device-internal Authentication based on Secret Sharing

Fig. 9 shows an example where a device uses a secret-sharing scheme internally. The device key used for device authentication is determined during runtime by combining the different shares. This can be achieved by distributing the secret key (private key) in shares between device components. One approach for sharing may utilize Shamir's secret key sharing:

$$f(x) = s + a_1x + a_2x^2 + \ldots + a_{t-1}x^{t-1} \mod p$$

with

- s as the secret key (here, the private key),
- a_i randomly chosen values,
- x_i may be public values.

Following Shamir's Scheme, the polynomial $f(x)$ is constructed in a way that the order of the polynomial is t-1. Now n nodes can be calculated with $n \geq t$ and based on that the initial secret can be split into n parts x_i, $s_i = f(x_i)$, (with $x_i \neq 0$), which in turn can be distributed to n different components of the device. To reconstruct the polynomial and thus the secret, the Lagrange interpolation is used.

Determining the value for the case $x=0$ leads to the constant part of the polynomial, which constitutes the secret.

Note that for the reconstruction, not all n parts are necessary, t parts are sufficient. This leads to the possibility to determine, which parts of the system need to be available to enable usage of the private key, e.g., in a challenge response authentication.

In contrast of sharing the private key directly, a secret, typically used to protect access to the private key, may be shared instead. This may be beneficial, if the private key is stored on dedicated security hardware.

In a variant the device may use the X.509 certificate to authenticate to other peers without making them aware of the internal dependencies to access the private key. In a further variant, the dependency is made public through an extension of the certificate. The extension may contain abstract information, e.g., threshold of device components necessary to access the private key or specific by listing the components necessary to access the private key.

Thereby, the device may use an X.509 certificate to authenticate towards a peer or the infrastructure. As the access to the private key is bound to the existence of a certain threshold of original components, however, the authenticating site is able to authenticate the device, and additionally gets information about the system integrity.

V. EVALUATION

The security of a cyber system can be evaluated in practice in various approaches and stages of the system's lifecycle:

- Threat and risk analysis (TRA) of cyber system
- Checks during operation to determine key performance indicators (e.g., check for compliance of device configurations).
- Security testing (penetration testing)
- Security incident and event management (SIEM)

During the design phase of a cyber system, the security demand is determined, and the appropriateness of a security design is validated using a threat and risk analysis. Assets to be protected and possible threats are identified, and the risk is evaluated in a qualitative way depending on probability and impact of threats. The effectiveness of the proposed enhanced device authentication means can be reflected in a system TRA. The proposed enhancements to simple cryptographic device authentication can lead to a reduction of the probability and/or the impact of a threat, so that the overall risk for successful attacks is reduced.

Two exemplary threats affecting a device are given (using for this example a simple qualitative assessment metric of low/medium/high):

- An attacker obtains device authentication credential by attacking the authentication protocol (probability: medium, impact: high; risk: high).
- An attacker succeeds in exploiting an implementation vulnerability of a device to get root access to the device and manipulate the device functionality (probability: high, impact: high; risk: high).

With selected additional protection measures, the risk can be reduced to an acceptable level: A device authentication credential cannot be used by an attacker for a successful attack as the device credential alone does not allow for a successful device authentication. With functional verification of device capability, a manipulated device can be detected. For a successful attack, the attacker would have to ensure continuously the correct operation of the device as verified by the capability check, which increases the effort for the attacker. While in real-world attack models, it is never possible to prevent all attacks, the presented countermeasures help to increase the required effort for a successful, undetected attack.

The obtained information can be used also by SIEM tools, and to perform forensic analysis. Big data analytics using artificial intelligence can analyze the data to detect suspicious behavior of devices.

VI. RELATED WORK

Authentication within the Internet of Things is an active area of research and development. Gupta described multi-factor authentication of users towards IoT devices [35]. The Cloud Security Alliance published recommendations on identity and access management within the IoT [36]. Ajit and Sunil describe challenged to IoT security and solution options. Authentication systems for IoT where analyzed by Borgohain, Borgohain, Kumar, and Sanyal [38].

Al Ibrahim and Nair have combined multiple PUF elements into a combined system PUF [39].

An "automotive thin profile" of the Trusted Platform Module TPM 2.0 has been specified [40]. A vehicle is composed of multiple control units that are equipped with TPMs. A rich TPM manages a set of thin TPMs, so that the vehicle can be represented by a vehicle TPM to the external world.

For electric vehicle charging, a vehicle authentication scheme has been described by Chan and Zhou [41] that involves two authentication challenges, sent over different communication links (wireless link, charging cable) to the electric vehicle.

Host-based intrusion detection systems (HIDS) as SAMHAIN [42] and OSSEC [43] analyze the integrity of hosts and report the results to a backend security monitoring system.

Continuous user authentication, i.e., the checking during a session whether the user is still the same as the authenticated one, has been described by [32] and [33].

Haider at al. describe a multi-factor memory authentication that combines hardware-based memory integrity verification and software-based bounds checking [44].

VII. CONCLUSION

Robust and practical device authentication is an essential security feature for cyber physical systems and the Internet of Things to verify the identity of devices that communicate over open networks. The security design principle of "defense in depth" basically means that multiple layers of defenses are designed. This design principle can not only be applied at the system level, but also at the level of a single security mechanism.

This paper proposed means for advanced device authentication to increase the attack robustness of device authentication. A well-known cryptographic device authentication can be extended with additional validations to check the device identity. The paper described how concepts known from advanced human user authentication like multi-factor authentication and continuous authentication can be applied to device authentication. They can be used to improve the security level for device authentication in an industrial control system and in an industrial IoT environment. Also, the concept of authentication of a single entity, as a single human user, a single device, or a single process, is expanded to the authentication of a system that comprises a multitude of entities.

The consequent next step is to setup pilots to integrate a selection of enhanced device authentication means as proof of concept, allowing to verify the concepts as such in a realistic application environment, and to analyze the advantages and the applicability of these advanced authentication technologies in a real-world setting. With the upcoming cloud-based platforms for industrial Internet of Things supporting cloud-based apps executable in the IoT backend [46], it is possible to realize advanced device authentication technologies flexibly by setting-up specific cloud apps that implement advanced device authentication functionality. So, a cloud-based industrial IoT backend, which can also be called the industrial IoT operating system, provides the technical basis for a quick introduction of new research-oriented technology developments into productive use.

REFERENCES

[1] R. Falk and S. Fries, "Advanced Device Authentication: Bringing Multi-Factor Authentication and Continuous Authentication to the Internet of Things," The First International Conference on Advances in Cyber-Technologies and Cyber-Systems (CYBER 2016), pp. 69-74, 9 -13 October 2016, Venice, Italy, Thinkmind, available from: http://www.thinkmind.org/index.php?view=article&articleid=cyber_2016_4_20_80029, last access: May 2017

[2] R. Falk and S. Fries, "New Directions in Applying Physical Unclonable Functions," The Ninth International Conference on Emerging Security Information, Systems and Technologies (SECURWARE), pp. 31-36, 23-28 August 2015, Venice, Italy, Thinkmind, available from: https://www.thinkmind.org/index.php?view=article&articleid=securware_2015_2_20_30028, last access: May 2017

[3] IEC 62443, "Industrial Automation and Control System Security," (formerly ISA99), available from: http://isa99.isa.org/Documents/Forms/AllItems.aspx , last access: May 2017

[4] ISO/IEC 62351-8, "Role-based access control for power system management," June 2011

[5] NIST IR 7628, "Guidelines for Smart Grid Cyber Security," Sep. 2014, available online http://dx.doi.org/10.6028/NIST.IR.7628r1, last access: May 2017

[6] BDEW, "Requirements for Secure Control and Telecommunication Systems," whitepaper, February 2015, available online: https://www.bdew.de/internet.nsf/id/232E01B4E0C52139C1257A5D00429968/$file/OE-BDEW-Whitepaper_Secure_Systems%20V1.1%202015.pdf, last access: May 2017

[7] ISO, "Road vehicles - Vehicle to grid communication interface - Part 3: Physical and data link layer requirements," ISO 15118-3, 2015, available online: http://www.iso.org/iso/home/store/catalogue_tc/catalogue_detail.htm?csnumber=59675, last access: May 2017

[8] R. Falk and S. Fries, "Using Managed Certificate Whitelisting as a Basis for Internet of Things Security in Industrial Automation Applications," International Journal on Advances in Security, vol 8, nr. 1-2, pp. 89-98, 2015, Available online: http://www.iariajournals.org/security/ , last access: May 2017

[9] "IEEE Standard for Local and metropolitan area networks--Port-Based Network Access Control," IEEE standard, 802.1X-2010, available from https://standards.ieee.org/findstds/standard/802.1X-2010.html , last access: May 2017

[10] G. Horn and P. Schneider, "Towards 5G Security," 14th IEEE International Conference on Trust, Security and Privacy in Computing and Communications (IEEE TrustCom-15), Helsinki, Finland, 20-22 August, 2015, available from http://networks.nokia.com/sites/default/files/document/conference_paper__towards_5g_security_.pdf , last access: May 2017

[11] Wikipedia, "Security Assertion Markup Language," available from https://en.wikipedia.org/wiki/Security_Assertion_Markup_Language , last access: May 2017

[12] J. Richer, "User Authentication with OAuth 2.0," available from http://oauth.net/articles/authentication/ , last access: May 2017

[13] E. Gerck, "Overview of Certification Systems: X.509, CA, PGP and SKIP," MCG, 1998, available from http://mcwg.org/mcg-mirror/certover.pdf , last access: May 2017

[14] L. O'Gorman, "Comparing passwords, tokens, and biometrics for user authentication," Proceedings of the IEEE, vol. 91, issue 12, pp. 2021 – 2040, 2003

[15] C. Herder, Y. Meng-Day, F. Koushanfar, and S. Devadas, "Physical Unclonable Functions and Applications: A Tutorial," Proceedings of the IEEE, vol. 102, nr. 8, pp. 1126-1141, August 2014, available from: http://ieeexplore.ieee.org/stamp/stamp.jsp?arnumber=6823677, last access: May 2017

[16] R. Falk and S. Fries, "Advances in Protecting Remote Component Authentication," International Journal on Advances in Security, vol 5, nr. 1-2, pp. 28-35, 2012, Available online: http://www.iariajournals.org/security/ , last access: May 2017

[17] A. Costin, J. Zaddach, A. Francillon, and D. Balzarotti, "A Large-Scale Analysis of the Security of Embedded Firmwares," 23rd USENIX Security Symposium, August 20–22, 2014, San Diego, CA, available from https://www.usenix.org/system/files/conference/usenixsecurity14/sec14-paper-costin.pdf , last access: May 2017

[18] R. Santamarta, "Identify Backdoors in Firmware By Using Automatic String Analysis," 2013, available from http://blog.ioactive.com/2013/05/identify-back-doors-in-firmware-by.html , last access: May 2017

[19] J. A. Muir, "A Tutorial on White-box AES," Cryptology ePrint Archive, Report 2013/104, available from https://eprint.iacr.org/2013/104.pdf , last access: January 2017

[20] M. Balakrishnan, "Freescale Trust Computing and Security in the Smart Grid," Freescale white paper, document number: TRCMPSCSMRTGRDWP REV 1, 2013, available from

http://cache.nxp.com/files/32bit/doc/white_paper/TRCMPSC SMRTGRDWP.pdf , last access: May 2017

[21] Infineon, "Highly integrated and performance optimized 32-bit microcontrollers for automotive and industrial applications," 2016, available from http://www.infineon.com/dgdl/TriCore_Family_BR-2016_web.pdf?fileId=5546d46152e4636f0152e59a1581001d, last access: May 2017

[22] ARM: "Building a Secure System using TrustZone Technology," ARM whitepaper PRD29-GENC-009492C, 2005 - 2009, available from http://infocenter.arm.com/help/topic/com.arm.doc.prd29-genc-009492c/PRD29-GENC-009492C_trustzone_security_whitepaper.pdf , last access May 2017

[23] Atmel, "ATECC508 Atmel CryptoAuthentication Device," summary datasheet, 2015, available from http://www.atmel.com/images/atmel-8923s-cryptoauth-atecc508a-datasheet-summary.pdf , last access: May 2017

[24] Infineon, "Optiga Trust E SLS32AIA," product brief, 2016 available from http://www.infineon.com/dgdl/Infineon-OPTIGA%E2%84%A2+Trust+E+SLS+32AIA-PB-v02_16-EN.pdf?fileId=5546d4624e765da5014eaabac63f5a38, last access: May 2017

[25] Infineon, "SOLID FLASH™ SLE 97 Family," product brief, 2012, available from http://www.infineon.com/dgdl/Infineon-SOLID_FLASH_SLE_97_Family_32-bit_High_Performance-PB-v08_12-EN.pdf?fileId=db3a30433917ea3301392ec288fc4ff0, last access: May 2017

[26] Trusted Computing Group: "TPM Main Specification," Version 1.2, , available from http://www.trustedcomputinggroup.org/resources/tpm_main_specification, last access: May 2017

[27] Trusted Computing Group, "Trusted Platform Module Library Specification, Family 2.0," 2014, available from http://www.trustedcomputinggroup.org/resources/tpm_library_specification, last access: May 2017

[28] K. Pahlavan et al., "Taking Positioning Indoors, Wi-Fi Localization and GNSS," InsideGNSS, pp. 40-47, May 2010, available from http://www.insidegnss.com/auto/may10-Pahlavan.pdf , last access: May 2017

[29] B. Parno, " Bootstrapping Trust in a Trusted Platform," 3rd USENIX Workshop on Hot Topics in Security, July 2008, available from http://www.usenix.org/event/hotsec08/tech/full_papers/parno/parno_html/, last access: May 2017

[30] M. Braun, E. Hess, and B. Meyer, "Using Elliptic Curves on RFID Tags," International Journal of Computer Science and Network Security, vol. 2, pp. 1-9, February 2008

[31] T. Dierks and E. Rescorla, "The Transport Layer Security (TLS) Protocol Version 1.2," RFC 5246, Aug. 2008, available from http://tools.ietf.org/html/rfc5246 , last access: May 2017

[32] H. Xu, Y. Zhou, and M. R. Lyu, "Towards Continuous and Passive Authentication via Touch Biometrics: An Experimental Study on Smartphones," Symposium on Usable Privacy and Security (SOUPS) 2014, July 9–11, 2014, Menlo Park, CA, available from: https://www.usenix.org/system/files/conference/soups2014/soups14-paper-xu.pdf , last access: May 2017

[33] K. Niinuma and A. K. Jain, "Continuous User Authentication Using Temporal Information," available from http://biometrics.cse.msu.edu/Publications/Face/NiinumaJain_ContinuousAuth_SPIE10.pdf , last access: April 2016

[34] N. Costigan and I. Deutschmann, "DARPA's Active Authentication program," RSA Conference Asia Pacific 2013 available from https://www.rsaconference.com/writable/presentations/file_upload/sec-t05_final.pdf , last access: May 2017

[35] U. Gupta, "Application of Multi factor authentication in Internet of Things domain: multi-factor authentication of users towards IoT devices," Cornell university arXiv:1506.03753, 2015, available from: http://arxiv.org/ftp/arxiv/papers/1506/1506.03753.pdf , last access: May 2017

[36] A. Mordeno and B. Russel, "Identity and Access Management for the Internet of Things - Summary Guidance," Cloud Security Alliance, 2015, available from: https://downloads.cloudsecurityalliance.org/assets/research/internet-of-things/identity-and-access-management-for-the-iot.pdf , last access: May 2017

[37] J. Ajit and M.C. Suni, "Security considerations for Internet of Things," L&T Technology Services, 2014, http://www.lnttechservices.com/media/30090/whitepaper_security-considerations-for-internet-of-things.pdf, last access: May 2017

[38] T. Borgohain, A. Borgohain, U. Kumar, and S. Sanyal, "Authentication Systems in Internet of Things," Int. J. Advanced Networking and Applications, vol. 6, issue 4, pp. 2422-2426, 2015, available from http://www.ijana.in/papers/V6I4-11.pdf , last access: May 2017

[39] O. Al Ibrahim and S. Nair, "Cyber-Physical Security Using System-Level PUFs," 7th International Wireless Communications and Mobile Computing Conference (IWCMC), 2011, available from http://lyle.smu.edu/~nair/ftp/research_papers_nair/CyPhy11.pdf , last access: May 2017

[40] Trusted Computing Group, "TCG TPM 2.0 Automotive Thin Profile," level 00, version 1.0, 2015, available from http://www.trustedcomputinggroup.org/resources/tcg_tpm_20_library_profile_for_automotivethin, last access: May 2017

[41] A. C-F. Chan and J. Zhou, "Cyber-Physical Device Authentication for Smart Grid Electric Vehicle Ecosystem," IEEE Journal on Selected Areas in Communications, vol. 32, issue 7, pp. 1509 – 1517, 2014

[42] R. Wichmann, "The Samhain HIDS," fact sheet, 2011, available from http://la-samhna.de/samhain/samhain_leaf.pdf, last access: January 2017

[43] OSSEC, "Open Source HIDS SECurity," web site, 2010 - 2015, available from http://ossec.github.io/, last access: May 2017

[44] S. K. Haider et al., "M-MAP: Multi-Factor Memory Authentication for Secure Embedded Processors," 33rd IEEE International Conference on Computer Design (ICCD), Oct. 2015, IEEE, available from: https://eprint.iacr.org/2015/831, last access: May 2017

[45] Letsencrypt, letsencrypt.org, last access: January 2017

[46] Siemens, "MindSphere – Siemens Cloud for Industry," The Magazine, Siemens, 2015, available online: https://www.siemens.com/customer-magazine/en/home/industry/digitalization-in-machine-building/mindsphere-siemens-cloud-for-industry.html, last access: May 2017

A Systematic Approach to Agent-Based Dynamic Analysis of Social Media Communication

Jan Ole Berndt,
Fabian Lorig, Ingo J. Timm

Business Informatics 1
Trier University
54296 Trier, Germany
Email: [berndt,lorigf,itimm]@uni-trier.de

Christof Barth,
Hans-Jürgen Bucher

Media Studies
Trier University
54296 Trier, Germany
Email: [barth,bucher]@uni-trier.de

Abstract—**The omnipresence of information technology and the increasing popularity of online social networks (OSN) has led to a change in communication behavior. While companies benefit from this, i.e., through viral marketing campaigns, they are also challenged by negative phenomena, like Twitterstorms. However, existing empirical approaches and theories for analyzing the dynamics of social media communication processes and for predicting the success of a campaign have several shortcomings with respect to this change of communication. Agent-based social simulation (ABSS) provides approaches to overcome existing restrictions, e.g., privacy settings, and to develop a framework for the dynamic analysis of communication processes, e.g., for evaluating or testing OSN marketing strategies. This requires both a valid simulation model and a set of real world data serving as input for the model. In this paper, a systematic procedure for preparing and implementing such a model is developed. The paper describes an integrated process for collecting and analyzing the required data. In addition, it outlines the components of agent-based models for simulating OSN communication processes and demonstrates the necessary steps by examples.**

Keywords–Social Network Analysis; Networks of Communication; Data Collection and Handling; Agent-Based Modeling; Simulation Methodology.

I. Introduction

One of the most noticeable advances of this century is the omnipresence of information and communications technology which demands novel and innovative methods for analyzing and understanding new communicative phenomena [1]. The establishment of computer systems in various areas of our daily life and the connection of private households to the Internet has initiated and still promotes the *digital revolution* [2]. As a result, social media platforms have gained popularity and have become an inherent part of our private communication.

Nowadays, popular OSN, e.g., Facebook, Twitter, or Google+, have more than 1 billion registered users each and the tendency is still rising. Internet user spend approximately 28% of their online-time in OSN [3]. Companies have observed this trend, too, identified the potential of OSN as a platform of aggregated customer contact, and have shifted the focus of many business units to OSN, e.g., customer service or marketing. This has the benefits of facilitating the determination of the customers' demands, of decreasing the efforts of client contact, and of allowing for an identification of trends at an early stage.

A. Dynamics of Communication Processes in OSN

The high degree of connectivity between the users makes OSN beneficial for companies, e.g., in terms of word-of-mouth marketing. Moreover, it allows for fast direct communication and situation assessment by both companies as well as official authorities in cases of crisis [4]. OSN users are connected with a large average number of people which results in an increased speed of information distribution. Marketing strategies of companies utilize this to quickly reach a high level of awareness, e.g., in viral marketing campaigns [5]. The self-replicating process of gaining awareness for a certain product or brand is driven by messages which are spread by users and which contain information on the entity that is advertised.

However, the effects and mechanisms which are beneficial for companies in terms of viral marketing and for gaining a high level of awareness can also result in harmful consequences. Due to the fast diffusion of information in OSN, negative comments or criticism can be multiplied in an uncontrollable way and cause a storm of protest. As these storms often occur on Twitter, they are called *Twitterstorms*.

A recent example is the *#CrippledAmerica* Twitterstorm. In late 2015, Donald Trump, an American businessman, politician, and the 45th President of the United States, mocked a disabled reporter during a political rally while promoting his book "Crippled America". Stuttering stand-up comedian Nina G took this as an opportunity propose using the hashtag *#CrippledAmerica* for writing about experiences with disability [6]. As a result, the hashtag's focus shifted from promoting Trump's campaign and book to reports on peoples' experiences with disabilities and negative responses to his statement.

Currently, companies lack methods to influence or end Twitterstorms and thus sometimes inadvertently promote the distribution of negative statements. Nevertheless, the challenge is not only to avoid negative impacts. Also utilizing positive aspects of OSN communication is difficult as traditional concepts of communication can no longer be applied to analyze the dynamics of OSN. The reasons are multilateral communication behaviors as well as an increased number of interpersonal relationships in OSN. Furthermore, the lack of distribution barriers (*"death of distance"* [7]) and the increased size of the potential addressees of messages need to be considered.

This does not only challenge companies. Also from a scientific perspective, there is a lack of empirical methods for investigating and explaining complex social mechanisms and dynamics of communication processes [8]. Due to their characteristics, compared to traditional offline communication, innovative concepts and techniques are required for analyzing communication processes in OSN [9].

Related research questions arise from the fields of media studies and communication research. Here, contents and effects of mass media as well as human communication are in focus. Considering standard research methods from these areas, there are two major challenges: Firstly, operators of OSN restrict access to data and users applying privacy settings to protect their personal data. This prevents researchers from accessing relevant information. Thus, field studies can only be conducted when the communication is openly accessible. Secondly, anonymity and the large number of actors in OSN influence the behavior of the users. Hence, empirical experiments under laboratory conditions are unfeasible. It can be assumed that actors will not behave the way they would behave in real OSN when knowing they are part of an artificial network which is being observed in a scientific study. Consequently, alternative approaches are needed for analyzing communication dynamics in OSN, e.g., for evaluating Twitterstorm strategies in advance.

B. Agent-Based Social Simulation for Analyzing Communication Processes

Computer simulation is a commonly used technique for analyzing complex and inaccessible systems in many disciplines. Here, artificial systems are created by modeling and simulating actors and mechanisms which then can be studied using existing research methods. In contrast to real world systems, simulated systems can be fully accessed, modified, and recreated by the researchers as required. In social sciences, Agent-Based Social Simulation (ABSS) has been established as a special type of simulation for studying emergent social behavior [10]. By modeling the actors of the real world system as autonomous entities, individual decision-behavior can be simulated and global social phenomena emerge from local interactions of the actors.

For the use in OSN analysis, such a simulation must model social media users, their behaviors, and the emergent effects of their communicative activities. It has to be grounded on a real world data basis of actual online discourses as well as on sociological and psychological theory. Consequently, the data basis comprises data about the actors (the users of the OSN), the environment of the actors (the OSN itself), as well as the topics of conversations and their development (the contents and styles of OSN communication). This information regarding the types of actors, their actions and goals but also the structure and the opportunities for actions provided by the OSN are needed for creating a realistic simulation model.

That model can then be used to produce artificial communication scenarios which imitate or alter real discourses in a controlled experiment setting. These simulations provide various potential conversation flows as their results. This will allow for evaluating which media phenomena, e.g., Twitterstorms, are likely to emerge from a given situation. Moreover, simulations can serve as a method for evaluating communication strategies to cope with these phenomena or to take advantage from them.

To achieve these results, a systematic process of data handling, model development, and simulation experimenting is required. Hence, this paper presents a first step towards the development of a framework for analyzing communication dynamics in OSN and for testing communication strategies using an ABSS approach. It extends existing work [1] with systematic procedure models for gathering and analyzing data as well as for modeling social media communication.

Section II outlines the foundations of communication in OSN, conventional analysis methods, and related work. In Section III, agent-based dynamic analysis is introduced as the method being systematically explored in this paper. Section IV focuses on the automated collection, preparation, and selection of relevant communication data from OSN. The usage of that data for developing the components of a simulation model is subsequently discussed in Section V. In Section VI the implementation and evaluation of the approach is described. Here, particularly the syntactical context of the communication will be in focus with an outlook on requirements for additional analyses of its semantics. Using the example of Twitter, isolated tweets related to the same topic are selected, individual actors and messages sent by them are derived, and communication dynamics are reconstructed. To evaluate this approach, communication dynamics of Twitterstorms and political discourses are analyzed and discussed. Finally, Section VII provides a concluding summary of the findings.

II. Foundations

For analyzing the dynamics of OSN communication processes, the act of communication itself but also the structure of OSNs need to be considered.

A. Communication

Human communication can be considered a sequence of actions of individuals, where the behavior of a sender influences the behavior of a receiver [11]. It can be understood as a process, where the sender uses a set of characters to encode a message, which then is transmitted using an information medium. The receiver uses an own set of characters to decode and interpret the message and returns a feedback using the same mechanism but not necessarily the same medium [12]. However, a message does not necessarily need to be a verbal utterance but can also be nonverbal.

Each message consists of different layers of information (Figure 1). Without further knowledge, a message is only perceived as a set of characters. Syntax adds rules defining the relationship between characters. Hence, the characters become a message. The meaning of a message is determined by its semantics. A transfer of information can only be achieved if both the sender and receiver share the same semantics. Pragmatics reveal the intention of the message's sender.

The shifting of communication into technical media results in a loss of information. The transmission of messages is ensured, yet, the receiver does not know whether a message was interpreted correctly. On Twitter, e.g., the platform determines and restricts communication processes between users and influences understanding. The result of a communication can only be returned on the same technical way it has been received, by replying to a tweet using another tweet. Thus, we focus on the analysis and simulation of sequences of tweets and leave nonverbal communication out of account at first.

For that analysis, it is necessary to know the participating social actors, the structure of the network, and how communication is made possible. As pragmatics and semantics need to be abstracted for the simulation model, tools for the automated evaluation of messages are needed and are provided

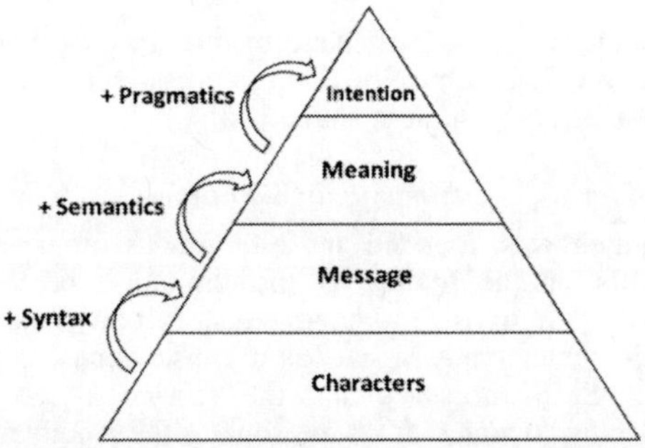

Figure 1. Pragmatics, semantics, and syntax of communication [13], [14].

by computer linguistics. Even though our example does not focus on the computer linguistic analysis of tweets, it is an essential part of the model building process as the large amount of data requires an automated approach.

B. Communication Platforms: Online Social Networks

Since the early 1980s, platforms which are now referred to as OSN exist. According to Boyd and Ellison [15], OSN are *webservices*, enabling users to create a profile, to maintain a list of other users they are in contact with, and to navigate through their own list as well as through the list of other users of the service. In 1980, *Usenet* was the first service to enable users to discuss certain topics with others sharing the same interests. 17 years later, in 1997, *SixDegrees.com* provided the first OSN according to [15]. In 2004 and 2006, Facebook and Twitter were started, respectively and made OSN popular. As of today, they are still two of the three most popular OSN, according to the number of active users. End of 2015, Twitter had 320 millions and Facebook had 1 billion active users [16][17].

In terms of graph theory, the structure of a social network can be described by a set of users (nodes) and relationships between the users (edges), connecting those nodes [18]. Depending on the direction of the relationship, graphs can be unidirectional, defining the direction of the relationship, or bidirectional, connecting two nodes without providing information regarding the direction of the relationship.

For assessing the importance of a node in a graph, e.g., the most influential users of an OSN, centrality measures can be used [19]. The *degree* of centrality corresponds to the total number of edges a node has and can be used as a measure of a node's interconnectedness in a graph. Nodes having a high *degree* (compared to other nodes) are classified as hubs in terms of information diffusion. When considering directed graphs, the *indegree* (number of inbound edges) needs to be distinguished from the *outdegree* (number of outbound edges).

In contrast to this node-specific measure, the *density* is calculated for an entire network or graph. Doing so, it can be used for comparing different graphs. The *density* of a graph is defined by the ratio of the number of existing edges and the maximum number of edges in case every pair of nodes would be connected by an edge (complete graph).

For simulating communication in OSN, the structure of the network needs to be recreated. A representation of a network using a graph defines the communication channels. In particular, the described platform-specific characteristics give indication of the conditions under which communication is taking place, e.g., who can send messages to whom and how their reach can be assessed.

C. Communication Actors, Activities, and Contents: Computational Linguistics

In addition to the structure, OSN consist of messages which are send between the users. For analyzing communication processes, the content of the messages is of relevance, too. It provides the researcher information about the intention as well as the context of communication. Thus, it is desirable to automatically classify the topic of individual messages and communication processes. Doing so, a first impression of the content of communication is given which facilitates the researcher's process of finding and selecting relevant communication processes. Furthermore, a basis for the abstraction of the content for the modeling process is provided. Yet, as the messages consist of natural language, analyzing the content in an automated way is challenging. *Computational linguistics* focuses on the modeling and processing of natural language and provides suitable techniques.

1) Machine Learning: A basic technology used in computational linguistics is *machine learning* which evolved from *artificial intelligence*. In contrast to other algorithms following hard-coded program instructions, *machine learning* algorithms learn from experiences gained from data or from models built from data [20]. There are three types of machine learning: supervised, unsupervised, and reinforcement learning. While supervised algorithms learn rules from example inputs and outputs, unsupervised learning approaches find patterns in data on their own. Reinforcement learning takes place in dynamic environments and will not be considered any further in this paper. For classifying data, supervised learning algorithms are commonly used, e.g., *support vector machines* (SVM) [21].

2) Content and Lexical Analysis: When using machine learning algorithms for processing natural language, the text first needs to be divided into its linguistic entities. These include words as well as phrases or even entire paragraphs of a text. For separating words, whitespace characters can be used in most segmented writing systems, e.g., those consisting of Latin characters. The entities received when dividing a text are called *n-grams* and are used for creating a model of the language. In this work, n-grams are used for analyzing the mood of messages, i.e., tweets.

For assigning attributes (tags) to words, *part-of-speech tagging* (POST) is applied [22]. Given a text, POST identifies the grammatical categories of each word, e.g., noun, verb, or adjective. This is challenging, as words may appear in different parts of speech at the same time. Yet, analyzing the mostly used nouns, verbs, and adjectives in a large data set, e.g., a set of tweets, may provide a first impression regarding the most commonly discussed topics.

When analyzing frequencies of words in a text or when indexing documents, a reduction of the words to their base form is needed. *Stemming* aims at reducing words with a similar or identical meaning, but which differ in its suffix, to its word stem. Here, each language requires own stemming algorithms. A commonly used algorithm for the English language is the *porter stemming algorithm* [23].

Summarizing it can be said that for evaluating communication processes in OSN, content and lexical analysis provide information regarding the topic of a conversation and allow for a first assessment of the tweet.

D. Related Work

There are several existing approaches to modeling and analyzing networks of communication and discourses in OSN. In the following, we discuss these works and relate them to our systematic procedure.

Information propagation aims at identifying a group of users which can propagate an unspecified information, i.e., a message, to as many users as possible [24]. These users are frequently modeled as agents with particular behavioral rules that fire if a certain activation threshold is reached. Such a threshold denotes the required strength of influence (e.g., a number of received messages) on an agent until it becomes active itself. This method is particularly relevant for planning advertising strategies in OSN as viral marketing campaigns make use of information propagation effects [25] [26].

However, information propagation frequently leaves the content of communication out of account or only focuses on a particular topic. Nevertheless, alternative approaches exist where the topics of communication within OSN are explicitly modeled for providing a topic-aware estimation of the propagation probability [24]. Thus, information propagation provides valuable ex-post approaches for analyzing networks of communication but lacks methods for integrating individual and more complex opinion making processes.

Cogan et al. [27] used Twitter data to reconstruct complete conversations around an initial tweet which is given. This enables a more detailed evaluation of conversation topologies, as social interaction models can be compared to OSN. Yet, only isolated and minor conversations lasting up to six hours were analyzed, not larger networks of communication as they occur in Twitterstorms.

For analyzing political discourses among Twitter users, Hsu et al. [28] examined their participation in discussions. The identification of key users was based on the users' public data, e.g., Twitter ID, location, number of tweets, and *follower-followee-networks*, instead of considering the communicative behavior of the users.

Maireder [29] described discourses on Twitter using three perspectives: networking topics, networking media objects, and networking actors. By connecting these perspectives, the author aims at understanding the process of political opinion-making through Twitter using empirical approaches by hand.

These approaches consider the collection and preparation of data as isolated processes for social network analysis. An integration of data handling in an entire research process for generating theories, testing hypotheses or deriving conclusions is not proposed. Additionally, an adoption of data handling and its impact on model development as part of a simulation study is not performed. Thus, the approach presented in this paper complements existing approaches such that an agent-based simulation of communication processes in OSN is facilitated.

III. Dynamic Analysis

For analyzing and modeling the dynamics of OSN communication processes, a data basis is needed. As the number of existing OSN is large and as OSN differ in structure and mechanisms, the process of data collection differs, too. In this paper, *Twitter* is used as an example platform due to the size of the OSN and the unrestricted access to data. Compared to other OSNs like Google+ and Facebook, Twitter's data is not as much affected by privacy settings and can be accessed using the provided API. Still, the communication processes which can be observed on Twitter are of relevance as they affect the general public and have resulted in cross-media phenomena in the past, e.g., the harlem shake [30].

A. Twitter as a Communication Platform

Twitter was founded in 2006 and, compared to other OSN, its unique feature is the limitation of the message ("*tweet*") length to 140 characters. Initially, the restriction to 140-character messages was a consequence of the limited size of SMS messages and the service aimed at sharing short status updates from personal life. Another difference is how friendships are represented. While most OSN consist of bidirectional relationships between users, meaning two users constitute the *friendship* together, a distinction between *followers* and *followees* is made on Twitter. Here, a user actively and voluntarily decides which other users to *follow* for receiving their status updates in an unidirectional way.

Following another Twitter participant makes the following user become a *followee*. Nevertheless, the user being followed does not need to follow its *followers*. Thus, a connection between two users does not imply that they exchange information in both directions. In consequence, for analyzing communication dynamics, the directions of the relationships need to be considered.

Besides the user network, the hashtag (#) emphasis Twitter provides is of special interest from a media studies and communication research point of view. When publishing messages, Twitter users can make use of two operators for classifying a message. The #-symbol is used for categorizing messages and for marking keywords of a tweet. This simplifies the researcher's assignment of tweets to a certain topic.

Furthermore, Twitter provides mechanisms for replying to other tweets and for addressing a tweet to a certain person. Using the @-symbol followed by the name of a user or by putting the prefix *"RT"* (retweet) at the beginning of a tweet, the identification of dialogs or conversations is supported. Due to these features, Twitter has been widely used for conducting studies of certain subjects or events, e.g., spread of news [31], the activity of diseases [32] or political communication [33].

B. ABSS of Communication Processes in OSN

For developing a dynamic analysis framework which makes use of simulation techniques, the simulation method needs to be chosen according to the phenomena to be analyzed. A special feature of phenomena occurring in OSN, e.g., Twitterstorms, is that they are emergent [34]. Due to the local interactions of the users on a micro level, global effects occur on a macro level as shown in Figure 2. Yet, they can not (entirely) be explained by the local actions.

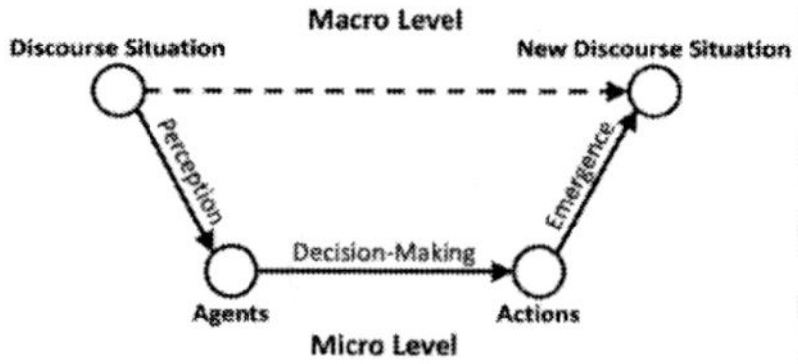

Figure 2. Emergence of macro level discourse dynamics from micro level agent interactions. Figure adapted from Hedström and Ylikoski [35].

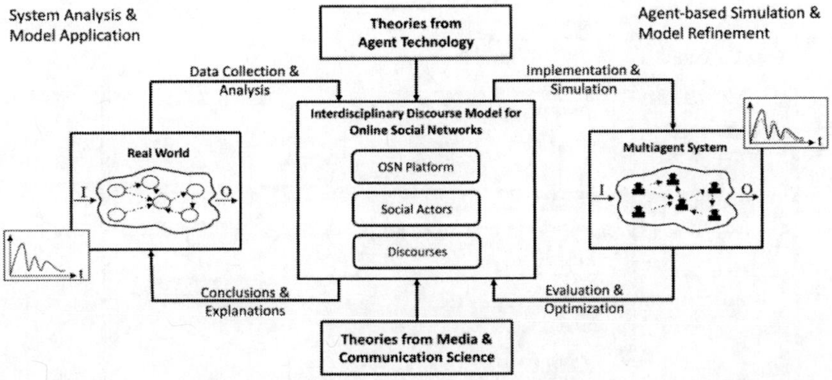

Figure 3. Integrated research method for creating and refining an interdisciplinary model of OSN communication.

For analyzing, reproducing, and investigating such emergent phenomena, agent-based computer simulation has been established as a standard means. By modeling real world actors, in this case the users of an OSN, as autonomous software agents, individual behavior and anticipation of behavior on the micro level can be simulated resulting in emergent effects on a macro level [36]. The observation of the global phenomena in combination with the knowledge of the actions and interactions of the actors can then be used for deriving as well as examining scientific explanations regarding the mechanisms of the system. In terms of social sciences, using agent-based actor models for doing social simulation studies is referred to as ABSS [37].

For using ABSS to analyze communication dynamics in OSN, three entities need to be modeled: the users of an OSN (actors), the decisions and actions of the users (behavior), and the connections between the actors (network). While actors and their behavior can be considered as the micro level of the model, the network is a macro phenomenon and can be observed in the real world. Accordingly, an understanding of the macro level needs to be established first, as a basis for further consideration of the actor-based micro level.

During the model development process, domain expertise is needed for modeling real world mechanisms and processes according to observations or results from discourse analysis. This information from sociology and media studies, enriched with theories from software agent technology, can then be technically formalized and used for specifying a multiagent system for simulating OSNs. As a result, different artificial scenarios and processes can be observed based on how stochastic events influence the mechanisms. Instead of using the real world system as an object of research, domain-specific research methods can then be applied to the artificial system.

Compared to the real world system, a more cost-efficient and restriction-free access to data is provided. Furthermore, variations of the spatial or temporal dimension as well as repetitions of experiments are possible and the real world system is not exposed to any risk or needs not be existent at all. Results of the simulation experiments will be used for refining the model. This enables domain experts to draw conclusions and implications from the model regarding the real world system using specific theories, e.g., to provide decision support for analyzing viral marketing or for preventing Twitterstorms.

The described process results in two interconnected loops of research where a central interdisciplinary model serves as intermediator. This model is improved and refined stepwise by both disciplines, i.e., agent technology and media studies, until a satisfying state is reached as depicted in Figure 3. The model can then be used in the dynamic analysis framework for simulating OSN and communication processes within them.

The following sections elaborate on the research process in Figure 3 in detail. Firstly, Section IV covers the data collection and processing aspects of its left hand side. This is necessary to develop a simulation model of OSN which allows for drawing conclusions about real world communication dynamics. In addition, Section V further explains the right hand side of the Figure. It describes an iterated modeling approach of OSN communication structures, users, and contents as a basis for conducting social media simulation experiments.

IV. Data Collection and Processing

The process of performing a simulation study for analyzing dynamics of communication in OSN can be divided into three major steps (see Figure 4): the acquisition of relevant data, the conduction of the simulation experiments, and the drawing of conclusions from the results of the experiments regarding the real world. In this paper, we focus on the first step, the acquisition of relevant data and the simultaneous development of an agent-based simulation model.

To decide which data is relevant for a specific simulation study, the experiments need to be designed in advance. This includes the determination of the methodology of the simulation study as well as the definition of research hypotheses to be tested. After the experimental design has been defined in consultation with the domain experts, e.g., PR experts, relevant data needs to be collected, prepared, and selected accordingly.

A. Data Collection

When gathering OSN data using APIs, most of the data is provided in standardized data formats, e.g., JSON or XML. Due to the structure of the data format, each message or contribution (e.g., tweet or Facebook posting) is transferred as a single piece of information. Additionally, each entity is described by meta data, e.g., a unique ID, the name of the author, a timestamp when it was published, and a reference to which other message it replies.

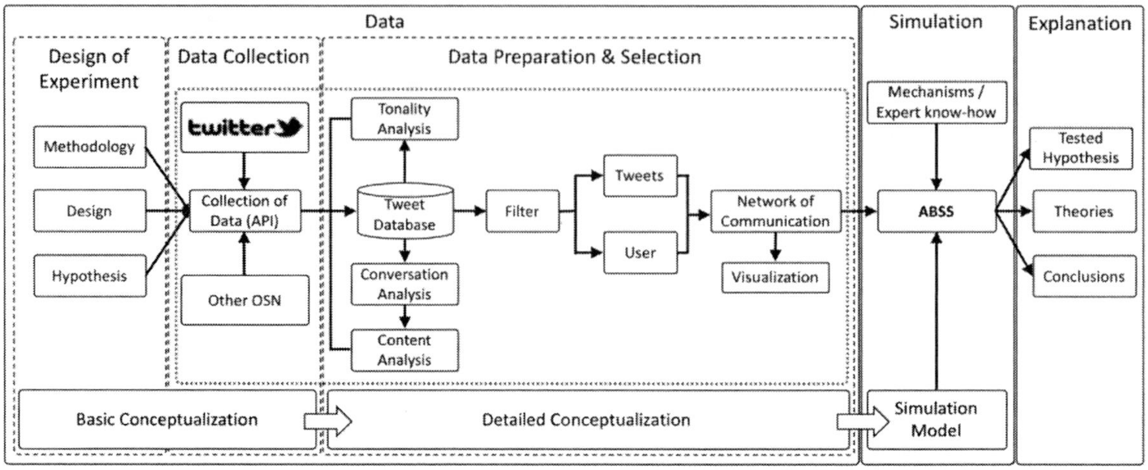

Figure 4. Procedure model for collecting, editing, and aggregating OSN data for ABSS studies.

Twitter provides REST APIs for reading and writing data. The access to the API is at no charge and the data can be downloaded as JSON files. Each tweet is characterized by up to 35 attributes, e.g., favorite count and geo coordinates. Up to 500 million tweets are sent per day. Two APIs are intended for the assessment of data. The *streaming* API provides access to the global stream of data and the *search* API allows queries against a subset of tweets from the past week. Both APIs need to be requested with a set of predefined keywords, i.e., hashtags, to restrict the results.

Here, the tradeoff is the extent of the data. The streaming API provides complete data regarding a hashtag, yet, this results in large datasets which need to be collected and stored in real-time. Technical problems during this process may result in a loss of data, as past data can not be accessed. In contrast to this, the *search* API provides relevant data only which decreases the size of the dataset. The data of the last week can be accessed, which enables a non-real-time collection of data, but the completeness as well as representativity of the provided data are questionable.

Certainly in terms of topics and events that are not discussed using a hashtag which is known in advance, e.g., a Twitterstorm, the advantages and disadvantages of the two APIs are noticeable. The keywords of the real-time streaming API need to be modified in order to capture the tweets of the storm of protest. Yet, when the Twitterstorm is recognized, the beginning has been in the past and thus can not be captured using a real-time API. The search API, in contrast, can be used to collect "popular" tweets of an event which has occurred up to one week ago. Yet, Twitter determines the popularity of a tweet without providing any information regarding the weighting function being used. Thus, the completeness of the dataset collected using the search API can not be assessed. Consequently, according to the design of experiment, the appropriate API needs to be chosen or a combination of both APIs needs to be used for the collection of data.

B. Data Preparation & Selection

After a dataset has been collected using the API provided by the OSN, it needs to be stored for further processing. In this phase of the data handling, communication processes are identified in the set of isolated tweets, and the content of the communication is analyzed. Furthermore, the network of communication is reconstructed representing related messages and conversations. That network of communication provides the basis for specifying, refining, and validating the agent-based simulation model.

1) Conversation Detection & Content Analysis: Topic-related communication processes, i.e., discourses, are considered as coherent dialogs between users or groups of users regarding a certain topic [38]. From a media studies and communication research perspective, the identification and analysis of these discourses within a network of communication is of high relevance. They are the foundation for reconstructing and evaluating topics and opinion-making processes over time.

For discovering discourses in a network of communication, both the conversations between users and the content of the messages need to be analyzed. A conversation is defined by the direction as well as the order of messages which were sent. First, the beginning of a discourse, i.e., the *initial tweet*, needs to be identified. The identification of this tweet in a dataset can be achieved by selecting all tweets, one after another, and checking the following two conditions: 1) Does another tweet exist in the dataset, which is a reply to the selected tweet? and 2) Is the selected tweet no reply to other tweets itself?

In case both conditions are fulfilled, a tweet is considered an *initial tweet*. Still, the dataset may contain only a part of a conversation. This might occur, if the initial tweet has not been part of the collection received from the API. In this case, the initial tweet is the one which is a reply itself, yet, the tweet it replies to is not part of the dataset. By iteratively applying this procedure (see Figure 5), communication processes can be identified as shown.

After identifying communication processes between users in networks of communication, an automated analysis of the conversation is desirable due to the large amount of data. Doing so, researchers can get a first impression regarding the type and topic of the conversation. On the one hand, the tonality of tweets can be determined using sentiment analysis, providing information about the mood expressed in

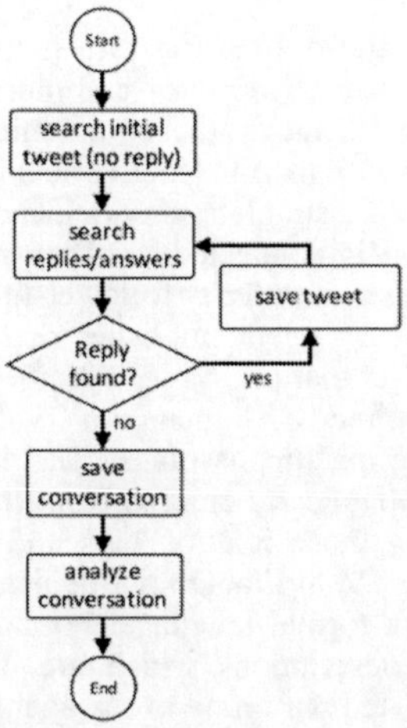

Figure 5. Conversation detection in Twitter dataset.

the tweets. Communication processes can be differentiated according to differences of opinion, i.e., pro and contra. In terms of discourses, an alternating tonality can be assumed, as two parties talk about the truth of a certain statement. On the other hand, an automated analysis of the discourse topic can be performed. Content analysis provides techniques for determining commonly used terms in tweets, giving a first impression regarding the potential topic of the conversation.

The tweets are analyzed in two ways. First, the hashtags used in the tweets are identified and collected. An overview of the most commonly used hashtags of a conversation provides a first impression regarding the topic of the conversation. As a second step, a POST approach is used for analyzing nouns and adjectives. For doing so, all tweets of the conversation need to be divided into single words. Hashtags can be removed from the set of words, as they have already been evaluated individually and as hashtags often consist of made-up words or abbreviations. Thus, the decision whether a hashtag is a noun or adjective is difficult. POST will then be applied to the remaining words to identify nouns and adjectives which occur multiple times. The outcome enables a first assessment of the conversations' topics.

Furthermore, the tonality of a tweet is another indicator for assessing its content. Tonality or sentiment analyses of tweets can be conducted by means of rule-based classificators [39]. Alternatively, applying supervised learning algorithms for classifying tweets according to their tonality requires a three-stage approach [21]. As a first step, classification algorithms require a set of training data, which has been classified by hand. Using this data, the learning algorithm is trained and configured for the third step, the automated classification of the remaining tweets.

To increase the algorithm's accuracy, the data should be preprocessed. As the mood of the tweet is assessed by analyzing natural language only, artificial constructs, such as links to websites, @-mentions, and the "RT" prefix can be removed. Doing so, disturbances of the algorithm can be reduced.

2) Network of Communication: At this point, the dataset contains a large number of individual communication processes. Yet, for analyzing the dynamics of communication, these conversations must not remain separate. Instead, the entire network obtained when merging all individual communication processes is of interest. It contains dependencies between different conversations and provides a chronological order of each conversation. In the following, this topic-specific network of users and messages sent between the users is referred to as *network of communication*.

When reconstructing networks of communication in OSN, the relationships between the users are of relevance. Generally, Twitter provides two kinds of relationships between users: communicative relationships expressed by the use of the *RT* or @ operator and social relationships which are represented by Twitter's *follower-followee-mechanism*.

Analyses of the communicative structure of past Twitter-storms have shown that a small amount of the involved OSN users operate as central nodes and drive the diffusion of the criticism (see Section VI). Thus, for reconstructing networks of communication, communicative relationships seem to be most relevant. Social relationships, in contrast, do not contain any information regarding the participation and intensity of communication. Yet, a user's "communicative power" [38] can be determined by the social interconnectedness of that user. This is relevant when analyzing scenarios that potentially can lead to Twitterstorms, i.e., prospective analysis. In terms of networks of communication, communicative power can be considered as the ability to gain a high level of awareness for a message due to the large number of users the writer is connected with. Accordingly, for reconstructing networks of communication, these types of relationships need to be extracted from the dataset.

Beginning with a large amount of separate tweets and related attributes derived from the Twitter API, a preselection regarding a defined hashtag of interest needs to be performed. At this point, additional filters can be applied for limiting the extent of data, e.g., structure, content or mood filters. Doing so, the dataset is reduced to the relevant tweets directly associated with the topic to be analyzed. Here, the assumption is made that the hashtags mentioned by the tweet imply the topics the tweet is related to, as intended by Twitter. Tweets, that are meant to be related to a topic, yet, do not mention the hashtag in particular, can not be considered as part of the study, as they are not recognized by the API.

As a next step, isolated users must be removed. They are not part of the network of communication. Accordingly, isolated tweets need to be removed as well. They are considered not to be of interest to other users. A tweet is *isolated* when neither addressing a certain user nor being a retweet or reply to a previous tweet. By considering retweets, circles may occur, as some users tend to retweet their own tweets. These tweets are irrelevant for the network of communication.

Based on this cleaned dataset, a directed graph can be generated. In this graph, the nodes represent the users of the OSN and the edges represent the tweets of the users. For simplification purposes, just one type of edges will be used for all three types of communication: retweets, replies, and @-mentions. If the type of communication becomes relevant, it is always possible to refer back to the contents of the particular tweets which provide that information. At that point, the calculation of centrality measures can be performed, e.g., degree or closeness centrality. When visualizing the graph, the researcher gets a first impression of the structure of the network of communication. This structure provides the validation target for the simulation as well as a basis for detailing the settings for the previously defined simulation experiments.

As the aim of this process is to create a realistic simulation model, the conceptualization of the simulation model is performed parallel to the data collection and preparation. This facilitates the coordination and enables a harmonization of these two interdependent processes. For one thing, the simulation model is created according to the dataset which has been collected and thus can take account of certain characteristics of the dataset, e.g., involved actor types or specifics of the topic. For another thing, the collection and preparation of data can be adapted to the model ensuring the suitability of the dataset.

Starting with a basic conceptualization of the model during the design of experiment and data collection phases, a more detailed conceptualization during the preparation and selection phase is done. This results in the creation of an applicable simulation model which matches the acquired data as it has been developed based on them.

V. Agent-Based Modeling of OSN Communication

The data collected and prepared in the previous steps can now serve as input for the simulation model. At this step, ABSS experiments can be conducted using the results of the previous process step. In addition, expert know-how is needed to validate and verify the simulation model as well as to interpret the results of the experiments. This includes proving or disproving of the hypotheses defined during the design of experiment phase as well as deriving conclusions or theories from the results.

As depicted in Figure 6, the conceptual model comprises three major components: The *platform structure*, the *agents* and their behaviors, as well as their available *communicative actions*. These components are interconnected and from their interplay emerge artificial communication processes in the simulation. However, this interconnectedness makes it difficult to construct and validate a simulation model. Hence, we propose an iterative modeling process. That process consists of three consecutive phases, each of which focuses on one component while only making those changes to the others that are necessary for maintaining a runnable simulation model. Each phase ends with a specific milestone. As explicated in the following, such a milestone denotes the availability of a validated simulation model with the required expressive power to dynamically analyze a particular kind of research questions.

A. Phase 1: Platform Modeling

The first modeling phase covers the development of an initial agent-based OSN model. In particular, it focuses on representing the OSN platform under consideration (e.g., Twitter) which provides the agents with various activity options. These options include abilities to address specific users, to reply to messages or comments, as well as to forward and distribute information to other users. Hence, the goal of this modeling phase is to enable the simulation of information diffusion by means of these different communication mechanisms (i.e., *how does communication take place?*).

With respect to Twitterstorms, the corresponding milestone encompasses the simulation of how protests can emerge from specific users utilizing particular channels of communication. This covers research questions like *who are the most important actors in communication processes?* and *how can information spread throughout the OSN?*

To address those questions, it is necessary to imitate the aforementioned networks of communication in the agent-based simulation. That is, the communicating users must be identified along with their respective social and communicative relationships. In the simulation model, each user is represented by an agent that is connected to other agents through social relationships (i.e., Twitter's follower-followee mechanism). Thus, each time an agent publishes or forwards a tweet, its followers receive that message. Additionally, an agent can address others directly by means of Twitter's @-mentions or it can listen to specific hashtags. The latter communicative relationships dynamically emerge from the agent activities.

Representing those relationships and enabling the agents to select among the available communicative options requires descriptions in a formal language. Formal ontologies provide such kinds of descriptions which are easily extensible and facilitate automated reasoning of the agents about their activity options [40]. In fact, ontologies for describing OSN structures and communication options are already available [41] [42]. These can be applied and extended in this context.

While those ontological descriptions allow for extensive reasoning about communication processes by the agents in a simulation, these agents can remain simple for the first modeling phase. In order to utilize the available options, it is sufficient to model their behavior through simple condition-action rules, in the same manner as existing threshold models for information diffusion [24]. As long as the agents make use of the *RT* and @ operators, these models are suitable for simulating the establishment of communicative relationships. In addition, the communicated content can be represented by means of one or more hashtags per tweet. They model the topics of each message as well as its visibility to further agents (other than an agent's followers). Hence, those hashtags enable analyses of information spread processes throughout the simulated OSN with respect to various topics.

To obtain realistic simulation results, the first iteration of the agent-based model must be calibrated and validated against the previously analyzed network of communication (see Section IV). To that end, activity selection rules of the agents have to be appropriately prioritized and their activation thresholds must be determined. In contrast to existing work, these calibrations can differ between the agents to model individual behavior as observed in real communication processes.

At this stage, the calibrated and validated model is then able to reproduce the results of retrospective communication analyses. However, it can also be used to prospectively identify potentials for rapid information diffusion from which Twitter-storms can emerge. That is, such a model allows for assessing the risk and extent of future Twitterstorms by means of systematically simulating various information spread scenarios (this being practically a reverse application of the influence maximization problem [25] [26]).

B. Phase 2: Agent Modeling

Subsequent to the platform modeling, the second phase focuses on the agents' decision-making. It replaces the initial threshold model with a more elaborate agent architecture to facilitate individual behavior. This phase models the agents' motivation for selecting particular activities in specific situations. Its goal is to allow for simulating the underlying cause of criticism diffusion (i.e., *why does communication take place?*).

Consequently, the respective milestone covers the sim-

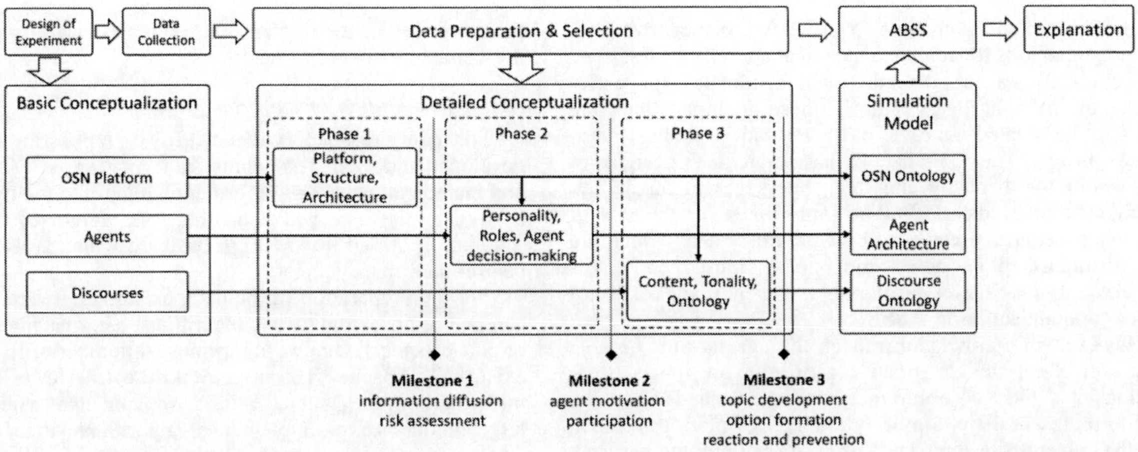

Figure 6. Procedure for modeling OSN structures, agent behaviors, and communicative actions in ABSS studies.

ulation of the OSN users' intentions which lead to them contributing to a Twitterstorm. It addresses research questions such as *who participates in a communication process for which reason?*, *which topic draws the attention of a particular user community?*, as well as *what would happen if a specific user did not participate in a Twitterstorm?*

Answering those research questions in a simulation requires a sophisticated model of the agents' decision-making [43]. As users either deliberately or affectively choose whether and how to participate in a communication process, the model must allow for representing various motivations and communicative roles. Candidates for such representations can be derived from psychological theory and cognitive science [44].

For instance, the *Big Five* of personality traits (sometimes also referred to as the OCEAN model) [45] [46] are a promising approach to analyze and understand human communication in OSN [47]. In an ABSS study, agents can be characterized by weighted combinations of these five personality traits which then determine their decision-making. In fact, we have successfully simulated social media phenomena by utilizing such a model in previous work [9].

Alternatively, agent decision-making models can be based on sociological theory. In contrast to personality-based approaches, sociologically inspired ones particularly emphasize the situational context, its effect on the interactions of individual actors, as well as the emergence of social phenomena from them [35]. Such a focus of the interplay between micro and macro social levels suits the modeling of agent behaviors in OSN simulations since it allows for connecting individual agent decisions with the emerging network of communications.

As an example, Dittrich and Kron [48] propose a sociologically derived agent architecture which parameterizes agents according to combinations of up to four basic social actor types. This kind of agent models even facilitates behavioral adaptation that results in self-stabilizing communication patterns [49] [36]. In dynamic OSN analyses, such methods can be utilized to investigate the emergence of topics and sentiments; e.g., in the early phases of a Twitterstorm.

While a refined agent model extends the scope and explanatory power of an ABSS, the first step to calibrate and validate that extension in the second modeling phase is to reproduce the behavior of the simple model from the first phase. The latter should already be capable of imitating the networks of communication observed from the real world. Therefore, calibrating the complex agent model accordingly makes it also applicable to analyses of information diffusion processes.

However, these processes now result from motivational dispositions instead of fixed behavioral rules. Consequently, the simulation becomes capable of the aforementioned research questions of this modeling phase. In particular, it is suitable for investigating hypothetic prospective scenarios like *would a Twitterstorm fail to emerge if a central actor did not participate in it or would another agent act in the same role instead?* Hence, the resulting model allows for deriving basic communication strategies, e.g., by predicting who might potentially become influential in a communication process for which reason.

C. Phase 3: Discourse Modeling

Finally, the third modeling phase focuses on the communication content and style in OSN. This extends the utilization of the previously developed complex agent model to its full extent. This is because an agent's motivation not only refers to whether or not communicate about a specific topic represented by a hashtag. It also allows for further differentiation between topics as well as for modeling the intentional or affective usage of specific sentiments and styles of content representation.

This phase covers that fine-grained modeling of topics, styles, and sentiments for both individual messages and discourses which connect them. Its goal is to facilitate the simulation of topic development and opinion formation in social media (i.e., *what is the subject and manner of communication?*). The milestone comprises the capability of simulating potential reaction strategies and interventions; e.g., for alleviating a Twitterstorm. Hence, it covers research questions such as *is self-mockery a sensible strategy for reacting to a Twitterstorm?* or *is it possible to draw attention to another topic?*

To achieve the aforementioned goal, it is necessary to extend the existing rudimentary representation of communication contents. Firstly, for individual messages (i.e., tweets) sentiment analysis methods can be applied to categorize the mood of communication as positive, neutral, or negative [39]. Secondly, methods for content and lexical analysis as described in Section II can provide additional candidates for topics besides the mere hashtags. Thirdly, these potential topics are likely to be related to each other instead of being mutually exclusive. This is reflected in hierarchical designs of *code books* for manually annotating messages in media and communication studies [50]. The same holds for the role of additional media like embedded pictures or videos which are also distinguished in those code books. Consequently, this provides a foundation for developing a content model of social media communication in ABSS.

However, in a simulation model, the agents must be able to reason about the described organization of topics, their relationships, their co-occurrence, and the embedded media used to represent them. Similarly to the OSN platform model, also the content is best modeled using formal ontologies. They are particularly suitable for reflecting the hierarchical design of the aforementioned code books. Hence, they provide a well-established means for abstracting from the contents and styles of human communication in OSN for its simulation.

In fact, ontologies are a standard method for encoding message contents in multiagent systems. In that context, *agent communication languages* (ACL) accompany the communication content itself with references to the ontology in use to represent that content [51]. Additionally, these languages model meaningful sequences of messages in terms of conversation protocols [52]. While those protocols are typically engineered to bring about an intended state of affairs, the can also be generated dynamically at runtime in the form of Markov chains [53]. This enables the agents to decide how to interact with each other and to adapt their decision-making about this interaction according to the current situation, their observations, and expectations [36]. By means of the same concept, it is possible to analyze and model the potential developments of topics, styles, and overall discourses in social media. Thus, we propose to use these techniques to represent the dynamics of communication in ABSS.

The resulting refined discourse model must, again, be calibrated and validated against the network of communication. This requires the tweets to be sufficiently annotated with topic, style, and sentiment information as described in Section IV. As that information should be encoded using the content ontology specified in the third modeling phase, the annotation must potentially be repeated or extended.

Given such a discourse model, the overall simulation still possesses the analytic capabilities obtained in the previous two phases. Moreover, its detailed representation of topics and sentiment as well as their potential development makes it suitable for testing elaborate prevention and intervention strategies for Twitterstorms. This complements the outcomes of phase two by modeling how influential users or groups would probably react to particular communicative acts. Additionally, this makes the simulation model transferable to other applications like the planning of social (viral) marketing campaigns as well as more sensitive communication areas like crisis management [4].

VI. Implementation and Evaluation

As a proof of concept and for evaluating the procedure model proposed in Section IV, the process of collecting and preparing data for ABSS studies is implemented. Furthermore, the feasibility of the implementation is evaluated by analyzing the datasets of two Twitterstorms.

A. Implementation of the Framework

For querying the Twitter API, a *PHP* script has been developed and used. The results are formatted as *JSON* objects and include all necessary information regarding the tweet itself as well as the user which has been the author of the tweet. The data is stored in a *MySQL* database which is used for the central data management.

For the preparation of the data, existing software packages can be used providing basic algorithms, e.g., machine learning or part-of-speech tagging algorithms. A number of frameworks exist, e.g., Apache Mahout or Scikit-Learn. However, due to the programming language it is implemented with and the large amount of preimplemented algorithms, the *DatumBox* framework [54] has been chosen for this implementation. *DatumBox* is a framework which provides natural language processing and classifying services written in *JAVA*. It focuses on social media monitoring as well as text analysis and quality evaluation in online communities.

The learning algorithms of the *DatumBox machine learning framework* have been used for this implementation, as the framework can handle large datasets and is open-source. The implementation of the *support vector machine* uses *LIBSVM* [55], a widely used open-source implementation of SVM. Furthermore, *Apache Lucene* [56] is used as text search engine, which is open-source and used by large companies, e.g., Twitter, for real-time search.

After collecting raw communication data, this implementation allows for performing tonality conversation analyses. To obtain the required training data, a number of tweets needs to be classified by human beings, after they have been edited. This training data as well as SVM, n-gram, and stemming algorithms provide a classification of the tweets regarding their mood. In addition, the conversation detection has been implemented as shown in Figure 5, followed by an analysis of the conversations' topics. The results of both analyses are then saved in the central database.

As a next step, for reconstructing networks of communication, the tweets of the database are filtered regarding the hashtags of interest. That is, the analyst has to identify hashtags associated with the topic to be analyzed. These are then used to query the database for any matching tweets. Additionally, the involved users are loaded from the database and a graph is created. The users serve as nodes, while each tweet is illustrated as a directed edge indicating the direction of the communication. For a reply, the edge would point from the user who replied to it to the author of the original tweet.

B. Analysis of the #pegida Twitterstorm

For evaluating the proposed approach, Twitter data has been collected since the beginning of 2015. For doing so, the hashtags of current topics of online news media have been used as keywords. Overall, 18 Mio. tweets containing 8 Twitterstorms have been recorded. Both *#pegida* and *#deflategate* are hashtags of considerable communication processes which took place on Twitter during this period of time.

The evaluation of the conversation analysis method requires a highly discursive topic, providing conversations with a high depth. For this reason, the social media echo of the *Pegida* protests has been chosen as dataset containing 3.2 Mio. tweets

[57]. Pegida is a right wing political movement that was founded in Dresden, Germany in October 2014 and opposes the perceived "Islamisation" of the Western world. Hence, due to the formation of opposing interest groups supporting or rejecting Pegida's point of view, opinions are divided and the formation of discourses is facilitated.

Analyzing the dataset, 19 685 conversations were identified consisting of nearly 51 000 tweets. Conversations can be classified by the number of replies as well as by the depth (steps) of the conversation. Figure 7 shows the distribution of the conversations by number of replies and depth. Conversations of a depth higher than 10, meaning that two users wrote 5 messages each replying to the previous message of the other user, are not existing whereas 136 conversations have more than 10 replies.

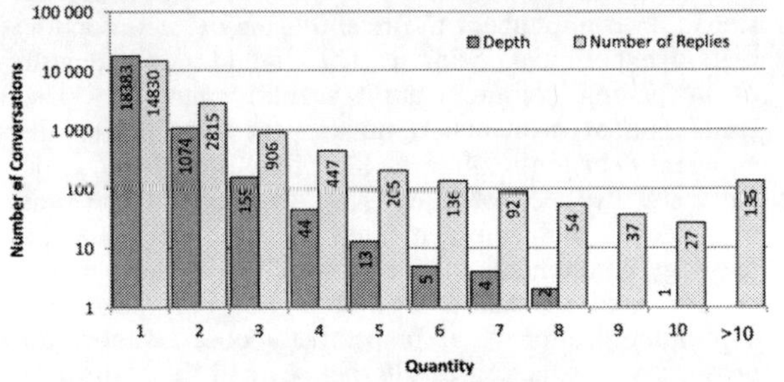

Figure 7. Distribution of conversations by number of replies and depth of conversation frm the #pediga analysis.

The structure of conversation trees can be divided into two major groups: *paths* and *stars* [27]. A *star* is defined by a low depth of the tree combined with a high number of tweets, consequently, a high amount of replies to one or a few tweets. In contrast, *paths* have a high depth while the total number of tweets is low.

Further analysis of the data showed that two types of *stars* exist in the dataset that differ in the number of involved users. The most extensive conversations of the dataset, consisting of 107 and 100 tweets, are the result of only 3 resp. 2 users. On closer examination, these conversations were classified as spam. Thus, we assume that for conversations on Twitter the ratio between the number of tweets and the number of involved users can serve as an indicator for spam. This assumption was strengthened by a manual analysis of the dataset. For most spam conversations, the ratio between users and tweets was at least 1 to 10. Accordingly, this type of star can be referred to as *spam star* and is only relevant for further analysis and modeling if it affects the behavior of users participating in the actual discussion.

A second type of stars exists where the ratio is inverted. In this case, the number of tweets and the number of users is almost equal implying that the majority of users commented on the conversation only once. In over 90% of the conversations which were detected in the dataset, 90% of the tweets have been written by different users. Consequently, most of the tweets have not been replied to. Even though these stars represent relevant conversations, they may not be considered as discourses, as the *"back-and-forth"* character of discourses is missing. Nonetheless, they indicate a motivation for uttering opinions that can be used to derive simple agent behaviors and the relations of subtopics with the main focus of the protest. In fact, this type of communication can potentially start more elaborate discourses and should therefore be included in an agent-based simulation model as a starting point for possible communication flows.

The paths, in contrast, are what we consider to be discursive behavior. Two or more users respond to each other's tweets and constitute a conversation. By merging both stars and paths, the network of communication can be reconstructed for further analysis. Furthermore, for the modeling of agent behavior, it appears that the communication rather than the exchange of opinions is in focus. This is triggered by an initial tweet and results in a *Fire-and-forget* behavior of the users. Such a setting indicates that agents in a simulation should act according to their internally modeled motivation if triggered by an observed tweet without closely following the progress of the evolving conversation. It further suggests that it is important to carefully model the (objective and subjective) visibility of communication for individual agents since users evidently often do not take notice of reactions to their tweets.

C. Analysis of the #deflategate Twitterstorm

The reconstruction of the networks of communication is evaluated using the dataset of the *#deflategate* Twitterstorm. Due to the limited timespan of a Twitterstorm, the collection of a complete dataset is simplified. Furthermore, analyzing a Twitterstorm's network of communication is of interest, as central users or tweets can be identified.

The *#deflategate* storm started three days after the 49th NFL Super Bowl and was triggered by a tweet of the journalist Chris Mortensen, claiming 11 of the 12 footballs were under-inflated [58]. As each team plays with separate footballs and as the hosting team supplies the balls, this appeared to have happened on purpose, to influence the behavior of the ball when thrown, kicked or caught. 17 621 tweets from 9 870 users have been collected during the *#deflategate* storm. Out of this, 41 tweets reply to themselves and 4 577 users are isolated and thus were removed. Consequently, the network of communication consists of 5 293 users and 6 067 tweets as shown in Figure 8 (left).

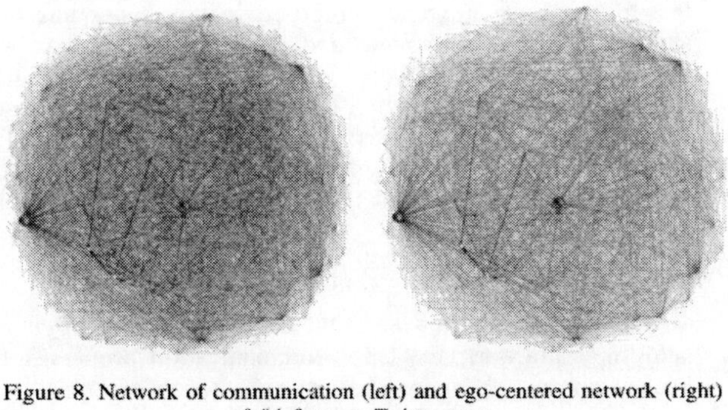

Figure 8. Network of communication (left) and ego-centered network (right) of *#deflategate* Twitterstorm.

Two central nodes can be identified in the network of communication. This observation is confirmed when comparing the *degree* centrality of the nodes. While the average *degree* is 1, a user named *TomBradysEgo* (Twitter User-ID: 317170443) is having the maximum *degree* of 509. *TomBradysEgo* is a parody account on Tom Brady, the quarterback of the New England Patriots, having 235 000 followers and posting an average of 113 tweets per month. During the Twitterstorm, 39 tweets were published by the account. Due to the high *outdegree*, 97.4% of the total *degree* of the node, in combination with the low number of published tweets, it can be assumed that the user's tweets have often been retweeted. Thus, a central role of *TomBradysEgo* can be implied and the account can be classified as a hub.

Similarly, the user named *brownjenjen* (Twitter User-ID: 2453787236) has a *degree* of 485 and is an American blogger. Having only 23 000 followers, *brownjenjen* published 43 tweets during the Twitterstorm. Due to the *outdegree* of 100%, a large number of retweets can be assumed, too. As the account does not reply to other tweets and participates in different topics, it can be classified as a hub, as well.

The important role the two accounts play for the Twitterstorm clarifies, when removing the two nodes and the related communication from the network of communication. Doing so, the density of the graph is reduced by 12.46% which can be compared to a reduction of the communication by the same extent. Figure 8b shows the union of the *ego-centered networks* of the two central nodes of the Twitterstorm. An ego-centered network places one node in the center and only includes those other nodes directly or indirectly connected to the central one. Consequently, such a network describes the communicative reach of a user. Here, 69.69% of the communication of the storm is linked to the two central nodes, showing their overall impact. Thus, a more detailed consideration of these two users seems promising in terms of social network analysis.

When modeling such a kind of network of communication, the agents representing these two users have a great influence on all other agents. However, the aforementioned observation of a large amount of communication being related to those users gives rise to the question whether the Twitterstorm would also have happened if they had not participated in it. That question can only be answered by simulating that communication in order to evaluate whether other influential users could have replaced them. The method we have proposed in this paper facilitates such a simulation.

To conclude, for both topics, *#pegida* and *#deflategate*, the feasibility of the approach proposed in this paper has been shown. In terms of content and discourse analysis as well as reconstruction of networks of communication, preliminary results assisting the selection of relevant data for subsequent studies were generated. Thus, when simulating emergent OSN phenomena, the different reach of agents needs to be considered. Some agents need to serve as hubs for pushing the diffusion of messages.

VII. Conclusions and Future Work

In this paper, the systematic development of a dynamic analysis framework for OSN communication processes has been proposed. A major challenge is the collection as well as the preparation and selection of relevant data, which is addressed by the presented approach. Currently, the analysis of a set of collected data for interesting phenomena for further consideration is done by hand. Our concept aims at providing assistance functionalities, by automating the handling of data for the preparation of simulation studies.

For gaining a first overview of the dataset of isolated messages, conversations between users are detected, the content and tonality of the messages are assessed, and the network of communication is reconstructed. This forms the basis for developing, calibrating, and validating an agent-based simulation model. This paper has proposed a three-phase iterated process extending from a simple initial version to a sophisticated detailed simulation model of OSN communication. Using the examples of *#deflategate* and *#pegida*, the process of data collection as well as data preparation and selection has been implemented and evaluated. The network of communication has been visualized and central nodes of the communication graph have been identified automatically as a foundation for the agent-based modeling process.

This work is a first step towards an agent-based modeling method for analyzing the communication dynamics of OSN. While it provides guidelines and techniques for systematic data collection, analysis, and simulation modeling, the next steps are to implement the resulting model and conduct simulation experiments with it. This includes the identification of interesting communication scenarios and the design of simulation experiments. Using our method, first results with an agent decision-making method based on social actor types have already been obtained [59]. However, these must still be extended and complemented with the OSN and discurse ontology components of our proposed simulation model.

The goal of that extension is not only the replication of communication as retrospectively observed, but also the prospective evaluation of alternatives and their impact on the communication dynamics. Such a simulation can then provide evidence about the expected robustness of phenomena such as Twitterstorms against intervention and point out possibilities to influence the communication dynamics. Thus, it can serve as a decision-making aid for developing strategies in social media communication.

Acknowledgments

We would like to acknowledge our master students Nils Dammenhayn, Stephanie C. Rodermund, Christopher Schulz and Nicolas Schulz for contributing to this work.

References

[1] I. Timm, J. Berndt, F. Lorig, C. Barth, and H.-J. Bucher, "Dynamic analysis of communication processes using twitter data," in Second International Conference on Human and Social Analytics (HUSO 2016). IARIA, 2016, pp. 14–22.

[2] W. R. Neuman, Y. Park, and E. Panek, "Tracking the Flow of Information into the Home: An Empirical Assessment of the Digital Revolution in the United States, 1960-2005," International Journal of Communication, vol. 6, 2012, pp. 1022–1041.

[3] J. Mander, "Daily time spent on social networks rises to 1.72 hours," https://www.globalwebindex.net/blog/daily-time-spent-on-social-networks-rises-to-1-72-hours, [retrieved: 09/16].

[4] V. Hoste, C. Van Hee, and K. Poels, "Towards a framework for the automatic detection of crisis emotions on social media : a corpus analysis of the tweets posted after the crash of germanwings flight 9525," in Second International Conference on Human and Social Analytics (HUSO 2016). IARIA, 2016, pp. 29–32.

[5] J. Kirby, Connected marketing: the viral, buzz and word of mouth revolution. Amsterdam: Butterworth-Heinemann, 2010.

[6] Nina G, "Disability Community Tweet-in," https://ninagcomedian.wordpress.com/2015/12/01/donald-trump-tweet-in-for-crippledamerica/, [retrieved: 09/16].

[7] E. Tranos and P. Nijkamp, "The death of distance revisited: Cyber-place, cyber-place, physical and relational proximities," Journal of Regional Science, vol. 53, no. 5, Dec. 2013, pp. 855–873.

[8] R. Mayntz, "Mechanisms in the analysis of social macro-phenomena," Philosophy of the social sciences, vol. 34, no. 2, 2004, pp. 237–259.

[9] F. Lorig and I. J. Timm, "How to model the human factor for agent-based simulation in social media analysis?" in 014 ADS Symposium (part of SpringSim multiconference). SCS, 2014, p. 12.

[10] D. Helbing, Social self-organization: Agent-based simulations and experiments to study emergent social behavior. Springer, 2012.

[11] C. R. Berger, "Interpersonal communication," The International Encyclopedia of Communication, 2008.

[12] C. E. Shannon, "A mathematical theory of communication," ACM SIGMOBILE Mobile Computing and Communications Review, vol. 5, no. 1, 2001, pp. 3–55.

[13] A. Church, "Carnap's introduction to semantics," The Philosophical Review, vol. 52, no. 3, 1943, pp. 298–304.

[14] C. W. Morris, "Foundations of the theory of signs," Journal of Symbolic Logic, vol. 3, no. 4, 1938, pp. 158–304.

[15] D. M. Boyd and N. B. Ellison, "Social network sites: Definition, history, and scholarship," Journal of Computer-Mediated Communication, vol. 13, no. 1, 2007, pp. 210–230.

[16] Facebook Inc., http://newsroom.fb.com/company-info, [retrieved: 09/16].

[17] Twitter Inc., https://about.twitter.com/company, [retrieved: 09/16].

[18] F. Vega-Redondo, Complex Social Networks. Cambridge University Press Cambridge, MA, 2007.

[19] L. C. Freeman, "Centrality in social networks conceptual clarification," Social networks, vol. 1, no. 3, 1978, pp. 215–239.

[20] D. E. Goldberg and J. H. Holland, "Genetic algorithms and machine learning," Machine learning, vol. 3, no. 2, 1988, pp. 95–99.

[21] S. Abney, Semisupervised learning for computational linguistics. CRC Press, 2007.

[22] A. Voutilainen, "Part-of-speech tagging," The Oxford handbook of computational linguistics, 2003, pp. 219–232.

[23] M. F. Porter, "An algorithm for suffix stripping," Program, vol. 14, no. 3, 1980, pp. 130–137.

[24] C. Zhang, J. Sun, and K. Wang, "Information propagation in microblog networks," in 2013 IEEE/ACM international conference on advances in social networks analysis and mining. ACM, 2013, pp. 190–196.

[25] W. Chen, Y. Wang, and S. Yang, "Efficient influence maximization in social networks," in 15th ACM SIGKDD international conference on Knowledge discovery and data mining. ACM, 2009, pp. 199–208.

[26] D. Kempe, J. M. Kleinberg, and É. Tardos, "Maximizing the spread of influence through a social network." Theory of Computing, vol. 11, no. 4, 2015, pp. 105–147.

[27] P. Cogan, M. Andrews, M. Bradonjic, W. S. Kennedy, A. Sala, and G. Tucci, "Reconstruction and analysis of Twitter conversation graphs," in First ACM International Workshop on Hot Topics on Interdisciplinary Social Networks Research. ACM Press, 2012, pp. 25–31.

[28] C.-l. Hsu, S. J. Park, and H. W. Park, "Political Discourse Among KEy Twitter Users: The Case Of Sejong City In South Korea," Journal of Contemporary Eastern Asia, vol. 12, no. 1, 2013, pp. 65–79.

[29] A. Maireder, "Political Discourses on Twitter: Networking Topics, Objects and People," in Twitter and Society. Peter Lang, 2013.

[30] J. Bollen, H. Mao, and A. Pepe, "Modeling public mood and emotion: Twitter sentiment and socio-economic phenomena." in 5th International AAAI Conference on Weblogs and Social Media, 2011, pp. 450–453.

[31] K. Lerman and R. Ghosh, "Information contagion: An empirical study of the spread of news on digg and twitter social networks." ICWSM, vol. 10, 2010, pp. 90–97.

[32] A. Signorini, A. M. Segre, and P. M. Polgreen, "The use of twitter to track levels of disease activity and public concern in the us during the influenza a h1n1 pandemic," PloS one, vol. 6, no. 5, 2011, p. e19467.

[33] A. Maireder and S. Schlögl, "24 hours of an# outcry: The networked publics of a socio-political debate," European Journal of Communication, 2014, pp. 1–16.

[34] J. Goldstein, "Emergence as a construct: History and issues," Emergence, vol. 1, no. 1, 1999, pp. 49–72.

[35] P. Hedström and P. Ylikoski, "Causal mechanisms in the social sciences," Annual Review of Sociology, vol. 36, 2010, pp. 49–67.

[36] J. O. Berndt and O. Herzog, "Anticipatory behavior of software agents in self-organizing negotiations," in Anticipation Across Disciplines. Springer, 2016, pp. 231–253.

[37] P. Davidsson, "Agent based social simulation: A computer science view," Journal of Artificial Societies and Social Simulation, vol. 5, no. 1, 2002.

[38] J. Habermas, Between facts and norms: contributions to a discourse theory of law and democracy, ser. Studies in contemporary German social thought. Cambridge, Mass: MIT Press, 1996.

[39] C. J. Hutto and E. Gilbert, "Vader: A parsimonious rule-based model for sentiment analysis of social media text," in Eighth International AAAI Conference on Weblogs and Social Media, 2014, pp. 216–255.

[40] P. Mika, "Ontologies are us: A unified model of social networks and semantics," in International semantic web conference. Springer, 2005, pp. 522–536.

[41] J. Golbeck and M. Rothstein, "Linking social networks on the web with foaf: A semantic web case study." in AAAI, vol. 8, 2008, pp. 1138–1143.

[42] U. Bojārs, J. G. Breslin, V. Peristeras, G. Tummarello, and S. Decker, "Interlinking the social web with semantics," IEEE Intelligent Systems, vol. 23, no. 3, 2008.

[43] U. Schimank, From "Clean" Mechanisms to "Dirty" Models: Methodological Perspectives of an Up-Scaling of Actor Constellations. Berlin, Heidelberg: Springer Berlin Heidelberg, 2005, pp. 15–35.

[44] T. Balke and N. Gilbert, "How do agents make decisions? a survey," Journal of Artificial Societies and Social Simulation, vol. 17, no. 4, 2014, p. 13.

[45] L. R. Goldberg, "An alternative "description of personality": the big-five factor structure." Journal of personality and social psychology, vol. 59, no. 6, 1990, p. 1216.

[46] ——, "The structure of phenotypic personality traits." American psychologist, vol. 48, no. 1, 1993, p. 26.

[47] S. Vandenhoven and O. De Clercq, "What does the bird say? exploring the link between personality and language use in dutch tweets," in Second International Conference on Human and Social Analytics (HUSO 2016). IARIA, 2016, pp. 38–42.

[48] P. Dittrich and T. Kron, "Complex reflexive agents as models of social actors," in SICE Workshop on Artificial Society/Organization/Economy, ser. Meeting of Systems Engineering, vol. 25. Tokyo: Gkajutsu Sougou Center, 2002, pp. 79–88.

[49] P. Dittrich, T. Kron, and W. Banzhaf, "On the Scalability of Social Order: Modeling the Problem of Double and Multi Contingency Following Luhmann ," Journal of Artificial Societies and Social Simulation, vol. 6, no. 1, 2003.

[50] K. A. Neuendorf, The content analysis guidebook. Sage publications, 2016.

[51] Foundation for Intelligent Physical Agents, "FIPA ACL Message Structure Specification," Standard, 2002, document No. SC00061G.

[52] ——, "FIPA Interaction Protocol Library Specification," Standard, 2003, document No. DC00025F.

[53] I. J. Timm and P.-O. Woelk, "Ontology-based capability management for distributed problem solving in the manufacturing domain," in German Conference on Multiagent System Technologies. Springer, 2003, pp. 168–179.

[54] DatumBox Framework, http://www.datumbox.com, [retrieved: 09/16].

[55] LIBSVM, http://www.csie.ntu.edu.tw/~cjlin/libsvm, [retrieved: 09/16].

[56] Apache Lucene, http://lucene.apache.org/core, [retrieved: 09/16].

[57] E. Crecsi, "How Germans documented Pegida's far-right protests on social media," http://www.theguardian.com/world/2015/jan/06/how-germans-documented-pegidas-far-right-protests-on-social-media, [retrieved: 09/16].

[58] A. Jaafari, "The goodell, the bad, and the ugly: The minimal level of integrity in the NFL's disciplinarian of players," Social Science Research Network (SSRN), 2016.

[59] J. Berndt, S. Rodermund, F. Lorig, and I. Timm, "Modeling user behavior in social media with complex agents," in Third International Conference on Human and Social Analytics (HUSO 2017). IARIA, to appear 2017.

Toward Next Generation Social Analytics: A Platform for Analysis of Quantitative, Qualitative, Geospatial, and Temporal Factors of Community Resilience

Dennis J. Folds, C.J. Hutto, Thomas A. McDermott

Georgia Institute of Technology, Atlanta, Georgia

Email: dennis.folds@gatech.edu; clayton.hutto@gtri.gatech.edu; tom.mcdermott@gtri.gatech.edu

Abstract— **Social science stands on the brink of a revolution – or of failure. It needs powerful new tools, methods, and paradigms in order to succeed. These will include advances in computational capabilities, machine-based knowledge assimilation, quantitative analysis, and measurement. Human social analytics in the next generation will need to embrace more multifaceted representations of human behavior with more complex models. Such models will need to integrate data of disparate forms, using disparate units of measure, collected from disparate sources, at disparate scales. The development of a complex model of societal well-being (an inherently qualitative construct) forms the basis of research for a next-generation societal resilience model. The model combines traditionally separate socio-environmental and psychological constructs of resilience, a representation that requires large scale quantitative, geospatial, and temporally referenced data of disparate forms, units, sources, and scales. The research forms a framework for the development of data analytic experimentation platforms in the social sciences. The platform will be used to demonstrate tools and methods that facilitate the progression towards next generational social analytics at large scales. These concepts, tools, and methods are intended to empower social science in transformative ways.**

Keywords- Computational social science; human social analytics; human-centered data science; sociotechnical systems.

I. A Vision for the Next Generation of Social Science and Analytics

In a special session on Next Generation Social Analytics, held as part of the HUSO 2016 conference in Barcelona, Spain, a call to action and two papers were presented that discuss the challenges faced by, and payoffs expected from, the tools and methods that will facilitate future conduct of social science research [1][2][3]. The results of that session along with additional related research activities are discussed herein.

Social science is under intense scrutiny from politicians, funding agencies, leaders of scientific societies, and from within the constituent disciplines [4][5]. Well-publicized instances of fraud and misconduct may dominate popular headlines, but underlying problems with replicability, poor generalizability, poor methods, and biased interpretation of results are larger problems, and do not involve malfeasance. Into this domain, the internet's global interconnectivity and massive data availability provide an opportunity to transform social science methods. Next generation social analytics can take advantage of the internet's massive reach and information capacity to produce families of new methods and tools that address these underlying problems.

However, it is dangerous to just assume that today's connectivity and access to information will improve formal social science methods. New approaches to study human behavior in real time using social media analysis are relevant but must be placed in the context of larger behavioral theories with decades of longitudinal study. Adding to this, even with decades of studies of human behavior at the individual and group levels, comprehensive theories that adequately account for behavior in real world conditions remain illusive. Behavior is indeed complex, but at the root of social science is the conviction that behavior is lawful. Much of basic psychology (sensation and perception, for example) is well established. But studies of such constructs as beliefs, political action, and organized violence lack unifying theories that have any success in accounting for wide ranges of social phenomena. Methods that correctly use the internet to study and create new theories of social behavior must be linked.

Study after study is trumpeted in the popular media, as long as it fits the ideological preferences of the media gatekeepers, despite ongoing lack of replication and obvious failures in generalizability. Whether these shortcomings are largely the result of poor methods, poor interpretation, or simply the complexity of the phenomena studied, is not known.

Many other sciences, notably astronomy and biology, have come under intense scrutiny and criticism when results contradicted the received wisdom, often from religious authorities. Methods were questioned, interpretations of results were challenged, and scientists were attacked when science threatened to undermine religious and civil authority. In most circles, though, these sciences prevailed because the soundness of the methods, data, and interpretation withstood objective scrutiny. Social science has not yet achieved that status.

What accounts for the difficulty in achieving robustness in social science theory? Is it the very complexity of social behavior? Problems with the way data are collected, analyzed, and interpreted? Or is it that much of the subject matter of social science is at the heart of political and religious spheres of interest? Astronomy may have benefited from the fact that the power of political and religious authorities did not in fact reside in whether the earth was at the center of the universe. Biology faced a stronger challenge, but it, too, benefited when political and clerical leaders realized that the origins and evolution of species were not central to their sphere. Social science, though, must address topics that are at the heart of political and religious discourse. Many of these are also at the heart of today's debates on facts/alternative facts, fake news, etc. It is imperative that the social sciences harness the power of the internet to make the underlying science more robust and transparent.

Moreover, scientists are also human beings, behaving in social situations, as they practice science. A physicist who changes her position on, say, string theory may face social pressure for and against the change, but string theory does not lie at the heart of public policy debates. But social scientists who study violence in inner cities, for example, are studying issues that do affect elections. To proclaim theories that question the wisdom of public policies related to reduction of inner-city violence is to court opposition from supporters of those policies, and adulation from those who wish to change them. There is little reason to think that either side is particularly interested in science for science's sake.

The disciplines that seek to address social phenomena include experimental psychology, social psychology, sociology, cultural anthropology, cognitive science, medicine, evolutionary biology, and political science. The computational sciences are increasingly interested in addressing social phenomena, and environmental sciences are also quite relevant in this arena. It is daunting to imagine theories and methods that could satisfactorily span these disciplines.

A. *Revolutionary Concepts Needed*

With respect to reproducibility, repeatability, and generalization of experiments, social scientists must accept that there is a problem and mount efforts to address it [6]. As other sciences matured, repeatability of results became expected, and lack of repeatability besmirched both the scientist who reported the study and the theory it supported. Social science must reach this point of maturation.

To reach this point, social science must develop a culture of sharing data, and agreement on methods of measurement and analysis. The infrastructure is in place, the methods are not matured. Repeatability of results cannot be expected when constructs are not defined the same way and measured the same way across studies. Results from studies that lack internal validity cannot be expected to have external validity, that is, to be generalizable beyond the specific conditions under which those results were obtained. Thus, long-term success in social science must address construct definition, measurement methods, and theoretical frameworks that span multiple academic disciplines, not just sharing of results and underlying data.

A revolution in connectivity and computational resources available to support social science is underway. "Big data" gives rise to the need for big platforms that support collection, maintenance, and sharing of social science data. Advances in machine-based text processing will produce methods to automatically scour the world's literature for new findings, new methods, and new interpretation of vast repositories of social science data. Cognitive systems may well scrutinize published studies and identify the topic studied (even if called by different names in different studies), results and interpretation, and potential errors and biases in the study. This will allow for ongoing meta-analyses of prior studies and assimilation of multiple diverse data sets. For social scientists to understand these analyses, new visualization techniques are needed, and machine-generated interpretations expressed in natural language must accompany those visualizations.

We can envision, then, a future in which social science studies are routinely conducted in the context of massive, ongoing collection of data about human behavior around the globe. These data sets will include everything from casual social media utterances to economic and policy decisions made by corporate and government leaders. One source of enabling technology is what is being called the Internet of Things (IoT): data from cyber physical objects such as mobile phones, automobiles, and home appliances will provide data about the behavior of people using those things. These data sets can be continuously updated. New hypotheses can be generated by scientists and by software systems, and competing theories can be subjected to ongoing tests as new data arrive.

A comparable situation emerged in meteorology as the community converged on the attributes to measure, the measurement methods, data representation conventions, and protocols for sharing. Nowadays, a typical study in meteorology does not necessarily involve developing new measurement capability and collecting new data (although such studies do exist). Rather, a typical study might simply involve formulating a new hypothesis about causal mechanisms in weather patterns, and testing that hypothesis using massive data sets freely available across the community.

Perhaps social analytics will follow a similar pattern. Perhaps the globe will be instrumented with data collection capability for social phenomena the way that it is instrumented for local temperature, wind, and precipitation. These social data will be validated and loaded into accepted registries, and will immediately be used to update ongoing studies. New studies can be implemented in those registries, to test new hypotheses about causal mechanisms in human social behavior. These could be exciting times for social scientists.

Even more exciting is how these capabilities can positively impact the human condition – not just the advancement of science. These new capabilities can help us address social problems more effectively – not just measure them more reliably. Problems related to human health, standard of living, and subjective well-being (SWB) are intricately related to the phenomena studied by social scientists. In the developed democracies, re-election of incumbents is also affected by these phenomena. Politicians and business leaders alike will have a vested interest in the integrity of the social sciences and will therefore be more likely to keep them properly resourced.

B. *A Timely Case Study: Well-being and Societal Resilience*

The fitness and function of infrastructure in cities – with shelter, water, energy, transportation, and social interaction perhaps the most primal – is critically important for the development, survival, sustainability, resilience, and overall success of communities. Sustainability and resilience of critical infrastructure, and the related human concepts of livelihood and SWB, are becoming the subject of greater and greater scientific study. Human communities and their city infrastructure and institutions are strongly coupled interdependent systems, and the concept of community resilience cannot be evaluated predictively using simple indices or optimization of individual components. There is a need to model these systems using complex representations of human and community development, participatory methods that address system complexity to engage communities and planners, and next generation social analytics tools to evaluate predicted, short-term, and long-term effects of resilience building. In other words, this is a perfect opportunity for revolutionary development of new methods and tools.

Our research on societal resilience is investigating four necessary features of future community resilience models that effectively address contextual factors and predicted emergence:

1. they accurately reflect the complexity of the problem of resilience building in the desired context, taking advantage of emerging computing methods to build complex social analytics;
2. they focus a set of core constructs and measurement models that scale effectively from local to regional to national level;
3. they can be used easily in decision analysis tools that exploit emerging large volume data analysis and machine learning algorithms; and
4. they provide predictive guidance to community planners on likely outcomes of community redevelopment projects including associated stress scenarios.

Each one of these features is a need driver in the opportunity space of next generation social analytics. However, the current state of research in this domain is not taking full advantage of emerging capabilities. Community development practice still recommends reduction into a few simple to understand (by stakeholders) measures. As a result, the complexity of the environment is lost and the effectiveness of the intervention becomes a debate. At the national level, planners still struggle to find measures that are meaningful at both local and national levels [7]. In today's era of big data analytics and social network analysis, much richer measures and deeper understanding of results are possible. Our community resilience case study includes a complex structural equation model (SEM) that relates over 130 human capital development measures to measures of critical infrastructure redevelopment [2]. This model is novel in that it captures a rich representation of the combined constructs of standard of living and SWB in the context of city infrastructure change. A challenge problem for next generation social analytics is to model the optimization of these disparate measures and predict likely outcomes of interventions in decision analysis tools used in participatory community design.

C. *We Should Not Miss Out on the Future*

The latest calls from researchers and city planners for simplified measures and independently defined interventions in resilience development continue [8]. This viewpoint represents continuation of business as usual in the social sciences. Studies will continue to be conducted with students or other convenient samples of small size, and results will continue to lack robustness. And city planners will still be searching for tools that help them predict the broader impact of their designs. A significant program that develops and tests the next generation of social science and social analytics methods and tools is sorely needed.

Funding for machine learning and data analytics is exploding, and true cross-disciplinary research is needed to meet the scale necessary for social science to succeed. Researchers in engineering, science, and computing disciplines are finding large and varied uses for these new technologies in socially related problem spaces. These communities are and will continue to study social phenomena themselves, and will attract funding and other forms of support in part due to the lack of acceptance of next generation technologies and methods of the established social sciences.

As a result, some of the core challenges of the human condition will continue to evolve without the benefits that rigorous science in the social domain could potentially provide. Community resilience is just one area. Throughout the developing world, and in many population segments in the developed world, such problems as infant mortality, vulnerability to crime, malnutrition, unemployment, financial insecurity, and mental illness remain rampant. Vulnerable populations continue to be at higher risk in terms of health outcomes, economic outcomes, and social outcomes because of these problems. Policy makers might well be willing to help alleviate those problems if only they could get guidance on the steps to take. Widespread adoption of vaccination for childhood diseases occurred once medical science was able to identify and understand the disease and to develop effective methods of prevention. Until then, policy makers were divided on approaches to address such problems as polio. Once an effective vaccine was developed, policy fell in line, and those problems were greatly reduced. Similar advances are needed in the social sciences for the social problems that plague humanity across the globe. Until then, social science will continue to have a diminished place in the public forum.

The connectivity and ability to access data in today's internet connected society, along with continually evolving solutions to make that access more broad and agile, creates a huge opportunity space. However, this must be addressed broadly across the social science community as an opportunity to transform methods and tools, not just enable individual studies. In this paper, we describe a conceptual approach and a computational platform that is intended to facilitate conduct of social science research in the age of "big data". Section II provides a general overview. In Sections III and IV we present a complex model of individual and societal well-being and the computational tools that support testing and extending that model. In Section V we briefly discuss the various issues and questions surrounding conduct of such research. Then, in Sections VI – IX we describe large-scale data sharing and analytic platforms that are emerging in other disciplines and discuss how they could be used in social science. Section X summarizes our conclusions.

II. Next Generation Social Analytics

All sorts of new human social and behavioral data are now available, and on unprecedented scales. Of course, social scientists still rely heavily on traditional sources of social and behavioral data such as in-person, telephone, or computer assisted interviews, questionnaires and survey instruments, and sources of "thick descriptions" [9] of human behavior compiled from ethnographic or anthropological observation research. However, new sources of human social behavior data are now available due to our increased use of mobile phone, GPS technology, and personal wearable technology (such as fitness trackers), as well as the digital traces of technology-mediated communications and online social interactions. These new data sources will allow researchers to conduct human social analytics for extraordinary levels of insights ranging from intra-individual scale investigations, through inter-personal and group level interactions, to organizational and even population scale research. Over the next 25 years (a generally accepted duration of a generation), social scientists and data analysts will need to modernize their ways of thinking about and interacting with human behavior data, else risk their research becoming obsolete and irrelevant.

The research goal is to address issues facing the next generation of social data scientists. In Section III, we present our case study, in which we progress beyond simple representations of human social behavior by constructing a complex model of individual and societal well-being. We describe the integration and analysis of data of varying forms, collected via diverse methods from a variety of sources by different groups, consisting of varied units of measure, spanning a temporal range of more than 40 years, and representing human behavioral data at disparate scales. In short, we present a case study of blending quantitative, geospatial, and temporally diverse data for the purpose of advancing human social analysis for an inherently qualitative construct using a more complex (and, we argue, more representative) model of human social behavior.

In Section IV, using the case study, we describe how new methods borrowed from the field of computer science can be leveraged to support next generation human social analysis of qualitative data. Computational natural language processing (NLP) and statistical machine learning (ML) techniques have the potential to be extremely useful for blending *thick data* (which is most commonly qualitative in form: e.g., descriptive text, audio, imagery, video, or similar multimedia) with the concepts of *big data* (typically more quantitative in nature). Here, we discuss three specific "tools" that embody NLP and ML techniques to support large-scale human social analysis on qualitative data. The first tool, called VADER (**V**alence **A**ware **D**ictionary and s**E**ntiment **R**easoner), provides researchers the ability to quantify both the direction (positive or negative) and magnitude of affective expressions in textual documents ranging from word-level to tome-level scales, processing millions of sentences in a matter of seconds [10]. The second tool, CASTR (**C**ommon-ground **A**cquisition for **S**ocial **T**opic **R**ecognition), produces supporting text-based information needed to establish so called *common ground*, whereby sharing mutual facts and knowledge generally facilitates faster, better understanding [11][12]. The third tool, EAGLE-ID (**E**thnicity, **A**ge, **G**ender, **L**iteracy/**E**ducation **Id**entifier), automatically aids in characterizing demographic features of individuals based on social profile data. Finally, we discuss how digital crowdsourcing economies such as Amazon Mechanical Turk (a massive, distributed, anonymous crowd of individuals willing to perform human-intelligence micro-tasks for micro-payments) can be leveraged as a valuable resource for the next generation of social science research and practice [13].

In Section V, we discuss several open questions with regards to human social analytics, including those related to ethics, data ownership and use, and personal privacy concerns. We then look at the concept of federated data platforms to accelerate the social science community development and learning of these new constructs.

III. Increasing Representational Complexity of Data Models for Human Social Analytics

Traditional social scientific models of human behavior are often over-simplified representations of what in actuality are very complex aspects of the world. Human social analytics in the next generation will need to embrace more multifaceted representations of human behavior with more complex models. Such models will need to integrate data of disparate forms, using disparate units of measure, collected from disparate sources, at disparate scales. In this section, we contribute an example in which we develop a complex, system-of-systems representation of societal well-being.

A. *From Simple to Complex Modeling of Well-being*

Individual and societal constructs of well-being are well established in traditional social science and economic literature as a person's assessment of their own general *happiness* and overall *satisfaction* with their personal life [14][15]. Following from [16], we further posit that happiness and satisfaction are themselves complex social constructs, which holistically comprise four principal constituents:

1. Affective Experiences: the longer-term experiences of pleasant affect (as well as a lack of unpleasant affect) as indicated, for example, via their general perceived happiness in life, in their marriage, and with their cohabitation companion (e.g., partner or roommates).
2. Global Life Judgements: a person's overall belief regarding how interesting they find their own life in general (e.g., whether they consider life to be dull, routine, or exciting), as well as a judgement about the general nature of humanity (whether they believe most other people to be trustworthy, fair, and helpful).
3. Cognitive Appraisals: a person's subjective self-assessment of their own current socioeconomic state relative to their life goals, as well as broader social comparisons. Determinants include financial status self-appraisals, social status self-appraisals (e.g., social rank and social class), and self-appraisals regarding their health, the relative quality of their domicile, and aspects of the city in which they reside.
4. Domain Specific Satisfaction: the degree of fulfillment or contentment with important social elements such as satisfaction with their family life, friendships, hobbies and recreational interests, job/career, and their wages.

Traditional social analytics tend to focus on a narrowly scoped subset of the above constituents. While such studies do provide useful insights, they are limited precisely because they are narrow; due to the inherent interconnectedness of these constituents, complex interactions abound. Nevertheless, they hold much greater analytical value when they are considered in conjunction with one another. The whole is greater than the sum of its parts, and aggregate-level insights may never emerge unless and until the underlying relationships are expressly represented.

To this end, we present an example in which we incorporate 130 different manifest indicators for- and correlates of- individual and societal well-being. This is represented in the "Community Population" oval of Figure 1. To do so, we blend qualitative, quantitative, geospatial, and temporal data from several sources. While detailed model specification is beyond the scope of this paper, we find the model useful as a reference for discussing next generation social analytics.

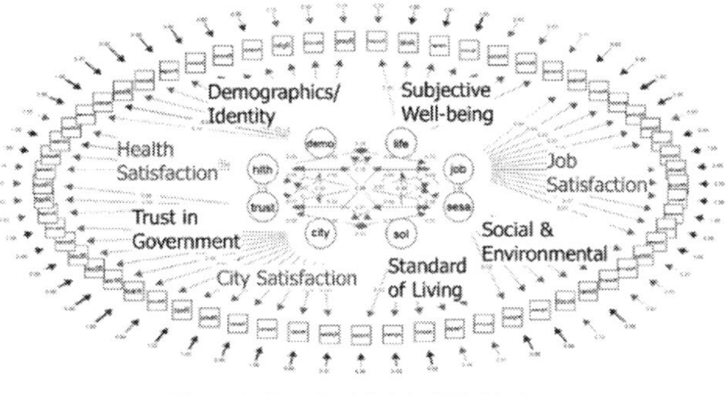

Figure 1. Complex Model of Well-being.

B. Blending Qualitative, Quantitative, Geospatial, & Temporal Data

The data for our complex model of well-being are drawn from several public data sets comprising records from 30 different collection activities spanning 42 years (from 1972 to 2014) across nine different divisions of the United States Census Bureau [17]. This data integrates 25 manifest indicators of societal well-being, organized into latent variable constructs representing the four principal constituents described in Section II-A. An additional 17 indicators provide data providing more objective measures of individual *quality of life and standard of living*, such as highest education level attained, number of people living in a household, type of dwelling (and whether owned or rented), various employment characteristics (part time, full time, student/homemaker, unemployed, retired, etc.), and constant (i.e., annual inflation adjusted) income in dollars. Also included are data capturing information about each respondent's *demographic* details, the *general political climate* (public opinion regarding amount of taxes paid, the efficacy of the courts, and national programs related to healthcare, transportation, and public transit), established local and regional *geographic boundary data*, annually recorded data regarding the *general economic climate* of the nation (such as inflation rates, consumer price indices, prime lending rates, and annual gross domestic product (GDP) per capital growth), and data characterizing the *general security climate* (e.g., individual and community exposure to crimes, perceptions of fear, etc.).

As one might imagine, the data are operationalized in multifaceted ways, taking multiple forms, units, and scales of measurement. In all, we integrate data from nearly 60,000 respondents spanning 42 years with regard to 130 different variables of interest, where each variable puts (on average) potentially 7 unique degrees of positive or negative pressure on individual and/or societal well-being. All told, this leverages approximately 55 million data points for our model, allowing for a very rich and complex representation of well-being – much more sophisticated than many other typical, prevailing social science models.

We argue that this representation, as opposed to a simpler model (for example, one based primarily on measures of *happiness*) is a more accurate reflection of true societal well-being. To illustrate this point, consider Figure 2, in which we visually depict how a simplistic representation of well-being (happiness scales) compare to a more complex representation of societal well-being for different geographic regions in the United States. Different insights emerge (especially in the southern regions) when a more complex construct capturing affective experiences, global life judgements, cognitive appraisals, domain specific satisfaction, objective socioeconomic quality of life and standard of living data, the general political climate, general economic climate, and the general security climate are incorporated when considering societal well-being.

We can also demonstrate how the model produces interesting insights in relation to political aspects of the national population, especially when considered in conjunction with temporal information. For instance, in Figure 3 the scatterplot dots indicate national-level averages for each year of data collection (1972-2014) for each self-identified political

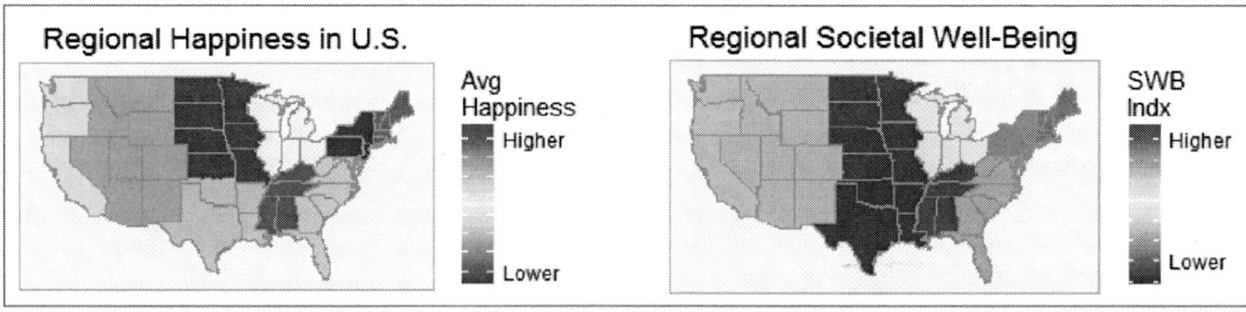

Figure 2. Comparing a simple representation of well-being (happiness scales, on left) to a more complex representation of societal well-being (on right) to derive different insights for different geographic regions in the United States.

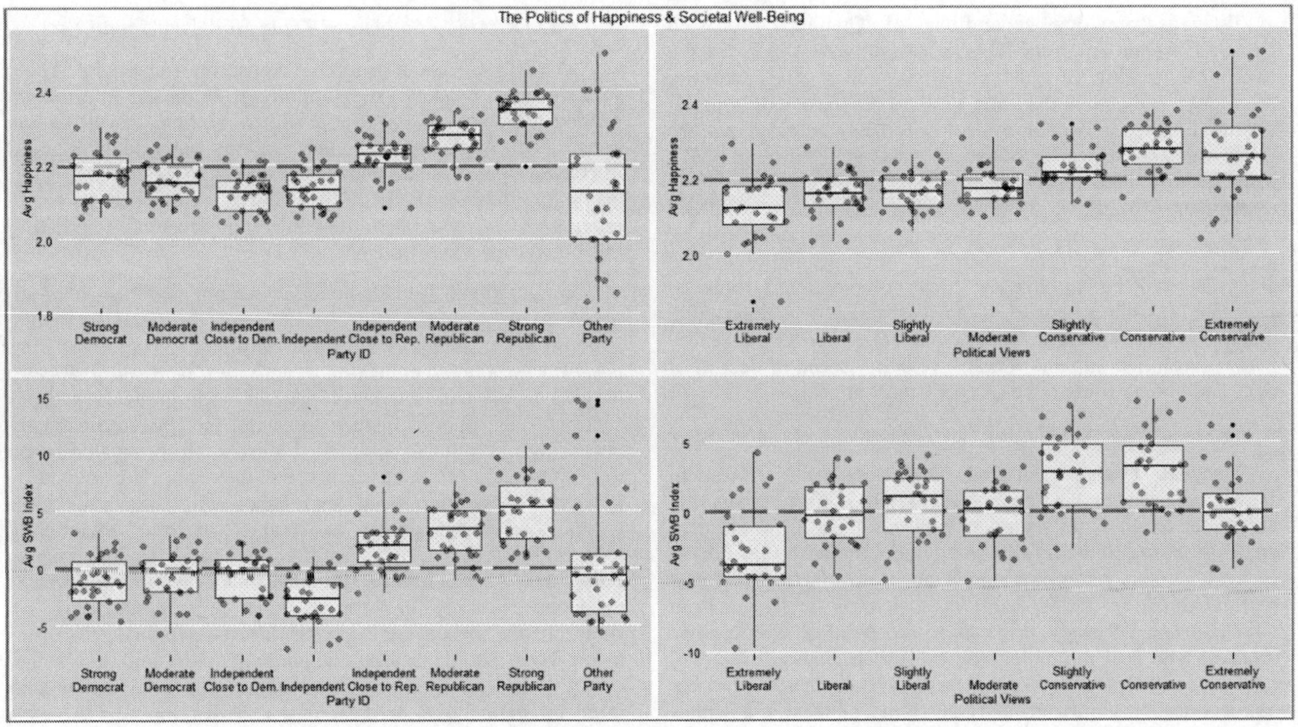

Figure 3. Aggregates of temporal data for political party and ideological views for a simplistic model of happiness versus a complex model of societal well-being.

community as measured by party affiliations in the left column plots (Party ID) or by ideological views in the right column plots (Political Views). The simple model of happiness (Avg Happiness) is plotted in the top row and the complex model of societal well-being (Avg SWB Index) is plotted in the bottom row. Boxes depict the middle fifty percent of the data (with mean lines) within each category, and whiskers show the range from minimum to maximum scores. The red dashed horizontal lines show overall means (across all categories). Especially interesting is how robust the results are for individual constructs; the general trends are qualitatively similar regardless of whether modeled with simplistic or complex representations of well-being.

C. *Monte Carlo Simulations and Predictions of Well-being*

The complex model, once derived as described in the previous section, may be used in Monte Carlo processes to explore the probability distributions associated with how potential changes in any subset of the input variables would impact societal well-being. The model can be extremely useful, for example, to government policy decision makers when the impacts of their decision alternatives could be vetted within a data-derived, model-driven trade space analysis tool. For example, Monte Carlo simulation modelers would be able to reliably quantify the effect that policy and funding decisions might have on societal well-being. Such considerations will enable next generation social analytics to generate better predictions, going beyond the prevailing social science policy of typically concluding a study upon reporting descriptive and inferential statistics.

IV. Methods, Techniques, and Tools for Next Generation Social Analytics of Qualitative Data

Next generation social scientists will also face issues related to developing methods and tools to help facilitate the collection, processing, analyzing, and visualizing of such multifaceted social data in near real-time. Our example model of individual and societal well-being is based on a static data set collected over many years. It is extremely valuable for generating structural equation models representing the interdependencies among the related input variables, and for paving the way for exploratory and predictive analyses.

Given the vast amount of qualitative data available in social media platforms such as Twitter, Facebook, and a host of blogging and microblogging technologies, it is possible to create "social sensors", which monitor important indicators of societal well-being, on massive scales, in near real-time. Traditional social science methods rely on labor and time intensive qualitative data analysis techniques to transform qualitative data into quantitative representations of affect (e.g., manually reading and coding individual text entries to determine if a person is expressing positive or negative affect). In contrast to most typical quantitative methods, qualitative data analysis methods do not easily scale up. Datasets are too large (consider the entire internet of social media, SMS/text messages, emails, blogs, etc.), and they are produced at extreme velocities (e.g., 500 million tweets per day, or status updates from 1.8 billion active Facebook users per day [18]). It is impossible for human researchers to even look at all the data, much less analysis it in a timely manner.

Whereas previous generations of Computer Assisted Qualitative Data AnalysiS (CAQDAS) software supported the traditional toolkit of qualitative researchers, i.e., sorting, searching, and annotating, the newest generation of tools is adding features powered by computerized natural language processing (NLP) and statistical machine learning (ML) techniques to enable automated rapid, massively large scale assessment of digital text, audio, video, and other multimedia traces of people's affective experiences as portrayed in their social media posts. The norm for next generation social analytics will be to employ such computational tools to facilitate blending of social media *thick data* (rich, descriptive qualitative data) with *big data* (i.e., data that is characterized by massive volume (amount of data), velocity (speed of data in or out), and variety (range of data types and sources)).

A. VADER: Automated Analysis of Affect in Social Media

VADER (**V**alence **A**ware **D**ictionary and s**E**ntiment **R**easoner) [10] is a computational tool for conducting automated large scale sentiment analysis [19][20]. Sentiment analysis is useful to a wide range of problems that are of interest to next generation social analysts, practitioners, and researchers from fields such as sociology, marketing and advertising, psychology, economics, and political science. The inherent nature of microblog content - such as those observed on Twitter and Facebook - poses serious challenges to practical applications of sentiment analysis. Some of these challenges stem from the sheer rate and volume of user generated social content, combined with the contextual sparseness resulting from shortness of the text and a tendency to use abbreviated language conventions to express sentiments. VADER is a simple rule-based algorithm and model for general sentiment analysis. In previous work [10], we compared VADER's effectiveness to eleven typical state-of-practice benchmarks for automated sentiment analysis, including LIWC [21][22], ANEW [23], the General Inquirer [24], SentiWordNet [25], and machine learning oriented techniques relying on Naive Bayes, Maximum Entropy, and Support Vector Machine (SVM) algorithms. We used a combination of qualitative and quantitative methods to produce, and then empirically validate, a *gold-standard* sentiment lexicon that is especially attuned to affective expressions in microblog-like contexts. VADER combines these lexical features with consideration for five generalizable rules that embody grammatical and syntactical conventions that humans use when expressing or emphasizing sentiment *intensity*. We found that incorporating these heuristics improves the accuracy of the sentiment analysis engine across several domain contexts (social media text, NY Times editorials, movie reviews, and product reviews). Notably, the VADER affective sentiment lexicon performs exceptionally well in the social media domain. The correlation coefficient shows that the VADER computational engine performs as well ($r = 0.881$) as individual *human* raters ($r = 0.888$) at matching ground truth (i.e., the aggregated group mean from 20 human raters for sentiment intensity of each text-based affective expression). Surprisingly, when we further inspect the classification accuracy, we see that VADER ($F1 = 0.96$) actually even outperforms individual human raters ($F1 = 0.84$) at correctly classifying the sentiment of tweets into positive, neutral, or negative classes.

B. CASTR: Aid to Automated Topic Models of Social Text

CASTR (**C**ommon-ground **A**cquisition for **S**ocial **T**opic **R**ecognition), produces the supporting text-based information needed to establish so called *common ground*, a well-known construct from psycholinguistics whereby individuals engaged in communication share mutual facts and knowledge in order to be better understood [11][12]. CASTR is intended to aid in *computational topic modeling* [26] by automatically acquiring this background knowledge.

Computational topic modeling techniques are used to uncover the hidden, or latent, concept-based semantic structures (i.e., topics) within text documents. Topic modeling is useful for a broad collection of activities, from automatically tagging newspaper articles with their appropriate newspaper sections (e.g., sports, finance, lifestyle, etc.) to automatically clustering like-minded social media users into groups based on the similarity of their expressed interests. Unfortunately, however, these automated approaches will sometimes infer topics that match poorly to – and are less semantically meaningful than – human inferred topics [27]. The issue is compounded when mining so-called *social text*, i.e., sparse text produced explicitly for informal social consumption (e.g., via social media, instant messages, SMS/texts, personal email, and so on where people rely on one another's common knowledge, rather than extended textual documentation, to understand intended meanings). In designing and developing CASTR's algorithms, we qualitatively assess the unique characteristics of social text, which present challenges to computational topic models, and which are not prevalent in other typical (non-social) text corpora like newspaper articles, scientific publications, or books. We find that a) constraints imposed by typical social media technologies, b) implicit social communication norms, and c) evolving conventions of use often confound typical computational topic modeling techniques for social text. For example, tweets are much terser than other kinds of text documents, and this sparsity is troublesome for computational topic modeling algorithms that perform posterior inference of the text. Also, tweets are often laden with a great deal of social communication "noise" (such as emoticons, emojis, hashtags, and URL links) that confuse computational models, and yet present very little trouble to humans.

CASTR leverages the concept of common ground to present a theoretically informed social and cognitive psychological framing of we refer to as the "human interpretability problem" as observed in computationally-produced topic models of text mined from social media. Additionally, CASTR employs a well-established theory from the field of Human-Centered Computing, namely Distributed Cognition (DCog) [28][29], as a basis for mitigating the issues of developing common ground for computational topic modeling efforts. DCog is a theoretical perspective that proposes knowledge and cognition are not confined to any single individual or referent resource; instead, they are distributed across individuals, objects, artefacts, and tools in the environment, and constructed in context.

As an example of how CASTR implements the DCog inspired mitigation strategies, consider a fictitious (but representative) social media post that expresses a person's positive affective experience related to attending a musical concert at a popular venue near Atlanta, Georgia: "*Headed to Stone Mountain to see the Rolling Stones. Mick Rocks! www.rollingstones.com/band/ #StonesOnFire*". Although it is a relatively simple thing for humans to immediately understand the meaning of this social text (most Americans know who The Rolling Stones are, most people from Georgia know what Stone Mountain is, and most people understand what it means when "rock" is used as a verb in this context, even if they are not immediately sure who Mick refers to, and most people recognize the conventional use of hashtags, as well as URL links). However, the shared, socially constructed knowledge (common-ground) necessary to understand the intended meaning of the above example social text is often not readily available to computational topic models.

CASTR automatically retrieves the (previously missing) background distributed knowledge about key words, phrases, and named entities (proper nouns) within the terse text, and provides this information to the computational topic model processes. The result is a much more accurate representation of which topic(s) a particular short social media document should be belong. For example, the social text above would be appropriately grouped with music and entertainment related topics, rather than geological science related topics.

C. *EAGLE-ID: Automated Demographic Profiling*

EAGLE-ID (**E**thnicity, **A**ge, **G**ender, and **L**iteracy/**E**ducation **Id**entifier) automatically aids in characterizing important human social demographic features based on social media profile data. The EAGLE-ID system consists of software (currently in beta stage) that performs automatic classification of a person's ethnicity (given the person's surname), their likely age range and gender (based on their first name), and their literacy and education level based solely on information mined from the person's digital social media data (including user profile data as well as shared content). The majority of this is done via text-based computational linguistic processing (in conjunction with comparisons to data from the U.S. Census Bureau database, Social Security Administration records, and U.S. Dept. of Health and Human Services data), but it also uses computer vision for image processing on profile pictures to boost ethnicity/age/gender classification accuracy.

In addition to the obvious uses for user profiling and user modeling, the EAGLE-ID software could be useful for automatically collecting and associating demographic information with particular social media accounts. When used in conjunction with VADER and CASTR, EAGLE-ID facilitates rapid, large scale analysis of social data for use in real-time monitoring of individual and societal well-being with realistically representational complex models.

While the design and development of tools such as VADER, CASTR, and EAGLE-ID is not necessarily in the direct purview of social science, the employment and use of such tools will almost certainly be a significant part of next generation social analytics. It is already a major part of the new field of Computational Social Science. Eventually, the word "computational" will be dropped, and methods, tools, and techniques like the ones discussed in this section will be commonplace in social science research – integrated into social science education right alongside experimental study design, research ethics, and statistical analysis.

D. *Crowdsourcing for Scaling-Up Qualitative Data Coding*

An interesting interim step preceding fully automated artificial intelligent machine learning algorithms for conducting large scale qualitative data analyses are the emergence of digital crowdsourcing economies such as Amazon Mechanical Turk. These platforms are typically comprised of a massive, distributed, anonymous crowd of individuals willing to perform general human-intelligence micro-tasks for micro-payments, and they can be leveraged as a valuable resource for the next generation of social science research and practice. Indeed, in the past half-decade, Amazon Mechanical Turk has radically changed the way many social science scholars do research. The availability of a massive, distributed, anonymous crowd of individuals willing to perform general human-intelligence micro-tasks for micro-payments is a valuable resource for researchers and practitioners.

In other work [13], we addressed many of the challenges facing researchers using crowd-sourced platforms. Particularly, we reported on how to better ensure *high quality* qualitative data annotations for tasks of varying difficulty from a transient crowd of anonymous, non-experts. Crowdsourcing has already had a significant impact on social analytics, and we believe it will continue to play a substantial role in the next generation of social analytics.

V. From Traditional to Next Generation Social Analytics

The complex model of well-being described earlier differs from traditional social science in several meaningful ways:

1. *Representational complexity*: In next generation social analytics, model complexity will increase beyond what is typical for much of social science research today. Our example integrates more than 130 indicators for- and correlates of- individual and public well-being. These data are garnered from many sources, measured in numerous different units, stored using many data types at different scales representing individuals, communities, and entire societies. Just as other disciplines such as systems engineering, economics, and computer science have embraced the notion of incorporating "big data" into their typical data models, the next generation of social analytics will need to likewise expand their scope such that social analytics like the ones we illustrate are the norm, rather than the exception.
2. *Large-N and Multiple-T*: In order to achieve useful statistical power while incorporating the expanded scope resulting from increased representational complexity, and at the same time preserving broad generalization and application capacities, next generation social analysts will need to design and conduct studies with much larger sample sizes (i.e., "Large N" studies) collected over multiple instances in time (i.e., "Multiple T", or longitudinal studies). In our example, we integrate data

from nearly 60,000 respondents spanning 42 years with regard to 130 different variables of interest, where each variable puts (on average) potentially 7 unique degrees of positive or negative pressure on individual or societal well-being. All told, this leverages approximately 55 million data points for our model. Such study designs will eventually become more prevalent for social analytics.

3. *Extending exploratory and predictive analytics*: Our example model lays the foundations for predictive analysis (e.g., via Monte Carlo simulations), which would be extremely useful to government policy decision makers because the impacts of their decision alternatives could be vetted within a data-derived, model-driven trade space analysis tool. For example, we would be able to answer important questions such as: *in order to improve overall community/public well-being, should government decision makers invest tax dollars in a better public transportation system, economic development program, roads, schools, or security services*? Such considerations will enable next generation social analytics to generate better predictions, going beyond the prevailing social science policy of typically concluding a study upon reporting descriptive and inferential statistics.

Combining the increase in representational complexity with the methods, techniques and tools, a vision of how next generation social analytics will be conducted begins to emerge in which large-scale, individual and national-level, near real-time analysis of the following are common:

- social media data
- mobile and GPS technology data
- personal wearable technology data
- internet of things data

We outlined how new tools and techniques could be leveraged to marshal in the next generation of qualitative social analytics on heretofore unprecedented scales. VADER provides researchers the ability to automatically quantify both the direction (e.g., positive or negative) and magnitude of affective expressions in textual documents ranging from word-level to tome-level scales. In a matter of seconds, VADER is capable of automatically transforming millions of rich qualitative social media documents (e.g., tweets) into quantified measures of positive and negative affect for a given Twitter user. This capability alone allows us to produce a simple representation of well-being on a national scale in near-real time [10]. When we combine it with the ability to also understand the topic towards which the affective expressions apply, we can begin to incorporate other elements of the more complex representation of well-being previously discussed.

For example, consider when a Twitter user laments (or praises) aspects of her job, her health, her family or friends, her city/community, or her financial situation. Or consider how often she might express satisfaction (or dissatisfaction) for aspects of the general political, security, or economic climate of her community or nation. Now consider how prevalent such expressions are in aggregate for all Twitter users. Next think about how many other publically available forms of such data currently exist (other social networks like Facebook and Snapchat, place-based platform Foursquare, review platform Yelp, internet chat rooms, topical blogs, and discussion forums such as Reddit). Next generation social analytics should embrace such resources, as well as the tools needed for analyzing them at internet scale.

Typically, these social media data are time-stamped, so that temporal aspects can be incorporated (c.f., [30]). Slower changing data variables such as a person's demographic characteristics (e.g., ethnicity, age, gender, literacy and education level) can also be automatically extracted from a person's social media data. In many cases, these data can be combined with meta-information regarding the geolocated origins of the content producers, or otherwise merged with GPS, mobile, or other location-aware wearable technologies. Real-time assimilation of national, regional, or local unemployment rates, crime data, housing market data, inflation, consumer price index, prime rates, and gross domestic product round out the capability to produce timely, realistically complex models of societal well-being.

To achieve the vision of next generation social analytics, further research is needed in the following areas:

1) Model Complexity vs Model Interpretability

Increasing representational complexity in the way we discuss in Section II, while more characteristic of real-world human social behavior, is not devoid of its own issues; complex models are by their very nature more difficult to interpret. We offer a brief discussion of three avenues for mitigating the challenge of interpreting complex models. First, social science data analysts will need simple and intuitive interfaces for exploring the trade-space of the data. Such tools will increasing model transparency, and incorporating interactive data exploration will aid analysts in easily and quickly uncovering complex interrelationships within and among the variables of any complex model. Second, analysts need simple interfaces that allow them to rapidly build and assess Monte Carlo simulations regarding how potential changes in input variables impact selected response variables of interest. Third, advanced interactive data and information visualization tools will be critical for next generation social analytics to make sense of data at varying levels of aggregation and combination.

2) Ethical Considerations of Widespread Human Social Data Analytics

Ethical considerations related to privacy and confidentiality are often cited when human social analytics are discussed. Privacy (not collecting data that is not needed for the study) and confidentiality (protecting identifiable information from inappropriate dissemination) are fundamental principles of ethical research with human subjects. These principles must find new implementation when the context of research is large, shared data sets. By extension, as on-going studies continue (including longitudinal studies), mechanisms for individuals to monitor how their data are being used, and to have appropriate safeguards, must be developed.

Other issues include data ownership and potential for financial gain – both for individuals (about whom the data are collected) and for institutions that otherwise possess the data of interest. Owning institutions must take care as data is updated over time that it does not become used or cited for purposes that are outside the agreed upon collection context, lest the whole dataset becomes discredited. Possible financial gain suggests possible financial loss, perhaps from liability that might arise from compromise of privacy or confidentiality, or perhaps from errors in algorithms or in other study methods. These issues, and others that arise from them, deserve careful attention, but are beyond the scope of the present paper.

3) *Skill Sets and Education for NGSA*

We must educate and train the next generation of social data analysts to be comfortable embracing representational complexity and incorporating methods, tools, and techniques like the ones discussed above. It will need to become standard parts of social science education, integrated into social science curricula right alongside research methods and experimental study design, research ethics, and statistical analysis.

4) *Collaborative study and experimentation*

We must build platforms where social scientists can come together and conduct joint experiments or related experiments in common contexts with next generation methods and tools. Such platforms are becoming a central component of biomedical research, and are expanding into other fields as diverse as international affairs, materials research, and system design. Digital network technologies supporting cloud computing, federated data architectures, knowledge graphs, data mining and machine learning, standardized web ontologies, digital annotation, experimental workflow sharing, computer visualization, crowdsourcing, and computer gaming are creating unprecedented capability for shared study of social behaviors. Emerging shared data experimentation platforms will provide a means to transform access to and sharing of social science research and social data analytics.

VI. Next-Generation Research Federations

Although data sharing platforms like Harvard Dataverse are available to share the detailed results of scientific studies, in this section we discuss the idea of federated data models for experimentation – platforms that allow geographically dispersed cohorts of researchers to work together on scientific experiments around a common problem or area of study. To our knowledge such platforms have not yet entered use in the social sciences community. We discuss the challenges and opportunities associated with an experimentation platform concept, methodologies that can support development of such platforms, and an example case where a shared experimentation platform would be useful.

Unlike many other scientific areas of study, social situations represent complex adaptive systems that are characterized by independent agents who self-organize, adapt, and learn. In complex adaptive systems, broadly applicable models of behavior are difficult to generalize. The situation under study and the context of the situation must be studied together, and generalization across multiple contexts is not always wise or possible. Adaptation often makes generalized results short-lived. Intervention in social situations focuses heavily on causal relationships, but generalizing to purely linear causal relationships is often unsuccessful. Study of such systems must eventually account for *linear causal* relationships and also *circular causal* relationships, self-organization or *adaptive causal* relationships, and *reflexivity*, which acknowledges the act of studying the system can effect causal relationships [31]. Generalization of results using linear regressions is most common and appropriate, but can only be accomplished by applying assumptions with respect to the other three causal models that are often not captured with the data. These assumptions are often about which of a number of potential causes aggregate to larger populations, making explanations of causality difficult.

Because of such "shifts in causality," reduction to linear models makes the generalization of effects across multiple contexts difficult. They can also limit the reproducibility and replicability of social science study [6]. Issues related to reproducibility can be reduced by use of common datasets with access to original study data, models, and tools. Study generalization requires access to sampling methods as well as both positive and negative results, and more difficult, the original assumptions and abstractions used by the researcher to conceptualize the study. However, because many of these assumptions are related to selection of causal factors, effective conceptual models that capture context in the form of broader causal factors with hypotheses related to context-specific selections can help. The ability to do this has been until recently limited by the time and effort required to collect and analyze data, a condition which is changing rapidly.

Designing data analytic and computational models that accurately reflect performance measures at different layers of society, and the aggregation of measures from one layer to the next, is the primary conceptualization problem in social analysis and policy practice. Behavioral aspects of complex sociotechnical systems can be influenced at any layer of the system, but initiatives that try to analyze and improve factors at one level do not necessarily translate into positive influence at other layers. Moreover, the timeframes for measuring effects can vary greatly across different factors and societal layers [32] [33]. Lack of common methods and tools to define model abstraction and aggregation of data create further barriers to generalization, which tie back to the original conceptualization of the study and related selection of constructs and dependent variables.

Figure 4 places our complex model of societal well-being in the context of a city, where the built environment, institutions, and shared infrastructure provide the capital necessary for people's livelihoods. This model expands the total dataset required to evaluate well-being tremendously, and also introduces causal feedback into the model of well-being. This is a complex adaptive system that can be explored via complex models but will have no deterministic solution sets. Issues and concerns with use of data analytic methods in social experiments reflect the complex adaptive systems aspects of social phenomena like this. These include determining appropriate context, understanding both linear and non-linear causality, representing differing time scales, uncertainty about what constitutes entities that affect the system, and issues with agency or agent identification [34]. These can be overcome by

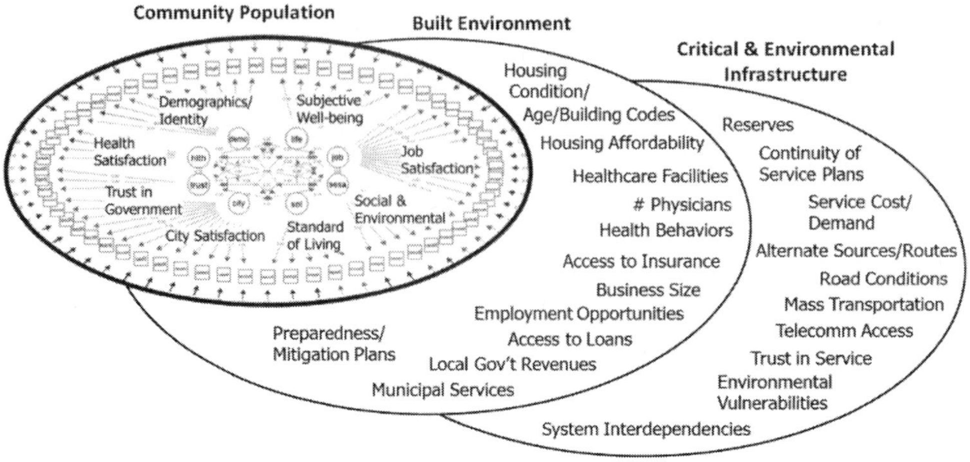

Figure 4. Complex Model of Human Capital in a Community Population situated in the Context of City Built Environment, Institutions, and Critical & Environmental Infrastructure.

viewing the social problem of interest as a system then conceptualizing both the problem system and response system as a set of conceptual and then dynamic models. Research related to enterprise systems of systems and sociotechnical systems analysis introduces a methodology to address these issues.

Shared experimentation implies agreement on paradigms that reflect the problem definition and contexts of interest, as well as the semantic descriptions of the sociotechnical system of interest, and the conceptual model of the current systems' behaviors and future states. The concept of an experimentation platform implies a set of methods and tools to define and address these agreements, which we discuss prior to descriptions of the tool framework.

In Section VII, we introduce the concept of an experimentation platform, using references from a United States Air Force concept as an appropriate framework for this application. We describe emerging computer platforms that make this concept a viable approach, and a methodology for building community-wide models in these platforms. In Section VIII, we describe the characteristics of a tool platform for experimentation, and the technological approaches that might be used to build it. We do not at this point describe a complete toolset, but a call for research to create these tools. In Section IX, we discuss early work in next generation social science study design tools necessary to complete the experimentation process.

VII. Experimentation Platform Concept

A shared data federation combined with a shared research and experimentation platform can serve to rapidly distribute knowledge and accelerate the development of new knowledge in scientific study. The concept of "System Level Experimentation" combined with next generation analytics is an approach that has not been explored yet in the social science domain, but is gaining prevalence in other areas of study. We discuss this first as a conceptual platform, then describe some of the emerging technology that can be used for implementation in the social science domain.

A. *System Level Experimentation*

Alberts et al. [35][36] captured a useful vision for information age transformation of social theories and related analytics in pursuit of a set of methods we refer to as System Level Experimentation. The authors define this as a "campaign of experimentation," or a "set of related activities that explore and mature knowledge about a concept of interest." Although developed as an approach for transforming military command and control, the general model of such a campaign provides a framework for joint experimentation in any social decision making domain. The framework is a scientific method for experimentation, which includes theory development, conceptualization or conceptual modeling, formulation of questions and hypotheses, collection of evidence, and analysis. The approach views system transformation as a campaign of multiple experiments that produces a body of knowledge that creates a foundation for future experiments. Such campaigns have leaders and goals, research cohorts who use and create knowledge aligned with the goals, and a shared knowledge capture framework that allows federated cohorts and experiments against a common knowledge model.

With respect to reproducibility, repeatability, and generalization of experiments, the idea of a campaign focuses the research process on aligned goals with deliberate urgency and resource allocation. Alberts and Hayes note, "*reuse here applies to ideas, information about investigations conducted, data collected, analyses performed, and tools developed and applied. In terms of experiments, it implies replication. Reuse, and hence progress, is maximized when attention is paid to the principles of science that prescribe how these activities should be conducted, how peer reviews should be executed, and when attention should be paid to the widespread dissemination of findings and conclusions.*"

The authors stress the importance of a shared conceptual model as a key to generalization, reproducibility, and replicability. Although in many scientific studies there exists a shared paradigm of study and generally shared conceptualization, this is difficult to achieve in social situations where stakeholder perspectives, even those of research communities, are difficult to align. For example the community measurement paradigm for "standard of living" is moving from a Gross-Domestic Product (GDP)-based measure of production to more representative consumption-based representations. However, the GDP measure was conceptually simple, and consumption measures are conceptually complex. Although the community is accepting the paradigm shift, there do not exist common agreed upon conceptual models of standard of living that can drive shared and replicable experimentation. A debate over the conceptualization of our complex model of well-being would be counterproductive. We need a platform where the agreed upon factors can be organized and shared, research cohorts can experiment with models and empirical study in their contexts, and the common conceptualization in terms of factors, abstractions, and weightings can be updated over time via community experimentation. Thus an effective shared experimentation platform must address common conceptualization artifacts as well as data and potentially dynamic models. Such a platform will serve both cross-sectional and longitudinal studies. Longitudinal studies conducted in such a platform will have opportunity to use dynamically-computed weightings for different data collection epochs as new information is added to the platform.

B. Emerging Data Analytics Platforms

What we can do much more easily these days is collect the data. Public datasets that report social variables in both broad and localized contexts are becoming widespread. Shared community data warehouses and models for experimentation purposes are becoming more widely used in complex health and medical studies, leading one to believe that such approaches may also have use in social research and analysis. Notable examples of medical research platforms include the Global Alzheimer's Association Interactive Network (GAAIN) [37] and the Medical Informatics Platform (MIP) of the European Union's Human Brain Project [38]. Common features of these projects include a federated data model, shared schemas or data codings, community agreed upon ontologies and sematic tagging, machine learning tools for extraction and matching of data, and web-based interfaces to data, research cohorts, and visualizations. In all such projects, a shared database is created where an entity-relationship model defines the schema of the resultant "data warehouse," and agreed upon data codings provide a map between the larger sets of data and the phenomena of interest. We will further explore the possibility of designing similar projects for social data experimentation.

To reach this point, the community must develop not just common data, but also methods for agreement on research paradigms, related stakeholder perspectives of problem and solution spaces, associated viewpoints, and shared conceptualizations. Thus long-term success in social analytics must address the capture of both the data and conceptual relationship models that make the data meaningful. These conceptual relationships are often determined using soft systems approaches, which are appropriate, but existing methods and tools do not adequately connect the conceptual artifacts with the data-driven analytics. In the social analytics field, there is a need for research that connects the resulting collected data to its conceptual model artifacts. Without this problems with abstraction, generalization, reproducibility, and replicability cannot be resolved. Research from the systems engineering community centered on management of enterprise systems-of-systems provides a set of useful methods and tools.

C. Enterprise Systems of Systems Methodology

Sociotechnical systems analysis is a specific methodology that supports assessment of multiple factors across all layers of a complex enterprise or societal construct using sets of tools derived from system science and system modeling. The methods recognize that factors arise from the interaction of many and diverse enterprises that can be defined by their entities, relationships, established processes, pursued strategies, and emergent phenomena. The sociotechnical systems analysis attempts to capture the combined conceptual, data, and analytical modeling artifacts necessary to completely describe the problem [39][40].

With respect to social situations, the method produces a set of artifacts that describe the system context and boundaries, system entities and relationships, primary construct variables, potential causal variables, and phenomena of interest. The process is conducted such that insight can be fed into dynamic computer models. Hypotheses that intervene in lower level causal factors can then be viewed as they aggregate up into larger population behaviors. The sociotechnical systems analysis produces artifacts that communicate the abstractions and aggregation of behaviors across different scales, helping to explicitly document both the assumed and modeled variables.

At the core of a sociotechnical systems model are entities and their relationships, which can be organized into associated databases and warehouses. The entity-relationship model can be created, modified, and refined over periods of short and long term study. Standardized codings of the data entities then make relevant data elements accessible to researchers and analysts. One use of this is for data collection and analysis, but the sociotechnical systems analysis methods are focused on development of experimentation platforms. Experimentation requires that not only the data but also the underlying conceptual models context of study be updated over time.

The conceptual model representations produced by the sociotechnical systems analysis serve as a bridge between the soft systems aspects of the problem (systems thinking) and the quantitative analysis approach (design). This is an area that needs significant additional research as related to methods and tool design. However, recent advances in machine learning and semantic graphs can bring the semantic model and mathematical model artifacts into the same toolsets. The bridge between the two is a conceptual model that uses semantic models to specify the analytical models. We identify these as metamodels as they should describe broader conceptual models and data, while individual experiments explore a subset of executable models and constructs related to central questions of interest. Figure 5 describes that bridge.

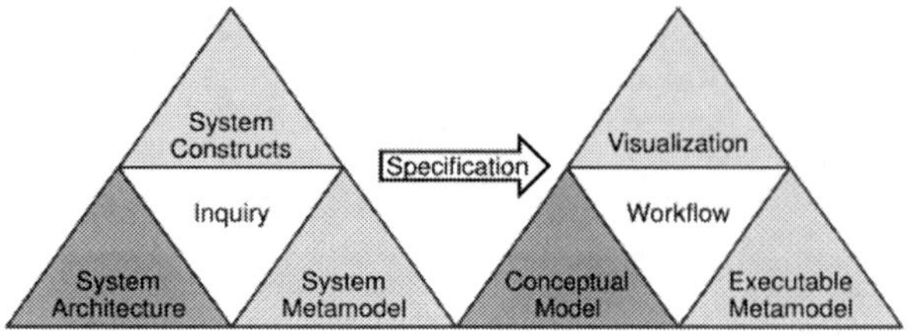

Figure 5. The bridge between soft systems analysis and social analytic model specification.

We define the soft systems aspects in Figure 5 as "*System Metamodeling*" using three fundamental abstraction approaches: system metamodels, system constructs, and system architecture models. These are determined in a participative, inquiry-based process. We describe hard system aspects as "*Executable Metamodeling*" determined by a specification and design workflow using conceptual models, executable metamodels, and data visualization. It is useful to think about this as a tool framework. The tools support structuring the systems metamodel, creating the conceptual models, creating the executable metamodels, analyzing and visualizing the decision space, and managing the contained knowledge over time [41].

The system metamodel is described as the set of constructs and rules used to define semantic relationships across information sets, associated data sets, and methodologies or processes [42]. The metamodel definition on the semantic side is an architectural description of the system using modeling views and stakeholder viewpoints. The executable metamodel is the dataset design and any associated computational models.

D. *Metamodels and Federated Data Models*

The emerging medical community models link together research cohorts by providing a common data model for integrating federated datasets. As experimentation platforms they provide a cohort discovery tool to link research communities, a federated data model integration architecture, and a common data visualization toolset that allows data exploration across multiple cohort data. The federated approach to data model integration allows individual cohorts to maintain their own working datasets while sharing and using data from other cohorts via a common data model representation. State of the art tools for data discovery, transformation, and integration automate most of the source data integration into the common data model. The common data model is implemented as a schema in a relational database using agreed upon codings for data tables and variables.

In a federated data model design, metadata or data descriptions are essential to data harmonization – integrating data from different sets and integrating experimental data back into the common data warehouse. Emerging data mining and machine learning tools can automate data harmonization assuming the metadata has a rich enough natural language description of the data elements to link multiple sets. Mapping variables between federated datasets and the common data model is accomplished by extracting and matching the data entities via descriptive data mapped from element descriptions in data dictionaries, a component of metadata. Adequate metadata provides a path to harmonizing the often cryptic tags placed on data elements in databases. Transformation tools are provided to map data between the common model representation and federated datasets [43].

The conceptualization of most existing common data model examples were developed initially from manual coding and integration of existing datasets [44][45]. In the social analytics area, a common conceptual definition of the data tables and entities would be a huge undertaking due to the tremendous differences in terminology, conceptual data relationships, and assumptions made around data generalizations across societal scales. Emerging approaches

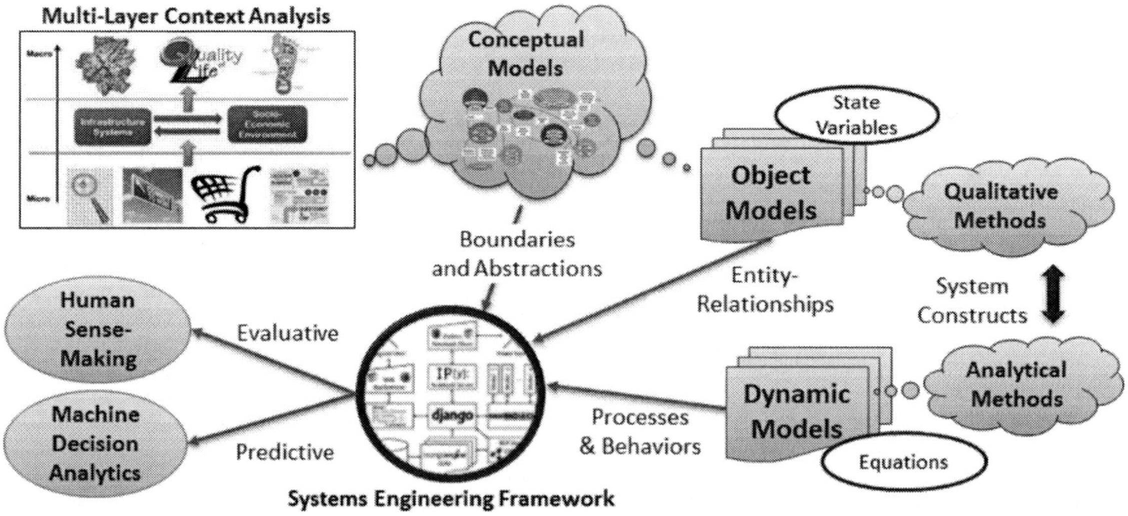

Figure 6. Conceptual Architecture Blending Qualitative and Quantitative Models into a Single Platform.

for graph representation of data entities and relationships should be explored in the social sciences arena as a tool for amassing large volumes of linked data and knowledge supporting both generalized and contextual research results.

VIII. Social Experimentation Tool Framework

We present a generalized concept for social experimentation and analytics using both bottoms-up software environment and top-down conceptual architecture descriptions. The purpose of this discussion is not to present the design of an existing tool (none exist), but to describe the characteristics and architectural constructs of future frameworks for social experimentation and analysis. Figure 6 presents our high level system and process architecture.

Alberts et al. note that "*For purposes of building knowledge, the most important elements are (1) consistent language (clear and operational definitions and measures), (2) explicit use of metatags (meta-data) on data, and (3) clear and complete descriptions of assumptions. These are part and parcel of an explicit conceptual model.*" [37]

A *consistent language* and *use of metatags* relate to the semantic model of the system of interest. This is often described as an ontology, but the term "System Metamodel" is more appropriate. The *description of assumptions* refers to appropriate documentation of construct variables and associated contextual assumptions of lower level abstractions.

The use of inconsistent language to name the data elements in the resulting database is the major limitation of a common data model, it can take years to agree on data element definitions and a static data schema can make the data model difficult to modify. Data element names are often useless to infer meaning. These issues can be abated by consistent mapping generated from data element descriptions in data dictionaries, a primary component of metadata. Data providers that create rich metadata and share this across the data federation will aid in effective model and data sharing. Metadata has additional benefit as it can hide the actual data if it is restricted, without impacting the federation [46]. Data value ranges and units must also be consistent or readable from the metadata.

Three general developments emerging from modern web standards aid in linking different data collections from different domains. The first is the Web Ontology Language (OWL) and widely used Resource Description Framework (RDF) stores such as Google's FreeBase. The standard subject-predicate-object or object-attribute-value framework and semantic linking ease in the standardization of semantic terms and relationships. Various domains are rapidly creating large RDF stores or web ontologies describing their domain. To date relatively little development and standardization of common web ontologies have been undertaken across the social sciences domain. However, as researchers opt to use existing ontologies and create domain specific ones, conditions will improve. A consistent language representation is the foundation of a good system metamodel.

A second development is extensive use of web linked data standards. Most database schemas remain defined in eXtensible Markup Language (XML) form but the web community is transitioning to JavaScript Object Notation (JSON) format for standard document annotation and linking of data to research. JSON is a computer language independent format for sharing objects and attribute-value relationships across different datasets, documents, etc. in addition, the use of annotated Hyper-Text Markup Language (HTML) documents to describe research experiments and link input data and results will aid in broader community sharing.

A third area of exploration is the evolution of linked graphs of semantic and mathematical information, an area that is rapidly developing due to Google's introduction of Knowledge Graph and similar entity-driven stores of large information sets. Graph structures support semantic integration and structuring of linked data by compiling text into linked nodes and then relating these to concepts that provide shared meaning to the text. In the graph structure the metadata of our data federation could be linked into a semantic network that can be grown over time with new data. This is an area of needed research; the ability to create large curated sets of community shared and agreed upon causal data and linked experimental results could transform social science research.

A significant hurdle in social science use of these tools is reconciling the linking of different actors' viewpoints to the standard object-attribute-value ontologies. Different actors assign different meaning to social entities and relationships, making contextual features of language by the actor an important variable. The specific meaning associated with the language used by different actors requires a different structuring of shared ontologies than used in most of these applications today. This is an area for further research.

The use of these new technologies does not inherently capture the conceptualizations that defined that data to be important in the first case, and it does not capture assumptions made about missing data elements in the graph. Discerning real causality from experimental measurement of a social construct often requires a qualitative analysis of the underlying causal variables that cannot be measured directly. This is an underlying conceptual model that is often not fully documented in the research results, particularly those potentially causal variables that were purposefully not assessed in the research. This is where context becomes critical – discussions of why these variables are assumed to be causal in this context versus different variables in another context – becomes a key component of the knowledge base. Existing computer-based data models and analytical models are not linked to their conceptual parent models, primarily because the available modeling tools have not been built. A related area of research is specific to this problem, which is how to formally link more freeform conceptual diagramming or facilitation artifacts with more constrained formal modeling and simulations tools.

The federation model recognizes the need to link in the dynamic aspects of predictive models with feedback and adaptation. Research cohorts should be able to extract the fundamental model from the central data model and conceptualization, apply their own dynamic or empirical results in their context, then provide updates back to the whole as new information and ideally new datasets. For example system dynamics models can provide a larger systems context by connecting key social and human capital factors from the societal well-being model with system dynamics models of infrastructure, spatial communities, and social communities. Medina-Borja and Pasupathy [45] demonstrated the combination of complex structured equation models for uncovering causal relationships in data-rich scenarios and elucidating these to stakeholders through system dynamics models. These dynamic models are going to be context dependent, and should not be considered part of the data federation itself, although they will produce evidence that matures the conceptual model over time.

The "clear and operational definitions and measures" noted by Alberts et al. in the military context is a difficult hurdle in less well governed social situations [36]. Operational definitions and measures in social situations tend to be an area of great debate between different communities of interest. A GAAIN-like common data model is doomed to fail unless we can also define methods and tools to reach agreement on the conceptual models that drive entities, relationships, data definitions, and assumptions. Much of this disagreement involves data conceptualization, definition, and abstraction/aggregation at different scales (for example macroscale measures like "GDP per capita" versus microscale measures like "owning a dishwasher" – both used to describe standard of living). Emerging computer approaches to semantic integration offer hope for much richer microscale measurement sets, as long as the community can clearly see the need for research in this area.

IX. Extending to Next Generation Social Science

The explosive growth of computational tools and methods for analyzing social science data are not limited to use only during the analytics stages of the scientific process. Such tools, along with the massive increase in global digital connectivity, has opened new possibilities for both designing and conducting social science research in addition to data analytics. In this section, we briefly discuss this research.

A. Next Generation Social Science Study Design

Technology in the next generation will aid social science researchers with many of the typical tasks required for sound study design by providing automated aid in finding and vetting authoritative sources; automatically summarizing, categorizing, and organizing the concepts and ideas within scientific texts; cueing researchers to emergent concepts; and helping to identify potential novel hypotheses based on prior literature (using, for example, Microsoft's Academic Graph [46] as a data source). This technology, which we refer to as the Study Design Tool (SDT), will utilize scientometric analysis to automatically ingest and parse scientific publications using computational natural language processing.

Current research and development efforts are underway to build the SDT. These efforts include a collaboration with the Open Science Framework (OSF) [47] in which we are working to develop a social science study schema, which captures relevant study design information in a structured format. To inform iterative design of the schema and associated metrics, the research effort involves eliciting information from researchers regarding their personal design process during each study cycle. Existing (traditional) research design processes and capabilities will be enhanced through the development of new annotation, search, and machine learning-based classification functions in the SDT to allow researchers to rapidly explore and discover social science studies stored in OSF according to topics, keywords, methods used, dependent/independent variables studied, sampling techniques employed, research subject pool demographics, hypotheses tested, cross-references, and/or forward/backward citation context mapping. For example, by having researchers provide keywords relevant to their studies and references to foundational studies, the SDT will report metrics based on a co-citation analysis that indicate the degrees to which foundational research may be biased – such as when it only cites particular subsets of past work (i.e., cliqued or clustered scientific communities, in a graph analytical sense). These analyses may be run over either external publication databases (e.g., Scopus [48] or Web of Science [49]) or over all data stored in OSF. Another function will be to suggest relevant journal articles to researchers based on unbiased sampling over a clustered topic space that may suggest new avenues for inquiry. SDT will also capture insights from researcher-conducted literature reviews, allowing for a reduction in labor for future studies. This technology will aid in novel hypothesis generation and innovative experimental methods (e.g., by cueing researchers to interesting, but as yet untested combinations of dependent/independent variables, methods, domain contexts, and so on) to advance rigorous, reproducible social science studies at scales necessary to develop and validate causal models of human social behaviors.

B. Next Generation Social Science Study Deployment

Once limited by practical constraints to experiments involving just a few dozen participants - often university students or other easily available groups - or to correlational studies of large datasets without any opportunity for determining causation, scientists can now engage thousands of diverse volunteers online and explore an expanded range of important topics and questions. New tools and methods for harnessing virtual or alternate reality and massively distributed platforms will be developed and objectively validated, helping to mitigate many of the vexing challenges in social science. By developing and applying new methods and models to larger, more diverse, and more representative groups of individuals - such as through globally connected web-based platforms - we seek to validate new tools that may empower social science in the same way that sophisticated telescopes and microscopes have helped advance astronomy and biology.

X. Conclusions

This paper serves both as a general call for new social science methods and tools, and as a review of several efforts across a number of domains that address the call. It is exploratory but also representative of current technology. Community resilience, in the face of climate change, aging infrastructure, migration, and other looming grand challenges, represents a perfect opportunity to test these new concepts. Community resilience is but one of the many societal issues that is need of enlightenment from social science. Issues of privacy and security must be acknowledged and addressed, but should not be insurmountable barriers to progress in the social sciences. We will be interested participants in and observers of the next generation in social analytics.

REFERENCES

[1] D.J. Folds, "Next Generation Social Analytics: Challenges and Payoffs," paper presented at HUSO 2016, The Second International Conference on Human and Social Analytics, 2016.

[2] C.J. Hutto, "Blending Quantitative, Qualitative, Geospatial, and Temporal Data: Progressing Towards the Next Generation of Human Social Analytics." Proceedings of HUSO 2016, The Second International Conference on Human and Social Analytics, 2016.

[3] T.A. McDermott, M. Nadolski, and D.J. Folds, "System-Level Experimentation: Social Computing and Analytics for Theory Building and Evaluation," Proceedings of HUSO 2016, The Second International Conference on Human and Social Analytics, 2016.

[4] Roberto Unger on what's wrong with social science today: http://www.socialsciencespace.com/2014/01/robertomangabeira-unger-what-is-wrong-with-the-social-sciencestoday/, accessed 31-May-2017.

[5] Open Science Collaboration, "Estimating the reproducibility of psychological science," Science. 349 (6251): aac4716. August 28, 2015

[6] K. Bollen, J Cacioppo, R.M. Kaplan, J.A. Krosnick, and J.L. Olds, Social, Behavioral, and Economic Science Perspectives on Robust and Reliable Science, Report of the Subcommittee on Replicability in Science, Advisory Committee to the National Science Foundation Directorate for Social, Behavioral, and Economic Science, May 2015.

[7] U. S. Federal Emergency Management Agency (FEMA), Draft Interagency Concept for Community Resilience Indicators and National-Level Measures, Published for Stakeholder Comment in June 2016.

[8] National Institute of Standards and Technology, NIST GCR 15-993, Community Resilience Workshop, February 18-19, 2015.

[9] C. Geertz, "Thick Description: Toward an Interpretive Theory of Culture," in The interpretation of cultures: selected essays, New York, NY: Basic Books, 1973, pp. 3–30.

[10] C.J. Hutto and E. Gilbert, "VADER: A Parsimonious Rule-based Model for Sentiment Analysis of Social Media Text," in Proceedings of the Eighth International AAAI Conference on Weblogs and Social Media, 2014, pp. 216–255.

[11] H.H. Clark, Using Language. Cambridge University Press, 1996.

[12] H.H. Clark and S.E. Brennan, "Grounding in communication," in Perspectives on socially shared cognition, L. B. Resnick, J. M. Levine, and S. D. Teasley, Eds. Washington DC: APA Books, 1991.

[13] T. Mitra, C.J. Hutto, and E. Gilbert, "Comparing Person- and Process-centric Strategies for Obtaining Quality Data on Amazon Mechanical Turk," in Proceedings of the 33rd Annual ACM Conference on Human Factors in Computing Systems, 2015, pp. 1345–1354.

[14] E. Diener, "Assessing subjective well-being: Progress and opportunities," Soc. Indic. Res., vol. 31, no. 2, pp. 103–157, Feb. 1994.

[15] E. Diener, E.M. Suh, R.E. Lucas, and H.L. Smith, "Subjective well-being: Three decades of progress.," Psychol. Bull., vol. 125, no. 2, pp. 276–302, 1999.

[16] D.J. Folds and V.M. Thompson, "Engineering human capital: A system of systems modeling approach," in Proceedings of the 8th International IEEE Conference on Systems of Systems Engineering (SoSE-13), 2013, pp. 285–290.

[17] T.W. Smith, P.V. Marsden, M. Hout, and J. Kim, "General Social Surveys, 1972-2014 [machine-readable data file]." NORC at the University of Chicago [producer and distributor], 2014.

[18] InternetLiveStats.com, "Internet Live Stats," Internet Live Stats - Internet Usage and Social Media Statistics, 2016. [Online]. Available: http://www.internetlivestats.com/, accessed: 31-May-2017.

[19] B. Pang and L. Lee, "Opinion Mining and Sentiment Analysis," Found. Trends Inf. Retr., vol. 2, no. 1–2, pp. 1–135, 2008.

[20] B. Liu, Sentiment Analysis and Opinion Mining. San Rafael, CA: Morgan & Claypool, 2012.

[21] J.W. Pennebaker, M. Francis, and R. Booth, Linguistic Inquiry and Word Count: LIWC 2001. Mahwah, NJ: Erlbaum Publishers, 2001.

[22] J.W. Pennebaker, C.K. Chung, M. Ireland, A. Gonzales, and R.J. Booth, The development and psychometric properties of LIWC2007. Austin, TX: LIWC.net, 2007.

[23] M.M. Bradley and P.J. Lang, "Affective norms for English words (ANEW): Instruction manual and affective ratings," NIMH Center for the Study of Emotion and Attention, Center for Research in Psychophysiology, University of Florida, Technical Report C-1, 1999.

[24] P.J. Stone, D.C. Dunphy, M.S. Smith, and D.M. Ogilvie, General Inquirer: A Computer Approach to Content Analysis. Cambridge, MA: MIT Press, 1966.

[25] S. Baccianella, A. Esuli, and F. Sebastiani, "SentiWordNet 3.0: An Enhanced Lexical Resource for Sentiment Analysis and Opinion Mining," in Proc. of LREC, 2010.

[26] D. Blei, A. Ng, and M. Jordan, "Latent dirichlet allocation," J. Mach. Learn. Res., vol. 3, pp. 993–1022, 2003.

[27] J. Chang, J. Boyd-Graber, S. Gerrish, C. Wang, and D. Blei, "Reading Tea Leaves: How Humans Interpret Topic Models," in Proceedings of the 23rd Annual Conference on Neural Information Processing Systems, 2009.

[28] J. Hollan, E. Hutchins, and D. Kirsh, "Distributed Cognition: Toward a new foundation for human computer interaction research," ACM Trans. Comput.-Hum. Interact. TOCHI, vol. 7, no. 2, pp. 174–196, 2000.

[29] E. Hutchins, "Distributed Cognition," in International Encyclopedia of the Social & Behavioral Sciences, N. J. Smelser and P. B. Baltes, Eds. Oxford: Pergamon, 2001, pp. 2068–2072.

[30] C.J. Hutto, S. Yardi, and E. Gilbert, "A Longitudinal Study of Follow Predictors on Twitter," in Proceedings of the SIGCHI Conference on Human Factors in Computing Systems, Paris, France, 2013, pp. 821–830.

[31] S.A. Umpleby, "Second-order science: logic, strategies, methods," Constructivist Foundations 2014, vol. 10, no. 1, pp. 16-23, 15 November 2014.

[32] J. Rotmans, R. Kemp, and M. van Asselt, "More evolution than revolution: transition management in public policy", Foresight, vol. 3, no. 1, pp. 15-31, February 2001. ISSN 1463-6689.

[33] F.W. Geels, "Technological transitions as evolutionary reconfiguration processes: A multi-level perspective and a case-study." Research Policy, vol. 31, pp. 1257–1274, 2002.

[34] R. Wagner-Pacifici, J.W. Mohr, and R.L. Breiger, "Ontologies, methodologies, and new uses of Big Data in the social and

cultural sciences," Big Data & Society, vol. 2 iss. 2, pp. 1-11, December 2015. DOI: 10.1177/2053951715613810.

[35] D.S. Alberts, R.E. Hayes, D.K. Leedom, J.E. Kirzl, and D.T. Maxwell, Code of Best Practice for Experimentation, Washington DC: CCRP Publication Series, 2002.

[36] D.S. Alberts and R.E. Hayes, Code of Best Practice for Campaigns of Experimentation: Pathways to Innovation and Transformation, Washington DC: CCRP Publication Series, 2002.

[37] www.gaain.org/ , accessed: 31-May-2017.

[38] www.humanbrainproject.eu/ , accessed: 31-May-2017

[39] W.B. Rouse and D. Bodner, Multi-level modeling of complex socio-technical systems – phase 1, A013 - final technical report, SERC-2013-TR-020-2, Systems Engineering Research Center, 2013.

[40] W.B. Rouse and M. Pennock, Multi-level modeling of socio-technical systems a013 - final technical report, SERC-2013-TR-020-3, Systems Engineering Research Center, 2013.

[41] T.A. McDermott and D. Freeman, Systems thinking in the systems engineering process: new methods and tools, in Systems Thinking: Foundation, Uses and Challenges, Eds. Frank, Shaked, Kordova, Nova Publications, 2016.

[42] J. Ernst, "What is metamodeling, and what is it good for," http://infogrid.org/trac/wiki/Reference/WhatIsMetaModeling, retrieved: November 2015.

[43] N. Ashish and A.W. Toga, "Medical data transformation using rewriting," Frontiers in Neuroinformatics, vol. 9, no. 2, pp. 1-8, 20 February 2015. doi: 10.3389/fninf.2015.00001

[44] N. Ashish, P. Dewan, J.L. Ambite, and A.W. Toga, GEM: The GAAIN Entity Mapper, in Data Integration in the Life Sciences, 11th International Conference, DILS 2015, Eds. Ashish, N. and Ambite, J., Springer 2015.

[45] A. Medina-Borja, K.S. Pasupathy, and K. Triantis, "Large-scale data envelopment analysis (DEA) implementation: a strategic performance management approach," Journal of the Operational Research Society, 58(8), 1084-1098, 2007.

[46] https://www.microsoft.com/en-us/research/project/microsoft-academic-graph/, accessed 31-May-2017.

[47] https://osf.io/ , accessed: 31-May-2017

[48] https://www.scopus.com/, accessed: 31-May-2017

[49] http://webofknowledge.com/, accessed: 31-May-2017

Detection of Japanese and English Tweets Where Birthdays are Revealed to Other People

Yasuhiko Watanabe, Naohiro Miyagi, Kenji Yasuda, Norimasa Mukai, Ryo Nishimura, and Yoshihiro Okada
Ryukoku University
Seta, Otsu, Shiga, Japan
Email: watanabe@rins.ryukoku.ac.jp, t120499@mail.ryukoku.ac.jp, t130522@mail.ryukoku.ac.jp,
t130514@mail.ryukoku.ac.jp, r_nishimura@afc.ryukoku.ac.jp, okada@rins.ryukoku.ac.jp

***Abstract*—These days, many people use a social networking service (SNS). When we use SNSs, we carefully protect the privacy of personal information: name, age, gender, address, telephone number, birthday, etc. However, we often reveal birthdays on SNS, not only ours but also of others. Birthday information can threaten our privacy and security when combined with other personal information. In this study, we investigated Japanese and English tweets where birthdays were revealed to other people, including unwanted audiences. We collected 1,000 Japanese tweets and 1,000 English tweets including word "birthday" and found about 30% of the collected Japanese tweets and 70% of the English tweets were tweets revealing someone's birthdays to other people. Furthermore, about 70% of Japanese tweets and 90% of English tweets revealing someone's birthdays to other people were ones where receivers' birthdays were revealed. We obtained 88% accuracy when we applied support vector machine (SVM) machine learning techniques to classify Japanese and English tweets including word "birthday" into ones revealing birthdays of senders, receivers, and others. However, the recall rate of Japanese and English tweets revealing senders' birthdays were only 17% and 30%, respectively.**

***Keywords*–birthday; personal information; Twitter; SNS; privacy risk.**

I. Introduction

These days, many people use a social networking service (SNS). These users, especially young users, tend to disclose personal information on their SNS profiles seemingly without much concern for the potential privacy risks. They seem to believe the benefits of disclosing personal information in order to use SNSs is greater than the potential privacy risks. Furthermore, they often reveal personal information on SNSs, not only theirs but also of others. For example, (exp 1) is a comment on a Facebook user profile.

(exp 1) I hope you had an amazing birthdayyy!

This comment was time-stamped. As a result, anyone, including unwanted audiences, could understand this user's birthday even if the user did not disclose his/her birthday on the profile. Also, we often find tweets where we can understand someone's birthday.

(exp 2) *Atashi no tanjyobi ha 8 gatu youka yo, Risshu tte itte 1 nen de mottomo atsui hi rashii wane–. Koyomi no ue deha dayo?*
(My birthday is August 8th, that is, the beginning day of autumn, and seems to be the hottest day of the year. Well, it is according to the calendar, you know?)

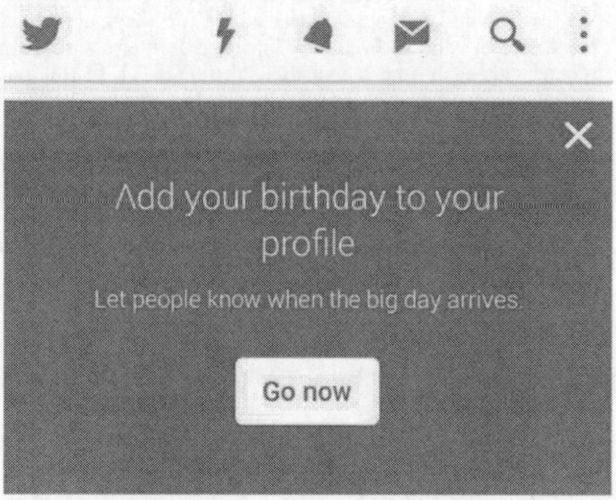

Figure 1. Twitter recommends us to add our birthdays to our profiles.

(exp 3) *@kahuhi kahuhi san tanjyobi omedetou gozaimasu!!*
(@kahuhi Mr. kahuhi, happy birthday!!)

Both (exp 2) and (exp 3) are tweets on Twitter. The sender of (exp 2) disclosed her birthday by herself. On the other hand, the sender of (exp 3) revealed his/her friend's birthday. In this paper, we focus on birthday information because we treat it different than other personal information. For example, if someone revealed our name, address, age, gender, telephone number, or social security number on a SNS, we would get upset with him/her for doing it. On the other hand, interestingly, if someone revealed our birthday in his/her birthday message on a SNS, like (exp 3), most of us would appreciate what he/she does, like (exp 4) and (exp 5).

(exp 4) *message kureta minna arigatou. yoi tanjyobi ni narimashita –* (*^^*)
(Thank you for birthday messages. I have a nice birthday – (*^^*))

(exp 5) *@taguma6 reina no mama no tanjyobi oboete kurete runyane, arigatou, sasuga*
(@taguma6 I'm glad to hear that you remember my mother's birthday. Thank you. Amazing.)

Birthday messages often give us opportunities to start new communications. As a result, as shown in Fig. 1, Twitter recommends us to add our birthday to our profiles. It is likely that these kinds of recommendations let SNS users discount the potential risks related to disclosing personal information. However, birthday information can be linkable to a specific individual when it is combined with other information. In order to deal with the privacy risks, it is important to investigate how we disclose or reveal personal information on SNSs, not only ours but of others. Birthday information especially should be investigated carefully because we treat it different than other personal information. Furthermore, it is important to investigate whether unwanted audiences can collect revealed personal information automatically. To solve these problems, we investigated Japanese tweets where birthdays are revealed to other users and showed how Japanese Twitter users communicate with each other about their birthdays [1]. In this paper, we investigate not only Japanese tweets but also English tweets where birthdays are revealed to other users. Furthermore, we discuss whether unwanted audiences can collect revealed birthday information from tweets by using machine learning techniques.

The rest of this paper is organized as follows: In Section II, we survey the related works. In Section III, we report how we disclose or reveal birthday information on Twitter. In Section IV, we discuss whether unwanted audiences can collect revealed birthday information from tweets by using machine learning techniques. Finally, in Section V, we present our conclusions.

II. RELATED WORK

Personally identifiable information is defined as information which can be used to distinguish or trace an individual's identity such as social security number, biometric records, etc. alone, or when combined with other information that is linkable to a specific individual, such as date and place of birth, mother's maiden name, etc. [2] [3]. Internet users are generally concerned about unwanted audiences obtaining personal information. Fox et al. reported that 86% of Internet users are concerned that unwanted audiences will obtain information about them or their families [4]. Also, Acquisti and Gross reported that students expressed high levels of concern for general privacy issues on Facebook, such as a stranger finding out where they live and the location and schedule of their classes, and a stranger learning their sexual orientation, name of their current partner, and their political affiliations [5]. However, Internet users, especially young users, tend to disclose personal information on their profiles, for example, real full name, gender, hometown and full date of birth, which can potentially be used to identify details of their real life, such as their social security numbers. In order to discuss this phenomenon, many researchers investigated how much and which type of information are revealed in SNSs, especially, in Facebook. Stutzman investigated Facebook profiles of University of North Carolina at Chapel Hill freshmen and found that 96.2% of them published their birthdays on their Facebook profiles, 74.7% their political views and 83.2% their sexual orientation [6]. Gross and Acquisti investigated Facebook profiles of Carnegie Mellon University students and found that 87.8% of them reveal their birth date on their profiles, 39.9% list their phone number, and 50.8% list their current residence [7]. Taraszow et al. observed Facebook profiles of 131 young people (68 females and 63 males, ages ranged from 14 to 29 years) and found that all participants disclosed their birthdays and 54.2% list their hometowns on their Facebook profiles [8]. Taraszow et al. also observed Cypriot Facebook users and found that they were willing to share personal information. All of them published their real names, 97% revealed their gender, 97% published their facial profile pictures, 51% indicated their hometowns and 88% published their date of birth [9]. Huffaker and Calvert studied 70 teenage bloggers and found that 70% of them published their first names, 20% list their full names, 67% list their ages, and 39% list their birthdays [10]. Based on these results, researchers discussed the reasons why users willingly disclose personal information on their SNS profiles. Dwyer concluded in her research that privacy is often not expected or undefined in SNSs [11]. Barnes argues that Internet users, especially teenagers, are not aware of the nature of the Internet and SNSs [12]. Hirai reported that many users had troubles in SNSs because they did not mind that strangers observed their communication with their friends [13]. Viseu et al. reported that many online users believe the benefits of disclosing personal information in order to use an Internet site is greater than the potential privacy risks [14]. On the other hand, Acquisti and Gross explain this phenomenon as a disconnection between the users' desire to protect their privacy and their actual behavior [5]. Also, Livingstone points out that teenagers' conception of privacy does not match the privacy settings of most SNSs [15]. Joinson et al. reported that trust and perceived privacy had a strong affect on individuals' willingness to disclose personal information to a website [16]. Also, Tufekci found that concern about unwanted audiences had an impact on whether or not students revealed their real names and religious affiliation on MySpace and Facebook [17].

Next, we survey studies that focus on the issue of potential privacy risks of disclosing personal information. Birthday information alone cannot threaten the privacy and security of users. However, it can expose users' identities and threaten their privacy when combined with other personal information disclosed in their profiles. Sweeney reported 87% of Americans can be uniquely identified from a birth date, five-digit zip code, and gender [18]. Acquisti and Gross reported the existence of a potential ability to reconstruct users' social security numbers utilizing a combination of information often found in profiles, such as their full name, date of birth and hometown [5]. Many banks and credit-card companies recommend their customers to select a personal identification number (PIN) that cannot be easily guessed, for example, birth date [19] [20]. Bonneau et al. investigated 805 participants and found that 23% of them chose their PINs representing dates [21]. Furthermore, Bonneau et al. asked users about the significance of the dates in their PINs: 29% of them used their own birthday, 26% the birthday of a partner or family member, and 25% an important life event like an anniversary or graduation. As a result, we should be aware of the potential privacy risks on SNSs and manage our personal information carefully. SNSs do not force users to reveal personal information. However, we think, they actually recommend and encourage them to do so. As shown in Fig. 1, Twitter recommended users to add their birthdays on their Twitter profiles. On the other hand, Twitter enables each user to set the visibility preferences for his/her birthday on the profile from options [22] [23]:

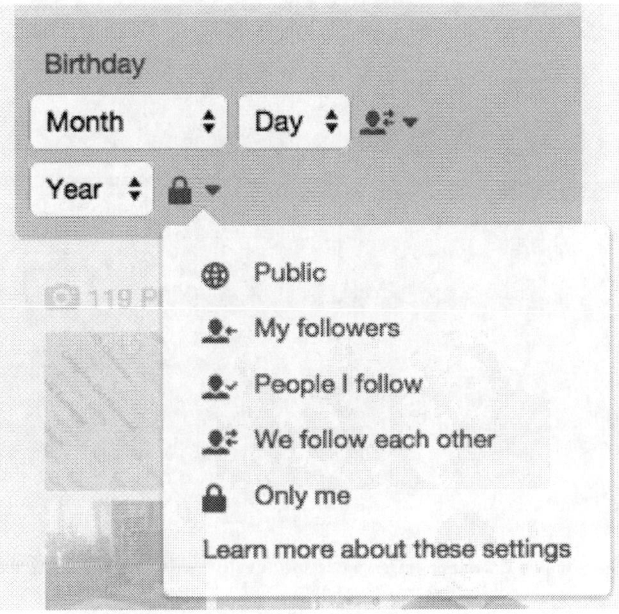

Figure 2. A Twitter user can set the visibility preferences for his/her birthday on the profile.

- public,
- limited audience, or
- closed.

Fig. 2 shows a Twitter profile where a user sets the visibility preferences for his/her birthday. However, even if a user set it closed, his/her birthday would be revealed to others when the following kind of tweets was submitted.

(exp 6) *@446xx110rn tanjyobi omedetou!!*
(@446xx110rn Happy birthday!!)

We found many tweets where someone's birthdays were revealed and linked to specific Twitter accounts. We may say that Fig. 1 and Fig. 2 show a disconnection between the Twitter's desire to protect their users' privacy and their actual behavior.

III. Investigation of Tweets Where Birthdays Are Revealed to Other People

In this section, we show how we disclose or reveal birthday information on Twitter.

A. *The investigation object*

We collected

- 1,000 Japanese tweets including word "*tanjyobi* (birthday)" in December 2015 and
- 1,000 English tweets including word "birthday" in December 2016.

We used these 2,000 tweets for investigating tweets where birthdays were revealed to other people.

Tweets can be classified into three types [24]:

- reply
  A reply is submitted to a particular person. It contains "@username" in the body of the tweet. For example, (exp 3), (exp 5), and (exp 6) are replies.
- retweet
  A retweet is a reply to a tweet that includes the original tweet.
- normal tweet
  A normal tweet is neither reply nor retweet. For example, (exp 2) and (exp 4) are normal tweets. Normal tweets are generally submitted to general public.

Fig. 3 shows the numbers and percentages of normal tweets, replies, and retweets in the 1,000 Japanese tweets. As shown in Fig. 3, there were no retweets in the 1,000 Japanese tweets. On the other hand, Fig. 4 shows the numbers and percentages of normal tweets, replies, and retweets in the 7,085,267 Japanese tweets obtained in November and December 2012 by using the streaming API [25]. The comparison of Fig. 3 with Fig. 4 shows that word "*tanjyobi* (birthday)" was used more frequently in replies than normal tweets. We classified these 1,000 Japanese tweets into three types:

TYPE S tweets where senders' birthdays were disclosed by themselves,
TYPE R tweets where receivers' birthdays were revealed by senders, and
TYPE N tweets where no one's birthdays were revealed.

Table I shows the classification result of the 1,000 Japanese tweets. We corrected the classification result reported in our previous study [1]. Especially, we carefully classified replies submitted to user accounts that were not open to the public. In our previous study [1], all the replies submitted to closed user accounts were classified into TYPE N. However, in this study, replies disclosing senders' birthdays and receivers' birthdays are classified into TYPE S and TYPE R, respectively, although they were submitted to closed user accounts. As shown in Table I, there were 326 tweets revealing senders' or receivers' birthdays. Furthermore, the number of tweets revealing receivers' birthdays (234 tweets) was more than twice the number of tweets revealing senders' birthdays (92 tweets). In this study, a tweet where someone's birthday was revealed but could not be linked to a specific Twitter account was classified into TYPE N: tweets where no one's birthdays were revealed. For example, the birthdays of *oniichan* (brother) in (exp 7) and *Chihiro Iwasaki* in (exp 8) were revealed but could not be linked to their Twitter accounts. As a result, in this study, these tweets were classified into TYPE N.

(exp 7) *kyou ha jikkei no tanjyobi! oniichan tanjyobi omedetou – ! 18 kin kaikin toka otona yana...*
(Today is my elder brother's birthday! Happy birthday, brother. Now, you can watch movies for adults only...)

(exp 8) *Iwasaki Chihiro san no tanjyobi nanoka*
(Today is the birthday of Chihiro Iwasaki.)

Chihiro Iwasaki was a famous Japanese artist.

Fig. 5 shows the numbers and percentages of normal tweets, replies, and retweets in the 1,000 English tweets. As with the Japanese tweets, Fig. 5 shows that there were no retweets in the 1,000 English tweets. On the other hand, Fig. 6 shows the numbers and percentages of normal tweets, replies, and retweets in the 31,253,241 English tweets obtained in

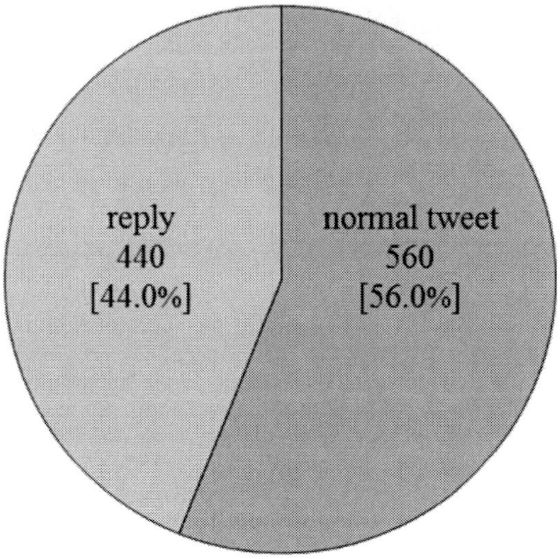

Figure 3. The percentages of normal tweets, replies, and retweets in the 1,000 Japanese tweets including "*tanjyobi* (birthday)" (in December 2015).

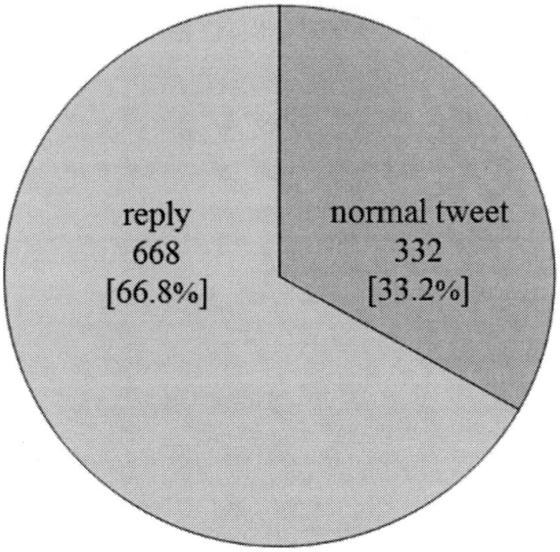

Figure 5. The percentages of normal tweets, replies, and retweets in the 1,000 English tweets including "birthday" (in December 2016).

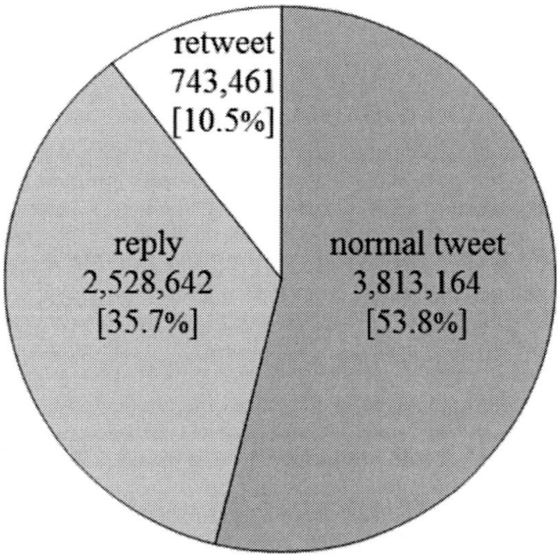

Figure 4. The percentages of normal tweets, replies, and retweets in the 7,085,267 Japanese tweets (in November and December 2012).

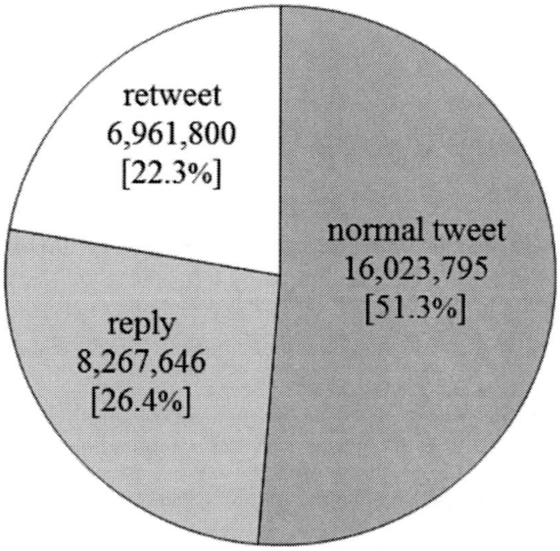

Figure 6. The percentages of normal tweets, replies, and retweets in the 31,253,241 English tweets (in November and December 2012).

TABLE I. THE CLASSIFICATION RESULT OF THE 1,000 JAPANESE TWEETS OBTAINED IN DECEMBER 2015 (BY HUMAN EXPERTS).

TYPE	whose birthday is revealed	normal tweet	reply	total
TYPE S	sender	56	36	92
TYPE R	receiver	0	234	234
TYPE N	no one	504	170	674
	total	560	440	1,000

TABLE II. THE CLASSIFICATION RESULT OF THE 1,000 ENGLISH TWEETS OBTAINED IN DECEMBER 2016 (BY HUMAN EXPERTS).

TYPE	whose birthday is revealed	normal tweet	reply	total
TYPE S	sender	62	21	83
TYPE R	receiver	0	604	604
TYPE N	no one	270	43	313
	total	332	668	1,000

November and December 2012. As with Japanese tweets, the comparison of Fig. 5 with Fig. 6 shows that word "birthday" was used more frequently in replies than normal tweets. Table II shows the classification result of the 1,000 English tweets. As shown in Table II, 70% of the 1,000 English tweets were tweets revealing someone's birthdays to other people. Furthermore, 90% of English tweets revealing someone's birthdays to other people were ones where receivers' birthdays were revealed.

B. Tweets where birthdays are revealed

1) Tweets where senders' birthdays are revealed (TYPE S): In order to start new communications on Twitter, many users submitted tweets where their birthdays were disclosed by themselves. The point is that senders disclosed their birthdays not only in normal tweets but replies. Both (exp 9) and (exp 10) were normal tweets where senders' birthdays were disclosed by themselves.

(exp 9) *kyou tanjyobi nanode dareka nonde kudasai!!!!*
(Today is my birthday. Does anyone keen to go drinking with me!!!!)

(exp 10) *shi-a-wa—se suggoi tanoshii tanjyobi deshita–!!! minasan no okagedesu. arigatou gozaimasu. toriaezu ashi itasugiru. hayo ie tsukan ka na-n*
(H-A-P-P-Y I had a very happy birthday!!! I do appreciate you. Thank you. Just say my foot hurts. I want to go home soon.)

On the other hand, (exp 11) was a reply where sender's birthday was disclosed by himself/herself.

(exp 11) *@takutwu_w takuto kun– kyou tanjyobi nanda oiwai rep hoshii na*
(@takutwu_w Takuto kun–, today is my birthday. Give me your birthday message, please.)

As shown in Table I and Table II, senders' birthdays were disclosed in normal tweets more frequently than replies. (exp 9) and (exp 10) were normal tweets and the senders of them wanted to communicate with anyone. On the other hand, (exp 11) was a reply and the sender of it wanted to communicate with a particular person (@takutwu_w). However, all of (exp 9), (exp 10), and (exp 11) were submitted for starting new communications on Twitter. On the other hand, (exp 12) was a reply where the sender disclosed her birthday not because she wanted to start a new communication but because she was asked when her birthday was.

(exp 12) *@kmns6_n teru-chan kon (*´ ∇ ` *) sou nano–kinou tanjyobi deshita. arigatoune– ♡ mata hitotsu toshi wo totte shimatta wa zutto nannimo itte kurenai kara akirame tetanda kedo, ureshii ♪*
(@kmns6_n Teru-chan hello (*´ ∇ ` *) Yes. Yesterday was my birthday. Thank you ♡ I got another year older again. I have got your birthday message out of my mind because you said nothing for a long time. I am happy ♪)

All of (exp 9), (exp 10), (exp 11), and (exp 12) were submitted within one day of senders' birthdays. On the other hand, (exp 13) and (exp 14) were not. The senders of (exp 13) and (exp 14) disclosed their birthdays by showing the dates.

(exp 13) *boku no tanjyobi ha, 2007 nen 9 gatsu 20 nichi goro da nya– (^^)*
(My date of birth is September 20, 2007 – (^^))

(exp 14) *@alex_hayate shigusa...uwame dukai toka? a, tanjyobi ha 8 gatsu nanoka desu*
(@alex_hayate gesture... up-from-under look? Oh, my birthday is August 7.)

The sender of (exp 15) disclosed his birthday by showing not the date but the festival day, *Tanabata*, when he was born.

(exp 15) *bokura no tanjyobi wa tanabata. orihime to hikoboshi ga, chotto shita kiseki wo purezento shite kurerun da.*
(Our birthday is Tanabata. Orihime and Hikoboshi will give us a little miracle.)

All of (exp 9), (exp 10), (exp 11), (exp 12), (exp 13), (exp 14), and (exp 15) were classified into TYPE S. On the other hand, (exp 16) was classified into TYPE N: tweets where no one's birthdays were revealed. This is because the sender of (exp 16) disclosed his birthday by using a metaphorical expression, mid-summer Christmas Eve. As a result, we determined that sender's birthday of (exp 16) was unclear. We shall discuss tweets classified into TYPE N later.

(exp 16) *@keirin55keigo @yuma123007 manatsu no Christmas Eve ga boku no tanjyobi!*
(@keirin55keigo @yuma123007 mid-summer Christmas Eve is my birthday!)

Sender's birthday of (exp 17) was also unclear. The sender of (exp 17) disclosed her birthday by showing not the date but whom she shared the same birthday with.

(exp 17) *masaka no furukawa yuuki kun to onaji tanjyobi ww majime ni ureshii desu*
(Oh, I share the same birthday with Yuuki Furukawa kun ww Very happy.)

Yuuki Furukawa in (exp 17) was an actor and his birthday might be published. However, we did not understand his birthday with just (exp 17). As a result, we determined that sender's birthday of (exp 17) was unclear. In this study, tweets where birthdays were revealed unclearly, such as (exp 16) and (exp 17), were classified into TYPE N.

2) Tweets where receivers' birthdays are revealed (TYPE R): As shown in Table I and Table II, tweets where receivers' birthdays were revealed by senders were all replies. Furthermore, almost half of Japanese replies including word "*tanjyobi* (birthday)" were ones revealing receivers' birthdays. Also, 90% of English replies including word "birthday" were ones revealing receivers' birthdays. Tweets revealing receivers' birthdays were almost birthday messages to them, such as (exp 18).

(exp 18) *@nami_1215_ nami tanjyobi omedetou!!!*
(@nami_1215_ Nami happy birthday!!!)

Birthday messages were mainly submitted into Twitter on receiver's birthdays. However, we often found belated birthday messages on Twitter, such as (exp 19).

(exp 19) *@identity_u 1 nichi okure desu kedo, tanjyobi omedetou gozaimasu?*
(@identity_u one day late, but anyway, happy birthday?)

Belated birthday messages can be classified into two types:

- belated birthday messages from which we can understand when receivers' birthdays were, and
- belated birthday messages from which we cannot understand when receivers' birthdays were.

For example, (exp 19) is classified into the former type. On the other hand, (exp 20) and (exp 21) are classified into the latter type. This is because it is unclear how late (exp 20) was submitted into Twitter from receiver's birthday. Also, it is unclear how early (exp 21) was submitted into Twitter before receiver's birthday. In this study, the former type of tweets were classified into TYPE R. On the other hand, the latter type of tweets were classified into TYPE N.

(exp 20) *@ayaka_li_u3u ayaka osoku natta kedo tanjyobi omedetou*
(@ayaka_li_u3u ayaka, belated happy birthday to you)

(exp 21) *@0218tom0 tanjyobi wa, mada, dakedo, tanjyobi omedetou?? ToMo ga, shiawase tte omotte kuretara, watasi ha, cho shiawase dayo??*
(@0218tom0 a little bit early, but, happy birthday?? If ToMo feels happy, I am very happy, aren't I??)

3) Tweets revealing no one's birthdays (TYPE N): Tweets where birthdays could not be linked to specific Twitter accounts, such as (exp 22), (exp 23), and (exp 24), were classified into TYPE N: tweets where no one's birthdays were revealed.

(exp 22) *ke-taman tanjyobi omedetou –*
(ke-taman happy birthday –)

(exp 23) *kyou ha daisuki na aya chan no tanjyobi!!!*
(Today is my favorite Aya's birthday!!!)

(exp 24) *@hokoa_a Valentine Day- yade w Jingu no tanjyobi ww tsuraa www watashi ha iroiro dashi sugite tsurai ww*
(@hokoa_a Valentine's Day w Jingu's birthday ww hard www I had a hard time of it ww)

(exp 25) was also classified into TYPE N. This is because it is unclear whether (exp 25) was submitted on sender's birthday or before.

(exp 25) *@AhyonCulturismo,@is9_miku N? ore heno tanjyobi puresento youi shite kureteru no ? sho–ga nai na–. morai ni ittya ou kana* (^o^)
(@AhyonCulturismo,@is9_miku Oh? Do you prepare a present for me? Oh, well. I'm gonna get it (^o^))

It is unclear whose birthday live streaming the sender of (exp 26) provided. As a result, (exp 26) was classified into TYPE N.

(exp 26) *kyou ha 0ji kara kossori tanjyobi oiwai CAS shimasu* (• ´ ω ` •)
(I will secretly provide a happy birthday live streaming from midnight tonight (• ´ ω ` •))

It is clear that the sender of (exp 27) and chiipopo shared the same birthday. However, it is unclear when their same birthday was. As a result, (exp 27) was classified into TYPE N.

(exp 27) *watashi chiipopo to tanjyobi onaji yawa*
(I share the same birthday with chiipopo.)

TABLE III. FEATURES USED IN SVM METHOD FOR DATA TRAINING AND CLASSIFYING JAPANESE TWEETS AND ENGLISH TWEETS INCLUDING WORD "*tanjyobi* (BIRTHDAY)" AND "BIRTHDAY", RESPECTIVELY.

$s1$	word unigrams of the tweet
$s2$	word bigrams of the tweet
$s3$	the number of words in the tweet
$s4$	word unigrams of the first sentence of the tweet
$s5$	word bigrams of the first sentence of the tweet
$s6$	the number of words in the first sentence of the tweet
$s7$	the last word of the first sentence of the tweet
$s8$	character unigrams of the tweet
$s9$	character bigrams of the tweet
$s10$	character 3-grams of the tweet
$s11$	the length of the tweet
$s12$	character unigrams of the first sentence of the tweet
$s13$	character bigrams of the first sentence of the tweet
$s14$	character 3-grams of the first sentence of the tweet
$s15$	the length of the first sentence of the tweet
$s16$	whether the tweet is a reply

The senders of (exp 28) and (exp 29) showed what had happened or would happen on their birthdays. However, they did not show when their birthdays were. As a result, (exp 28) and (exp 29) were classified into TYPE N.

(exp 28) *22 sai no tanjyobi ni* -20 °C *no yukiyama de fuhatsudan shori shiteta.*
(On my 22th birthday, I did bomb disposal work in a snowy mountain, minus 20 degrees.)

(exp 29) *tanjyobi ni intern kakutei shita shini tai*
(I have to work on an internship program on my birthday. I'd rather die.)

The sender of (exp 30) asked the receiver when her birthday was. We could not understand her birthday with just (exp 30). As a result, (exp 30) was classified into TYPE N.

(exp 30) *iku chan kyou tanjyobi jya nakatta?*
(Iku chan. Is today your birthday?)

Tweets dealing with topics related to "birthday", but not someone's birthday, such as (exp 31) and (exp 32), were classified into TYPE N.

(exp 31) *jissai, 2/29 umare no hito tte inno?? koseki ni 2/29 tte touroku shitara 4 nen ni 1 kai shika tanjyobi konai yona.*
(Actually, are there people born on Feb.29?? If the birthdays were registered correctly, they would have their birthday every four years.)

(exp 32) *@BBCNNHK douse nara suihanki to nanige nai kaiwa shite tanjyobi oboete kureru tekina yatsu ga eena*
(@BBCNNHK I might as well buy a rice cooker that deduces my birthday from a daily chat.)

IV. DETECTION OF TWEETS WHERE BIRTHDAYS ARE REVEALED TO OTHER PEOPLE

If we detect tweets revealing someone's birthdays automatically, we can give warnings to users before they submit their

TABLE IV. THE SVM CLASSIFICATION RESULT OF THE 1,000 JAPANESE TWEETS INCLUDING WORD "*tanjyobi* (BIRTHDAY)".

whose birthday is revealed	SVM result: sender	receiver	no one	recall
sender	16	5	71	0.17
receiver	0	212	22	0.91
no one	3	18	653	0.97
precision	0.84	0.90	0.88	

TABLE V. THE SVM CLASSIFICATION RESULT OF THE 560 JAPANESE NORMAL TWEETS INCLUDING WORD "*tanjyobi* (BIRTHDAY)".

whose birthday is revealed	SVM result: sender	receiver	no one	recall
sender	7	0	49	0.13
receiver	0	0	0	—
no one	1	3	500	0.99
precision	0.88	0.00	0.91	

TABLE VI. THE SVM CLASSIFICATION RESULT OF THE 440 JAPANESE REPLIES INCLUDING WORD "*tanjyobi* (BIRTHDAY)".

whose birthday is revealed	SVM result: sender	receiver	no one	recall
sender	9	5	22	0.25
receiver	0	212	22	0.91
no one	2	15	153	0.90
precision	0.82	0.91	0.78	

TABLE VII. THE SVM CLASSIFICATION RESULT OF THE 1,000 ENGLISH TWEETS INCLUDING WORD "BIRTHDAY".

whose birthday is revealed	SVM result: sender	receiver	no one	recall
sender	25	12	46	0.30
receiver	1	595	8	0.99
no one	28	34	251	0.40
precision	0.46	0.93	0.82	

TABLE VIII. THE SVM CLASSIFICATION RESULT OF THE 332 ENGLISH NORMAL TWEETS INCLUDING WORD "BIRTHDAY".

whose birthday is revealed	SVM result: sender	receiver	no one	recall
sender	20	0	42	0.32
receiver	0	0	0	—
no one	25	1	244	0.90
precision	0.44	0.00	0.85	

TABLE IX. THE SVM CLASSIFICATION RESULT OF THE 668 ENGLISH REPLIES INCLUDING WORD "BIRTHDAY".

whose birthday is revealed	SVM result: sender	receiver	no one	recall
sender	5	12	4	0.24
receiver	1	595	8	0.99
no one	3	33	7	0.16
precision	0.56	0.93	0.37	

tweets where someone's birthdays are revealed. In this section, we discuss whether we can automatically detect tweets where someone's birthdays are revealed by using machine learning techniques.

In this study, we used the support vector machine (SVM) for data training and classifying. Table III shows feature $s1 \sim s16$ used in machine learning on experimental data. $s1 \sim s7$ were obtained by using the results of morphological analysis on experimental data. In the experiments, we used a Japanese morphological analyzer, JUMAN, for word segmentation of Japanese tweets [26]. Also, we used the TreeTagger for annotating English tweets with part-of-speech and lemma information [27] [28] [29]. $s8 \sim s10$ and $s12 \sim s14$ were obtained by extracting character N-gram from experimental data. Odaka et al. reported that character 3-gram is good for Japanese processing [30]. $s4 \sim s7$ and $s12 \sim s15$ were obtained from first sentences of tweets. This is because, we thought, clue expressions of birthday messages are often found at first sentences of tweets.

In this study, we used the 1,000 Japanese tweets and 1,000 English tweets investigated in Section III for the experimental data. We conducted this experiment using TinySVM [31]. Table IV shows the experimental result of the 1,000 Japanese tweets. The experimental result was obtained with 10-fold cross-validation. As shown in Fig. 3, the experimental data of the Japanese tweets consisted of 560 normal tweets and 440 replies. We divided the experimental result of the 1,000 Japanese tweets (Table IV) into those of 560 normal tweets (Table V) and 440 replies (Table VI). On the other hand, Table VII shows the experimental result of the 1,000 English tweets. As shown in Fig. 5, the experimental data of the English tweets consisted of 332 normal tweets and 668 replies. We also divided the experimental result of the 1,000 English tweets (Table VII) into those of 332 normal tweets (Table VIII) and 668 replies (Table IX).

As shown in Table IV, 881 Japanese tweets were classified correctly and 119 tweets incorrectly in this experiment. 76 tweets out of the 119 incorrectly classified tweets were ones where senders' birthdays were revealed. As shown in Table IV, the recall of Japanese tweets revealing senders' birthdays were 17%. As shown in Table V and Table VI, many Japanese normal tweets and replies revealing senders' birthdays were classified incorrectly into tweets revealing no one's birthdays. On the other hand, as shown in Table VII, 871 English tweets were classified correctly and 129 tweets incorrectly in this experiment. 58 tweets out of the 129 incorrectly classified tweets were ones where senders' birthdays were revealed. As shown in Table VII, the recall of English tweets revealing senders' birthdays were 30%. As shown in Table VIII and Table IX, many English normal tweets and replies revealing senders' birthdays were classified incorrectly into tweets revealing no one's birthdays and receivers' birthdays, respectively. As a result, it is difficult to detect Japanese and English tweets revealing senders' birthdays and give warnings to senders before they submit tweets revealing their birthdays. On the other hand, Table IV shows the precision of Japanese tweets revealing senders' and receivers' birthdays were 84% and 90%, respectively. Also, Table VII shows the precision of English

TABLE X. THE CLASSIFICATION RESULT OF THE 500 JAPANESE TWEETS FOR TESTING (IN DECEMBER 2016) (BY HUMAN EXPERTS).

TYPE	whose birthday is revealed	normal tweet	reply	total
TYPE S	sender	34	14	48
TYPE R	receiver	0	168	168
TYPE N	no one	202	82	284
	total	236	264	500

TABLE XI. THE CLASSIFICATION RESULT OF THE 500 ENGLISH TWEETS FOR TESTING (IN DECEMBER 2016) (BY HUMAN EXPERTS).

TYPE	whose birthday is revealed	normal tweet	reply	total
TYPE S	sender	38	5	43
TYPE R	receiver	0	328	328
TYPE N	no one	120	9	129
	total	158	342	500

tweets revealing receivers' birthdays was 93%. Our method is useful for collecting tweets revealing birthdays, especially tweets revealing receivers' birthdays, precisely. As a result, it is easy for attackers to collect birthday information related to specific Twitter accounts by using our method.

Next, we discuss the number of tweets for data training. We conducted closed and open tests to measure the accuracy of the SVM classifier developed by using tweets investigated in Section III. In this experiments, we introduced the following data sets for the open tests:

- 500 Japanese tweets including word "*tanjyobi* (birthday)" (obtained in December 2016) and
- 500 English tweets including word "birthday" (obtained in December 2016).

Table X and Table XI show the classification results of the 500 Japanese and English tweets, respectively. There were no duplicate tweets between these data sets and tweets investigated in Section III. The accuracy values in Fig. 7 and Fig. 8 are ten times average values of the accuracy of classifying tweets into ones revealing birthdays of senders, receivers, and others. Fig. 7 and Fig. 8 show that, both in the closed tests and open tests, we obtained about 80% accuracy when we used only 100 tweets for data training. The accuracy was slightly improved as the number of tweets for data training increased. The point is that, as shown in Table IV and Table VII, the recall of tweets revealing senders' birthdays was low even if we used 1,000 tweets for data training. The recall rate of Japanese and English tweets revealing senders' birthdays were only 17% and 30%, respectively. As a result, it is difficult to develop an SVM detecting tweets revealing senders' birthdays.

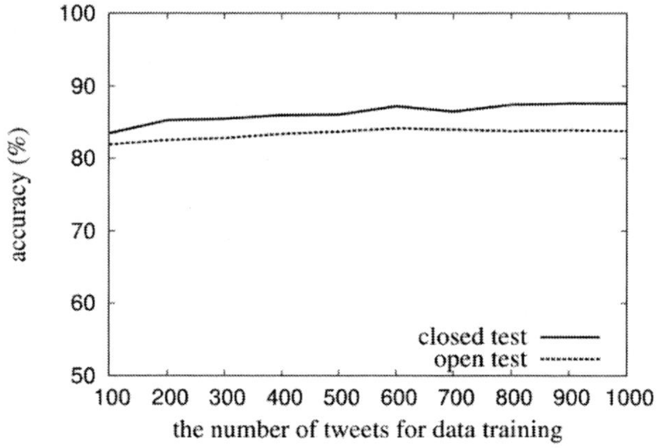

Figure 7. The accuracy of classifying Japanese tweets into ones revealing birthdays of senders, receivers, and others.

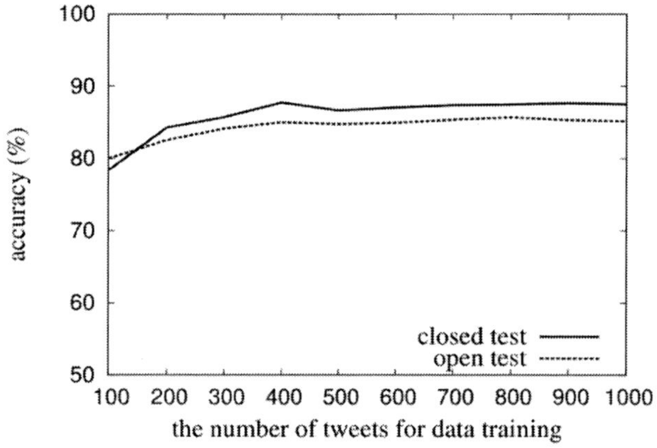

Figure 8. The accuracy of classifying English tweets into ones revealing birthdays of senders, receivers, and others.

V. CONCLUSION

Many people willingly disclose their birthdays on their SNS profiles and reveal others' birthdays on their SNS messages. They seem unaware of the potential risks of doing it. Birthday information alone cannot threaten their privacy and security. However, it can expose users' identities and threaten their privacy when combined with other personal information disclosed in their profiles. Interestingly, we treat birthday information different than other personal information. For example, if someone revealed our personal information except birthday on a SNS, we would get upset him/her for doing it. On the other hand, if someone revealed our birthday in his/her birthday message on a SNS, most of us would feel happy and appreciate what he/she does. However, we have not sufficiently investigated how we reveal birthday information on SNSs. As a result, the authors investigated how we reveal birthday information on SNSs, not only ours but of others.

In this study, we investigated tweets where someone's birthdays were revealed to other people. We collected 1,000 Japanese tweets including word "*tanjyobi* (birthday)" and found that about 30% of them were tweets where someone's birthdays were revealed to other people. Furthermore, about 70% of Japanese tweets revealing someone's birthdays were ones where receivers' birthdays were revealed by senders. We also collected 1,000 English tweets including word "birthday" and found that about 70% of them were tweets where someone's birthdays were revealed to other people. Furthermore, about 90% of English tweets revealing someone's birthdays were ones where receivers' birthdays were revealed by senders. In this study, we proposed a method of detecting tweets revealing someone's birthday by using machine learning techniques. The experimental results showed that our method was able to classify Japanese tweets including word "*tanjyobi* (birthday)" and English tweets including word "birthday" with accuracy of 88% and 87%, respectively. However, the recall of Japanese and English tweets revealing senders' birthday were only 17% and 30%, respectively. As a result, in our method, it is difficult to detect tweets revealing senders' birthdays and give warnings to senders before they submit them. On the other hand, the precision of Japanese tweets revealing senders' and receivers' birthdays were 71% and 82%, respectively. Also, the precision of English tweets revealing receivers' birthdays was 93%. As a result, in our method, it is not difficult to collect tweets revealing birthdays, especially tweets revealing receivers' birthdays, precisely. We recommend that birthday messages should not be sent via SNSs. This is because unwanted audiences can read and collect them. We are now investigating other language tweets where birthdays are disclosed or revealed to other people.

REFERENCES

[1] Y. Watanabe, N. Miyagi, K. Yasuda, R. Nishimura, and Y. Okada, "Detection of tweets where birthdays are revealed to other people," in Proceedings of the Eighth International Conference on Evolving Internet (INTERNET 2016), Nov 2016, pp. 30–35. [Online]. Available: https://www.thinkmind.org/index.php?view=article&articleid=internet_2016_2_30_40049 [accessed: 2017-5-25]

[2] C. Johnson III, Safeguarding against and responding to the breach of personally identifiable information, Office of Management and Budget Memorandum, 2007. [Online]. Available: http://www.whitehouse.gov/omb/memoranda/fy2007/m07-16.pdf [accessed: 2016-10-4]

[3] B. Krishnamurthy and C. E. Wills, "On the leakage of personally identifiable information via online social networks," in Proceedings of the 2Nd ACM Workshop on Online Social Networks, ser. WOSN '09. New York, NY, USA: ACM, 2009, pp. 7–12. [Online]. Available: http://doi.acm.org/10.1145/1592665.1592668 [accessed: 2017-5-25]

[4] S. Fox et al., Trust and Privacy Online: Why Americans Want to Rewrite the Rules, The Pew Internet & American Life Project, 2000. [Online]. Available: http://www.pewinternet.org/2000/08/20/trust-and-privacy-online/ [accessed: 2017-5-25]

[5] A. Acquisti and R. Gross, Imagined Communities: Awareness, Information Sharing, and Privacy on the Facebook. Berlin, Heidelberg: Springer Berlin Heidelberg, 2006, pp. 36–58.

[6] F. Stutzman, Student life on the Facebook, 2006. [Online]. Available: http://www.ibiblio.org/fred/facebook/stutzman_fbook.pdf [accessed: 2017-5-25]

[7] R. Gross and A. Acquisti, "Information revelation and privacy in online social networks," in Proceedings of the 2005 ACM Workshop on Privacy in the Electronic Society, ser. WPES '05. New York, NY, USA: ACM, 2005, pp. 71–80.

[8] T. Taraszow, E. Aristodemou, G. Shitta, Y. Laouris, and A. Arsoy, "Disclosure of personal and contact information by young people in social networking sites: An analysis using Facebook profiles as an example," International Journal of Media and Cultural Politics, vol. 6, no. 1, 2010, pp. 81–101.

[9] T. Taraszow, A. Arsoy, G. Shitta, and Y. Laouris, "How much personal and sensitive information do cypriot teenagers reveal in facebook?" in Proceedings of the 7th European Conference on E-Learning, 2008, pp. 606–611.

[10] D. A. Huffaker and S. L. Calvert, "Gender, identity, and language use in teenage blogs." Journal of Computer-Mediated Communication, vol. 10, no. 2, 2005. [Online]. Available: http://onlinelibrary.wiley.com/doi/10.1111/j.1083-6101.2005.tb00238.x/full [accessed: 2017-5-25]

[11] C. Dwyer, "Digital relationships in the "myspace" generation: Results from a qualitative study," in Proceedings of the 40th Annual Hawaii International Conference on System Sciences, ser. HICSS '07. Washington, DC, USA: IEEE Computer Society, 2007, p. 19.

[12] S. B. Barnes, "A privacy paradox: Social networking in the united states." First Monday, vol. 11, no. 9, 2006. [Online]. Available: http://firstmonday.org/article/view/1394/1312 [accessed: 2017-5-25]

[13] T. Hirai, "Why does "Enjyo" happen on the Web? : An Examination based on Japanese Web Culture," Journal of Information and Communication Research, vol. 29, no. 4, mar 2012, pp. 61–71. [Online]. Available: http://doi.org/10.11430/jsicr.29.4_61 [accessed: 2017-5-25]

[14] A. Viseu, A. Clement, and J. Aspinall, "Situating privacy online: Complex perception and everyday practices," Information, Communication & Society, 2004, pp. 92–114.

[15] S. Livingstone, "Taking risky opportunities in youthful content creation: teenagers' use of social networking sites for intimacy, privacy and self-expression." New Media & Society, vol. 10, no. 3, 2008, pp. 393–411.

[16] A. N. Joinson, U.-D. Reips, T. Buchanan, and C. B. P. Schofield, "Privacy, trust, and self-disclosure online." Human-Computer Interaction, vol. 25, no. 1, 2010, pp. 1–24. [Online]. Available: www.joinson.com/home/pubs/HCI_journal.pdf [accessed: 2017-5-25]

[17] Z. Tufekci, "Can You See Me Now? Audience and Disclosure Regulation in Online Social Network Sites," Bulletin of Science, Technology & Society, vol. 28, no. 1, 2008, pp. 20–36.

[18] L. Sweeney, "Uniqueness of Simple Demographics in the U.S. Population," LIDAP-WP4 Carnegie Mellon University, Laboratory for International Data Privacy, Pittsburgh, Pennsylvania, 2000. [Online]. Available: http://dataprivacylab.org/projects/identifiability/index.html [accessed: 2017-5-25]

[19] VISA, "Issuer PIN Security Guidelines," http://usa.visa.com/dam/VCOM/download/merchants/visa-issuer-pin-security-guideline.pdf [accessed: 2017-5-25], 2010.

[20] HSBC, "New service for HSBC cards — PIN (personal identification number) change via HSBC ATMs," https://www.hsbc.am/1/2/am/en/new-service-for-hsbc-cards [accessed: 2017-5-25], 2016.

[21] J. Bonneau, S. Preibusch, and R. Anderson, "A birthday present every eleven wallets? the security of customer-chosen banking pins," in The 16 th International Conference on Financial Cryptography and Data Security, 2012, pp. 25–40.

[22] Twitter, "Customizing your profile," https://support.twitter.com/articles/127871 [accessed: 2017-5-25].

[23] ——, "Profile visibility settings," https://support.twitter.com/articles/20172733 [accessed: 2017-5-25].

[24] Y. Watanabe, K. Nakajima, H. Morimoto, R. Nishimura, and Y. Okada, "An investigation of a factor that affects the usage of unsounded code strings at the end of japanese and english tweets," in Proceedings of the Seventh International Conference on Evolving Internet (INTERNET 2015), Oct 2015, pp. 50–55. [Online]. Available: https://www.thinkmind.org/index.php?view=article&articleid=internet_2015_2_40_40038 [accessed: 2017-5-25]

[25] Twitter, Inc. The Streaming APIs. [Online]. Available: https://dev.twitter.com/streaming/overview [accessed: 2017-5-25]

[26] S. Kurohashi and D. Kawahara, JUMAN Manual version 5.1 (in Japanese). Kyoto University, 2005.

[27] H. Schmid, "Probabilistic part-of-speech tagging using decision trees," in Proceedings of the International Conference on New Methods in Language Processing, Manchester, UK, 1994.

[28] ——, "Probabilistic part-of-speech tagging using decision trees," in New Methods in Language Processing, ser. Studies in Computational Linguistics, D. Jones and H. Somers, Eds. London, GB: UCL Press, 1997, pp. 154–164.

[29] ——, "Improvements in part-of-speech tagging with an application to german," in Natural Language Processing Using Very Large Corpora, ser. Text, Speech and Language Processing, S. Armstrong, K. Church, P. Isabelle, S. Manzi, E. Tzoukermann, and D. Yarowsky, Eds. Dordrecht: Kluwer Academic Publishers, 1999, vol. 11, pp. 13–26.

[30] T. Odaka et al., "A proposal on student report scoring system using n-gram text analysis method," The transactions of the Institute of

Electronics, Information and Communication Engineers. D-I, vol. 86, no. 9, sep 2003, pp. 702–705.

[31] Taku Kudoh. TinySVM: Support Vector Machines. [Online]. Available: http://chasen.org/taku/software/TinySVM/index.html [accessed: 2017-5-25]